PADDLEWAYS OF MISSISSIPPI

PADDLEWAYS OF MISSISSIPPI

*Rivers and People
of the Magnolia State*

Ernest Herndon and Patrick Parker

With maps by Elise and Patrick Parker

University Press of Mississippi / Jackson

The University Press of Mississippi is the scholarly publishing agency of the Mississippi Institutions of Higher Learning: Alcorn State University, Delta State University, Jackson State University, Mississippi State University, Mississippi University for Women, Mississippi Valley State University, University of Mississippi, and University of Southern Mississippi.

www.upress.state.ms.us

The University Press of Mississippi is a
member of the Association of University Presses.

Photographs by Ernest Herndon unless otherwise noted

Copyright © 2024 by University Press of Mississippi
All rights reserved

∞

Library of Congress Cataloging-in-Publication Data

Names: Herndon, Ernest, author. | Parker, Patrick (Travel/outdoor writer), author, cartographer. | Parker, Elise, cartographer.
Title: Paddleways of Mississippi : rivers and people of the Magnolia State / Ernest Herndon, Patrick Parker, with maps by Elise and Patrick Parker.
Description: Jackson : University Press of Mississippi, 2024. | Includes index.
Identifiers: LCCN 2023049662 (print) | LCCN 2023049663 (ebook) | ISBN 9781496840653 (hardback) | ISBN 9781496850812 (trade paperback) | ISBN 9781496850829 (epub) | ISBN 9781496850836 (epub) | ISBN 9781496850843 (pdf) | ISBN 9781496850850 (pdf)
Subjects: LCSH: Canoes and canoeing—Mississippi—Guidebooks. | Boats and boating—Mississippi—Guidebooks. | Outdoor recreation—Mississippi—Guidebooks. | Rivers—Mississippi. | Mississippi—Description and travel. | Mississippi—Guidebooks. | Mississippi—Social life and customs—Anecdotes. | Mississippi—History—Anecdotes.
Classification: LCC GV776.M7 H475 2024 (print) | LCC GV776.M7 (ebook) | DDC 797.12209762—dc23/eng/20231122
LC record available at https://lccn.loc.gov/2023049662
LC ebook record available at https://lccn.loc.gov/2023049663

British Library Cataloging-in-Publication Data available

Eventually, all things merge into one, and a river runs through it.
—NORMAN MACLEAN

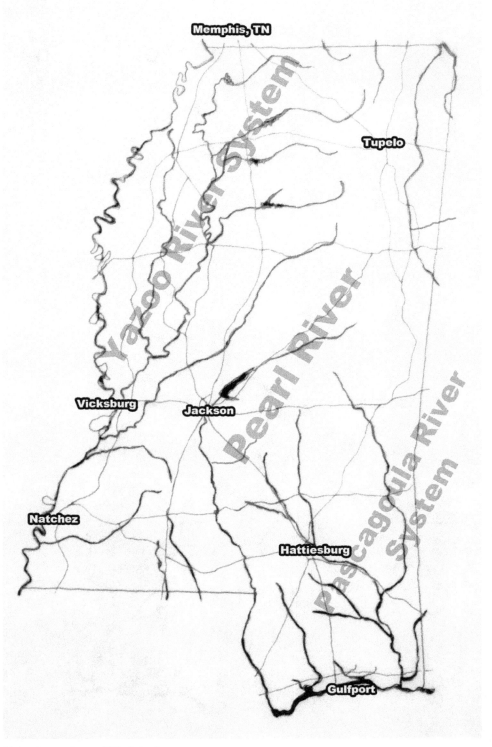

Major river systems of Mississippi

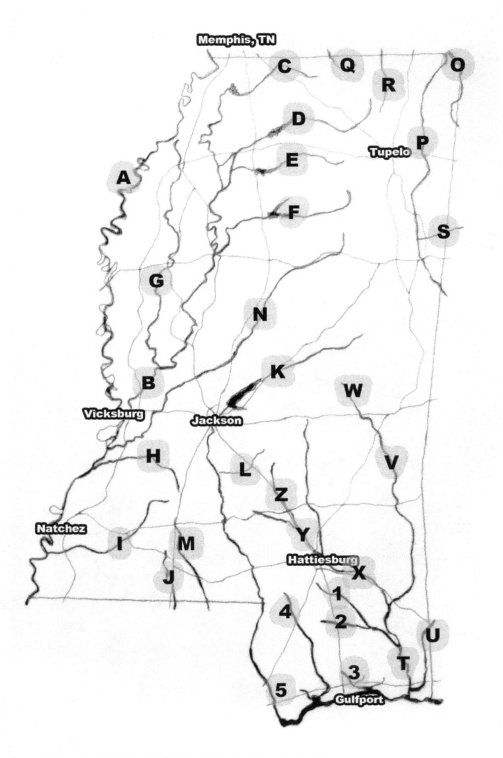

Navigable rivers of Mississippi* (*Map key is in the table of contents.)

CONTENTS

Acknowledgments xi
Introduction 3
The Mississippi River[A*] 7

THE DELTA 31

Yazoo River[B] 32
Coldwater River[C] 45
Tallahatchie River[D] 49
Yocona River[E] 55
Yalobusha River[F] 57
Big Sunflower River[G] 63

SOUTHWEST MISSISSIPPI 73

Bayou Pierre[H] 75
Homochitto River[I] 85
Tangipahoa River[J] 97

DOWN THE MIDDLE 107

Pearl River[K] 109
Strong River[L] 137
Bogue Chitto River[M] 143
Big Black River[N] 161

NORTHEAST MISSISSIPPI 171

Bear Creek[O] 173
Tennessee-Tombigbee Waterway[P] 175
Wolf River[Q] 183
Hatchie River[R] 184
Buttahatchee River[S] 185

Contents

SOUTHEAST MISSISSIPPI 189
Pascagoula River[T]   190
Escatawpa River[U]   201
Chickasawhay River[V]   205
Chunky River[W]   217
Leaf River[X]   223
Bowie Creek[Y]   239
Okatoma Creek[Z]   241
Black Creek[1]   247
Red Creek[2]   257

COASTAL MISSISSIPPI 261
Biloxi River[3]   263
Wolf River[4]   269
Jourdan River[5]   273
Gulf Islands   279

Index   287

*Superscripts refer to the map on page viii.

ACKNOWLEDGMENTS

> Rivers flow not past, but through us, thrilling, tingling, vibrating every fiber and cell of the substance of our bodies, making them glide and sing.
>
> —JOHN MUIR

The authors would like to acknowledge the contributions of the following people and organizations:

Our lovely and supportive wives, Angelyn Herndon and Elise Parker

Enterprise-Journal newspaper owner Wyatt Emmerich, publisher Jack Ryan, and managing editor Matt Williamson

Joseph Parker of the Scenic Rivers Development Alliance

Photographer Sam King

John "Driftwood Johnnie" Ruskey of the Quapaw Canoe Company

Mrs. Emma Crisler of Port Gibson

Robin Whitfield of Friends of the Chakchiuma Swamp

Cathy Shropshire, former executive director of the Mississippi Wildlife Federation

Andrew Whitehurst of Healthy Gulf

Libby Hartfield, former director of the Mississippi Museum of Natural Science

PADDLEWAYS OF MISSISSIPPI

INTRODUCTION

> I started out thinking of America as highways and state lines.
> As I got to know it better, I began to think of it as rivers.
>
> —CHARLES KURALT

The navigable rivers and creeks of the State of Mississippi have been foundational in every aspect of the state's geology, ecology, settlement, development, economy, and politics. These paddleways of Mississippi—its rivers, creeks, and streams as well as lakes, bays, and swamps—are its arteries, its lifeblood, and the connective tissue that holds its stories and histories together.

In prehistory, the area that would eventually become the State of Mississippi was covered by a shallow sea. As that sea receded, it left a low, largely flat plain that accumulated plant debris over the years. Wind rushing down what would become the Mississippi River Valley deposited fine glacier-ground dust to form many feet of loess soil, which was then cut into hills and hollows by rills and rivulets, leaving the terrain that is familiar to us throughout all of Mississippi, except for the Appalachian foothills in the farthest northeast corner of the state.

Native Americans traveled and settled along these waterways, which they used for drinking, cooking, and irrigation as well as for navigation. The Poverty Point culture grew up throughout the lower Mississippi River Valley and Gulf Coast region, only to be supplanted by other tribes and cultures including the Yazoo, Natchez, Choctaw, and Chickasaw. Nanih Waiya, the source of the Pearl River in central Mississippi, figures prominently in the origin stories of the Choctaw, Chickasaw, and other tribes.

European-descended Americans moved into the Mississippi Territory in steam-powered boats and paddlecraft, and they expanded into the territory on the smaller navigable waterways. French and Spanish explorers plied the navigable waters of Mississippi. Political treaties and boundaries were based on the locations of streams and rivers. Even the current political boundaries of the State of Mississippi were based to a large extent on the courses of the Mississippi, Pearl, and Tennessee Rivers.

Rivers and creeks dictated the construction and placement of roadways, because people could only ford or bridge or ferry a river at naturally occurring places of convenience. Settlers and soldiers traversed the Natchez Trace, the Three-Chopped Way, and the Old Federal Road, all of which passed over, around, or through countless streams to end at Natchez overlooking the Mississippi River. The construction of dams on the rivers and creeks of Mississippi further influenced the development of the communities around those rivers.

Commerce took place by way of rivers including, but not limited to, the mighty Mississippi, as evidenced by the legal definition of "navigable waters" in the Mississippi Code of laws: "[A]ll rivers, creeks and bayous in this state, twenty-five (25) miles in length, that have sufficient depth and width of water for thirty (30) consecutive days in the year for floating a steamboat with carrying capacity of two hundred (200) bales of cotton are hereby declared to be navigable waters of this state."

During the 1700s and 1800s, Natchez, situated in the southwest corner of the territory, became one of the major commercial centers of the hemisphere solely because of its location near prime cotton-growing land in Mississippi and Louisiana and near the commercial artery that was the Mississippi River.

A handful of the rivers of Mississippi played an outsized role in the Civil War. Decisive battles were fought at the Big Black and all along the Yazoo and its tributaries. Prisoners of war were kept for a short time at a horrific makeshift prison in a ruined covered bridge over the Pearl River in Jackson. Perhaps the most crippling blow of the entire war was dealt to the Confederacy at the confluence of the Yazoo and Mississippi Rivers when Vicksburg fell to a Union siege.

The rivers, especially the Mississippi, also influenced the movement and speciation of wildlife. A prime example is the black bear, populations of which thrived in Louisiana's Tensas River region on the west side of the Mississippi, but which declined east of the river until they were on the brink of extirpation in our state. Bears have since expanded back into Mississippi and are making a remarkable comeback, particularly along the river bottoms throughout the state. Panther, white-tailed deer, alligator, and bald eagle populations have followed similar patterns as black bears in the Mississippi River Valley.

Ecological issues also follow the courses of rivers, including erosion and habitat loss from clear-cutting and channelization, nitrate runoff followed by algal bloom, and dead zones as a result of agricultural overfertilization and sewage lagoon spillage. Any river that runs through a metropolitan area, like the Pearl River does through Jackson, will also have the problems of plastic and Styrofoam pollution as well as oil and gasoline runoff from roads and parking lots.

> Ecologically, things are looking pretty bright for the paddleways of Mississippi. Recent decades have seen improvements in forestry practices, erosion control measures, municipal and residential wastewater treatment, and pollution. However, considering that Mississippi's ribbons of water drain 48,430 square miles populated by three million people, they remain inherently fragile. The biggest threats currently include channelization, dams, erosion, flood control projects, invasive species, species decline, logging, and oil spills.

Because the rivers and creeks of Mississippi were so instrumental in the development of every aspect of the state, one of the best ways to understand Mississippi is to investigate the social, ecological, and oral histories of the peoples and communities that dot the state's navigable waterways.

These are the stories of the people of the paddleways of Mississippi.

> Some of the material for this book is adapted, updated, and restructured from content, articles, chapters, columns, and posts previously published in Ernest Herndon's books *Canoeing Mississippi* (2001, University Press of Mississippi), *Canoeing Louisiana* (2003, University Press of Mississippi), and *Paddling the Pascagoula* (2005, University Press of Mississippi, coauthored with Scott B. Williams); on Patrick Parker's blog, RoamingParkers.com; and in the outdoor and nature writing of both authors in local magazines and newspapers—particularly the McComb (MS) *Enterprise-Journal*.

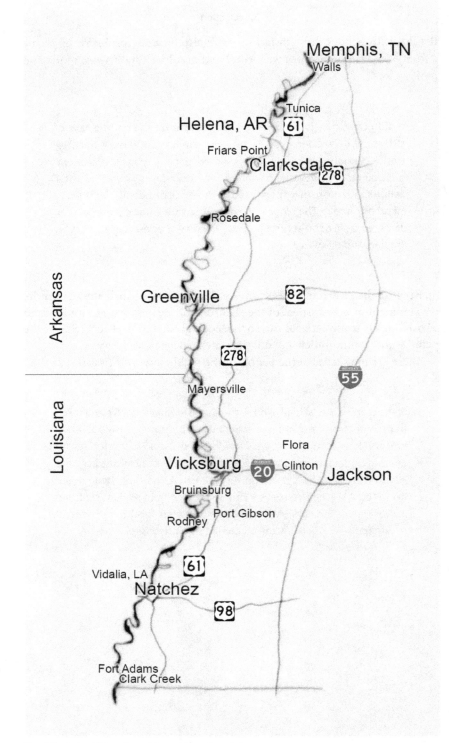

The Mississippi River from Memphis to Fort Adams

THE MISSISSIPPI RIVER

> With us, when you speak of "the river," though there be many,
> you mean always the same one, the great river, the shifting,
> unappeasable god of the country, feared and loved, The Mississippi.
>
> —WILLIAM ALEXANDER PERCY

The Mississippi River Basin is the one of the largest river systems in the world, draining thirty-one US states and two Canadian provinces totaling almost 1.3 million square miles; the river drains 41 percent of the area of the contiguous United States. Meandering more than 2,350 miles from its source at Lake Itasca in Minnesota to the Gulf of Mexico south of New Orleans, it defines the borders of ten US states, including Mississippi, which lays claim to about 410 miles of the namesake river's length.

At the headwaters at Lake Itasca, the river is quite shallow and is narrow enough to flow through a culvert, but it collects the waters of many tributaries including the Ohio, Missouri, Arkansas, White, Yazoo, and Red. As it nears its mouth at New Orleans, it sprawls more than a mile wide and two hundred feet deep in places.

> The word "Mississippi" is derived from an Ojibwe Indian phrase meaning, simply, Big River. Because many tribes lived along it, it has gone by many names, including Chucaga, Tamalisieu, Nilco, Mico, Okachitto, Olsimochitto, Namosi-sipu, Sassagoula, and Culata. Spanish explorers ignored the Native names, calling it Espiritu Santo or Río Grande, but when French explorers journeyed down the river from Canada, they took the label they'd learned from the northern Indians, for whom "mis" meant big and "sipi" was river.

Sunset over the Mississippi River

Over the course of millennia, the Mississippi River has wandered to and fro across the land, periodically flooding and receding, and relentlessly reshaping the terrain. It is easy to see on a modern satellite map just where the Mississippi has strayed eastward, then westward, back and forth, leaving snaky scars across what would become the southern United States.

> The Mississippi Petrified Forest in Flora, now almost fifty miles east of the river, contains fossils of ancient sequoia trees that could only have come from the extreme northwest parts of the Mississippi watershed. They probably washed here from the Dakotas via the raging, glacier-fed floodwaters that formed the Missouri River.

In its passing, the Big River carved steep bluffs and left behind a giant floodplain full of rich alluvial soil. In its current course, the river passes through two distinct geographic regions of the State of Mississippi—the floodplain largely north of Vicksburg, in places fifty to one hundred miles wide, and the loess bluffs to the south, in places two to three hundred feet high. In its endless shifting, the Mississippi helped carve what would become the Coldwater, Yalobusha, Tallahatchie, Yazoo, and Sunflower Rivers out of the floodplain east of the river—an area now known as the Mississippi Delta.

The endless flooding, receding, and shifting have also made human habitation along the river impermanent except for a handful of communities of the most tenacious people who settled in the most fortuitous spots along the river. As a result of these vagaries, right along the river you mostly find only ghost towns or tiny, unincorporated communities. Most of the larger, more permanent settlements lie either miles back away from the flooding meanderings of the river (north of Vicksburg) or else high above the river on bluffs (Vicksburg and south). Now only a few towns in the 410-mile-long Mississippi State segment actually border the waterway.

> The Mississippi River has been called a "wilderness between the levees," and the Audubon Society goes further and deems it a "River of Birds," as 60 percent of America's songbirds and 44 percent of migrating waterfowl use the Mississippi Flyway as a major migratory route. Audubon has designated Important Bird Areas throughout the state, including Yazoo National Wildlife Refuge, Vicksburg National Military Park, St. Catherine Creek National Wildlife Refuge, Shipland Wildlife Management Area, and Eagle Lake, among others. It's not uncommon to see herons, eagles, pelicans, and killdeer throughout the year.

RIVER MODELS

For the last couple hundred years, humans have tried, with varying degrees of success, to force the river to stay put in the course that is familiar and convenient to us. It has been said that in order to control something, one has to be able to measure it, and the US Army Corps of Engineers' attempts to measure and control the Mississippi River in the precomputer era involved elaborate physical hydraulic models of the river basin constructed from concrete and corrugated metal.

Once these accurately scaled models were built, engineers could flush hundreds of gallons of water at a time through them and see what flooded and what flowed like they wanted it to. They could make tiny physical changes to their models and predict the effects of construction projects on the actual river.

The River Flood Model at Vicksburg was constructed in the late 1930s as a proof of concept. A McComb (MS) *Enterprise-Journal* article dated January 9, 1939, describes the model as "[stretching] out over 245 acres . . . a perfect outdoor model of the Mississippi River covering 602 miles of the main river from Helena, Arkansas south to the Gulf, together with the five principal tributaries, all backwater areas, and the entire Atchafalaya Basin to the Gulf of Mexico covering a total area of 16,000 square miles."

Over the next three decades, the prototype Vicksburg model was used successfully to predict the results of flood control efforts, while a more extensive model was being constructed by thousands of German and Italian World War II prisoners of war and hundreds of Corps of Engineers employees at Clinton. In 1948, a *Popular Science* magazine article about this "largest scale model in the world" projected that "this effigy of Old Man River is expected to make him behave better."

When completed, the World War II–era Mississippi River Basin Model at Clinton accurately modeled the majority of the basin, accounting for the flow and drainage of everything from Nebraska to the Great Lakes and south to the Gulf of Mexico. The first official use of the completed model was in the spring of 1952 when it was put through sixteen days of twenty-four-hour nonstop testing to predict flood stages in Nebraska and Missouri. The results of this initial round of modeling are estimated to have prevented flood damages exceeding $65 million.

Despite being declared surplus with the advent of computer modeling, the hydraulic river model at Clinton was called back into operation as late as the mid-1970s in response to flood control questions. Now the remains of the long-mothballed model lie within the bounds of Buddy Butts Park in Clinton and are overgrown with trees and brush, scrawled with graffiti, and dotted with burned-out hobo campfires. In more recent years there have been efforts by university architecture and engineering students along with the Friends of the Mississippi River Basin Model group to clean and rehabilitate parts of the site for educational purposes.

Memphis also has an educational quarter-mile-long scale model of the lower third of the Mississippi River at a city park on Mud Island, as well as a museum of river history there. The city had this model built in concrete at a scale of thirty inches to the mile, which renders the entire river from Cairo, Missouri, to New Orleans.

In addition to the models at Clinton and Memphis, the Corps of Engineers (in collaboration with other government agencies) has the not-to-be-missed Lower Mississippi River Museum and Riverfront Interpretive Site on Levee Street in Vicksburg, with a theater, exhibits, a dry-docked boat to explore, and a quarter-acre flowing hydraulic model of a section of the river. Two blocks away, the floodwall is covered with hundreds of feet of historical murals.

NAVIGATION ON THE MISSISSIPPI

The Mississippi River is not the sort of place most paddlers go for a Saturday float. In fact, some folks advise against paddling it at all. However, humans have plied paddlecraft on the Mississippi River since time immemorial, and they're still doing it.

> The museum at the Poverty Point World Heritage Site in Epps, Louisiana, has copper artifacts that, according to metallurgical analysis, could have only come from the northern Midwest of the United States or from the eastern maritime provinces of Canada. So the people of the Poverty Point culture (1730 to 1350 BC) must have been navigating and trading along the Mississippi River Valley—certainly as far as the Great Lakes region and perhaps farther.

Around 1540, Hernando de Soto and his bloodthirsty army of gold-seeking Spaniards passed through north Mississippi. Contrary to popular opinion, De Soto did not "discover" the Mississippi even from a European perspective; earlier Spaniards had found it from the Gulf of Mexico. De Soto landed near what is now Tampa, Florida, hacked his way north to Tallahassee, veered northeast into the Appalachians as far north as Knoxville, Tennessee, then back south into Alabama near Montgomery, up the Tombigbee River, and across northeast Mississippi to the Mississippi River. He crossed the Mississippi River somewhere around Walls, Mississippi, just south of Memphis, then looped into Arkansas and back to the river around Port Gibson.

In 1682, French explorer Robert de La Salle came down the Mississippi River, celebrating Easter Mass on the high bluff at modern-day Fort Adams in Wilkinson County. In 1699, Pierre Le Moyne, Sieur d'Iberville, explored along the Gulf Coast and up the lower Mississippi River. In the Natchez area, he found the countryside pretty well settled by Native inhabitants, with fields, roads, and hamlets.

If you had paddled the river in frontier times, you'd have encountered dugout canoes, plank pirogues, log rafts, flatboats, keelboats, and shantyboats. Later, steamboats came along, littering the bottom with their wrecks, often due to fire from overheated boilers. Nowadays, in addition to towboats pushing barges, you'll encounter flat-bottom fishing boats, work boats servicing the usually stationary government dredges that keep the channel clear, paddlewheel cruise boats, moored gambling boats, and perhaps the occasional canoe, kayak, or yacht. All of these share the river with abundant birdlife such as white pelicans, hawks, seagulls, terns, ducks, geese, and turkeys as well as herds of deer and wild hogs, beavers watching from bank holes, and foxes.

A wooden canoe pulled into the shallows as a Mississippi River barge passes

In 1984, one father and son traveled pioneer-style from Idaho to New Orleans. The late Bob Hardison and his thirteen-year-old son Casey crossed the continent Lewis-and-Clark style wearing buckskins and carrying muzzle-loading weapons and other old-timey accoutrements. Traveling up the Spokane River, across Lake Coeur d'Alene and Lake Pend Oreille, and up Clark Fork River to the Continental Divide in Montana, the pair mounted their sixteen-foot cedar canoe to a homemade trolley, erected a mast and canvas, and literally sailed across the divide, walking alongside it. They struck the Jefferson River, floating into the headwaters of the Missouri, down into the Mississippi, and all the way to New Orleans.

CURRENTS AND TOWBOATS

The current of the Mississippi is so strong that paddlecraft headed downstream can easily cover twenty to thirty-five miles a day, while paddlers intent on making time could conceivably cover seventy-five to one hundred miles. Mississippi author Scott B. Williams averaged fifty miles a day in a sea kayak when he paddled from Minnesota to Vicksburg.

The Quapaw Canoe Company's John Ruskey prepares a camp meal.

Sometimes, upstream eddies can feel nearly as strong as the downstream flow. Dangerous whirlpools can occur where an eddy meets the main channel as the two currents collide. Whirlpools may also appear downstream from bridge pilings and rock jetties and at the mouths of rivers. Buoys marking the main river channel create miniature torrents as they bob up and down in the rushing current. Wind poses hazards, too, especially when it's out of the south against the current, whipping the river into whitecaps. The nearly constant stream of towboats pushing barges thirty or forty at a time, day and night, also contributes to the chaotic turbulence of the river.

DRIFTWOOD JOHNNIE'S RIVERGATOR GUIDE

The best source of information on paddling the Mississippi River, bar none, is John Ruskey's incredible Rivergator website (www.rivergator.org). The full title is "Rivergator: Lower Mississippi River Water Trail." The website has numerous segments on topics such as safety techniques, side trips, reading the river, avoiding towboats, and much more, along with maps and hundreds of photos. Although it's billed as a paddler's guide, it's of value to anyone who gets out on the big river, no matter the boat.

Ruskey admits right off that most people consider paddling the Mississippi River to be crazy. He writes in the introduction, "If you ask anyone who lives along the Lower Mississippi River, 'Is it safe to paddle on the Mississippi River?' the answer you're most likely to receive is, 'Are you nuts? Have you lost your mind? It's crazy to paddle on the Mississippi River! You won't come back!'"

He goes on: "Is this right? Well, yes—and no. Yes, the Mississippi River is notoriously hazardous. And yes, unfortunately a lot of people have gone out and not come back. The river and its tributaries have probably claimed more lives than all other rivers in North America put together. But, no, it's not crazy. Maybe it could be considered extreme. After all we're talking about the biggest volume river in this quadrant of the planet! You have to do it right."

Ruskey compares it to paddling places like the Great Lakes or the Colorado River through the Grand Canyon, or to climbing high mountains—dangerous but doable with the right know-how and equipment.

> John Ruskey began giving guided canoe tours on the Mississippi in 1992 and opened the Quapaw Canoe Company in Clarksdale in 1998. Ruskey, nicknamed "Driftwood Johnnie," is now considered a world-class expert on the Mississippi River. He has been featured in magazines such as *National Geographic Adventure*, *Outside*, and *Reader's Digest*. His customers come from all over the world to float the big river. He's formed a nonprofit organization, the Lower Mississippi River Foundation, to promote and preserve the river, and hosts a student apprenticeship program known as the Mighty Quapaws. The foundation's main work since completion of the Rivergator guide is producing the annual Mississippi River summer camps—the first-ever youth camps held entirely on the biggest river in North America. Ruskey has also taught workshops on building dugout canoes as far away as Washington State—and he is a talented blues musician, watercolor artist, mapmaker, and writer, having written articles, blogs, and a book.

> Black bears and white-tailed deer have been known to swim from one side of the river to the other. In 2010, Melanie Hill and Alex Mobley donned wetsuits and swam a mile and a half across the Mississippi River, with Ruskey—who has performed the feat himself more than once—filming from a nearby rescue boat.

> Ruskey acquired his knowledge the hard way. As a young man from Colorado, he rafted the Mississippi River—until he collided with a pylon. "After a five-month journey from Minnesota's North Woods in 1982–83 my best friend and I wrecked our 12 × 24–foot raft on a pylon supporting a TVA power line," he writes. "The snarling water wrapped our 'invincible' raft around the base of the tower and snapped it like a potato chip. It was February and we weren't in wetsuits. I shouldn't even be alive now to tell this story." Helping other people avoid such a fate is part of his reason for producing the Rivergator guide.

Ruskey said he considered writing a conventional guidebook at first. "But somehow, the more I got into it, the more I saw and realized what's there, and it just seemed a disservice to the river not to do a really good job," he said. "It's the Mississippi, and it seems like the Mississippi deserved as much attention as I could feasibly give and my family would allow me to."

> The Quapaw Canoe Company is named after the Quapaw people who inhabited the lower Mississippi River region. Quapaw is a Sioux word referring to "the people who went downstream," as opposed to Omaha, which means "the people who went upstream." The Quapaw and the Omaha were descended from the same Sioux-speaking group that lived in the Ohio River Valley. "I've heard and read that a fog descended on the last of the Siouxan peoples migrating down the Ohio," Ruskey said. "They missed the Mississippi confluence in the fog and kept going south. Hence, they became the Quapaw, the 'downstream people.'" Another legend has it that when the tribe migrated down the Ohio and got to the Mississippi River, some chose to go upstream and some downstream. Regardless, Ruskey says he feels a kinship with the Quapaw since they preferred the lower Mississippi.

Ruskey has also produced a series of colorful, artistic maps that accompany the Rivergator guide. The maps show a creative spirit reminiscent of the great Mississippi nature artist Walter Anderson—his biggest artistic influence—and a level of detail that recalls Mark Twain's *Life on the Mississippi*. To make his maps, Ruskey started by tracing the course of the river from US Geological Survey maps and double-checked them with Google Earth maps and aerial photos. Then came the art. "The last layer, which no one else can add to a project like this, is our personal experience on the river, seeing which channels are actually open and which actually exist," Ruskey said. "And feel, too. Like any maps, these are interpretations of what's there."

The maps, which come in a variety of sizes and are for sale on Ruskey's website, are on waterproof paper that can be rolled or folded. "I got the coloring from my many years of watercolor paintings of landscapes on the river," Ruskey said. "It's taken me almost two decades to come up with a palette that to me comes close to getting the colors and the feels of the landscape of the lower Mississippi River." He painted a base map of the river from St. Louis to the Gulf of Mexico. Separate maps break the river into sections.

> While relatively few people paddle the Mississippi, many anglers fish the river in motorboats. The fishing can be good if you know what to look for. The best action is often when the river is on a slow fall. When it's rising, the fish spread out and are less likely to bite. Try for catfish in areas where grain is loaded onto barges—such as Friars Point, Helena, Clarksdale, Rosedale, Greenville, and Mayersville. Catfish lurk near the bottom and will take worms or cut bait. Or use large silver or gray crankbaits to catch white and striped bass in places where water spills over rock dikes. White bass feed in schools and typically weigh from half a pound to two pounds. If you are after bream, head up oxbow lakes such as Lake Ferguson at Greenville and fish in the willow flats. The Lower Mississippi River Conservation Committee has an informative Mississippi River fishing guide that can be found at lmrcc.org.

OXBOW LAKES

Scattered here and there along the Mississippi River are crescent-shaped oxbow lakes formed when old meanders were cut off from the main flow of the river. These oxbows are realms of sugarloaf bluffs, flat beanfields, cypress trees, and Spanish moss; of white egrets, plopping turtles, thrashing gar, and catfish rolling slowly over in the murk. Many fishermen drive considerable distances to the string of lakes that lie alongside the Mississippi like the river's old footprints.

Major oxbows from north to south include Moon Lake, Desoto Lake, Lake Beulah, Lake Bolivar, Lake Ferguson at Greenville, Lake Lee, Lake Washington,

A shady, green backwater of the Mississippi River

Eagle Lake (plus nearby Chotard and Albemarle), and Lake Mary—and that's just in Mississippi.

There are two categories of oxbow: those still connected with the river if only seasonally, and those that are completely separate. "Lake Mary and Chotard and Larto and Deer Park are still controlled by the river, so you have favorable conditions sometimes and unfavorable conditions sometimes," said oxbow fisherman Marty Bass of Pike County. "St. John, Concordia, Bruin are separate from the river, so you have favorable conditions all year round for people who want [fishing] camps. They're cleaner lakes to me. They hardly ever get muddy. At Larto and Deer Park, people have no control. You can't go over there and build you a nice camp and plant you some St. Augustine grass and some yard plants and have it work."

Every spring the Mississippi River rises and spills over into the connected lakes via runouts or passes, recharging the fish population. While the water is high, catfishing is at its best as anglers set trotlines in areas that are normally dry. In April or May the river begins to drop, and the outflow of water stirs up the white perch, bream, and bass in those lakes. At least that's how it usually goes. Some years, to fishermen's dismay, the river stays up well into the summer.

MISSISSIPPI RIVER TOWNS

The northernmost portal to the Magnolia State's share of the Mississippi River is Mud Island Harbor at the foot of Beale Street in Memphis. As with most cities located on the riverbank, there are landings in the downtown vicinity. In fact, there are boat take-outs all along the river, but many are remote and seasonal, hard to find, and subject to flooding in high water. The surest stopping points are the cities of Helena, Arkansas; Mississippi's Rosedale, Greenville, Vicksburg, and Natchez; and Saint Francisville, Louisiana.

Downriver from Memphis, Tunica, Mississippi, is the first town of any size. Although it's located several miles from the river, it has quite a presence by the water with casinos and Tunica River Park, which includes a nature trail, observation tower, riverboat tours, and museum.

> Tunica was named for the Tunica Indians, who fled their Delta home as settlers encroached in the 1700s and sought refuge in southwest Mississippi. The Houma Indians took them in, only to be massacred and driven south to the vicinity of modern-day Houma, Louisiana. The Tunicas took over their turf, including the portion of southwest Wilkinson County and adjoining Louisiana now known as Tunica Hills.

South of Tunica lies a former port town that was once both the county seat of Coahoma County and the largest cotton-shipping port south of Memphis—Friars Point Landing. Although its heyday as a cotton port is long vanished, Friars Point remains one of the few sites in the Mississippi Delta with public access to the river. Friars Point is still alive and kicking, but the population is dwindling, and this once-booming port may be headed for ghost-town status. Probably the only thing keeping anyone's mind on Friars Point after the demise of King Cotton is the fact that numerous writers and musicians have referenced the town in their works—including William Faulkner, Tennessee Williams, Robert Johnson, Muddy Waters, and Sonny Boy Williamson. Friars Point is also the birthplace of famous country musician Conway Twitty.

A little farther south along Highway 61, the famous Blues Highway, lies Clarksdale, Mississippi. The Delta Blues Museum there features photos, 78-speed records, old guitars, even a life-size figure of the late bluesman Muddy Waters. A chart lists blues musicians from towns and counties throughout the state.

There's also a Delta blues archive, and an after-school educational program oriented toward Mississippi Delta youth but open to anybody. Local juke joints help keep the blues music alive with nightly live music offerings.

About fifty meandering river miles downstream of Clarksdale, but barely thirty miles as the crow flies, is Rosedale—home of Great River Road State Park, which pays tribute to the historic route that parallels the river from its headwaters to the Gulf of Mexico. In Mississippi, the Great River Road follows Highway 61 in the north, picks up Highway 1 in the middle, then rejoins 61 through Vicksburg, Natchez, and into Louisiana.

Farther south from Clarksdale, Greenville is home of the renowned Delta Blues Festival and the Hot Tamale Festival. Greenville is also known for its barbecue; just follow the smell of hickory smoke.

Another former port town of note is Mayersville. Originally known as Gipson's Landing, this spot south of Greenville was a hub for cotton speculators, saloon owners and patrons, riverboat gamblers, and showboat thespians throughout the 1800s. After the historic flood of 1927, a newly built flood control structure cut the town off from the river and ended its status as a port. Mayersville is also notable because it was there in the 1970s that civil rights activist, politician, and diplomat Unita Blackwell became the first Black female mayor of a city in Mississippi.

Vicksburg lies at the southern end of the floodplain that is typically called the Mississippi Delta and at the northern end of the loess (fine, crumbly soil) bluffs section of the river. The city is perched atop a bluff, which made it nearly impregnable during the Civil War. It took a tremendous amount of force and strategy before General Ulysses S. Grant's troops could capture it. Vicksburg National Military Park and Cemetery tells the story and also features a display of the USS *Cairo*, a Union ironclad vessel sunk during the war and later raised and restored.

> Vicksburg has a working scale-model replica of the Mississippi River and beautiful murals on the flood wall. Plus, there's the Biedenharn Coca-Cola Museum, located in the building where Coke was first bottled in 1894.

Grand Gulf Military State Park thirty miles downriver near Port Gibson provides a fascinating history of the area, as well as a campground. There's a public boat ramp a few miles from the park in the Claiborne County port, along with the Grand Gulf Nuclear Power Plant.

GHOST TOWNS AND RUINS

Between Port Gibson and Natchez, old county roads leading west of Highway 61 take sightseers deep into the past. The roads sometimes seem more like creeks—narrow, crooked, uneven, with steep banks and leafy ceilings. Like creeks, they once led ultimately to the Mississippi River. But the big river has long since moved west, leaving historical wonders behind—like the village of Rodney, the ruins of Windsor, and the Greek Revival Bethel Presbyterian Church.

Windsor was a magnificent mansion overlooking the Mississippi River when it still ran under the edge of these bluffs. The river is now more than two miles to the west, having changed course in the 1800s, as rivers are wont to do.

A short distance away, on the more modern Highway 552 north of Alcorn State University, stands Bethel Presbyterian Church, built in 1845 in Greek Revival architectural style. Its faded white walls give it a ghostly, Gothic look. The church is open to the public, with a guest register and plenty of brochures in the foyer. Beyond is a stark sanctuary with concrete floors, old pews, and a piano.

Rodney was once considered a riverside town with commercial potential equal to that of Baton Rouge until the river shifted away, leaving the community high and dry. Dr. Rush Nutt of Rodney ushered in the era of southern dominance in the cotton industry when he invented the steam-powered cotton gin.

> Fire seems to be the natural enemy of antebellum homes. Windsor survived the Civil War but burned in 1890 when someone dropped a cigarette. The only things left are twenty-three gigantic Corinthian columns amid the deep woods. Dr. Rush Nutt's Rodney home, named Laurel Hill, stood till 1982, when it burned while being restored.

Another of Rodney's claims to fame was Oakland College, the first US college south of Tennessee to confer a liberal arts baccalaureate degree. It operated for more than thirty years until it was shut down during the Civil War. After the war, Oakland College was never reopened, but it gave birth to two institutions that lasted through the twentieth century and beyond—Historically Black Alcorn University (now Alcorn State), and Chamberlain Hunt Academy.

The road from Port Gibson to Rodney takes a long downhill plunge through eroded, vine-covered loess bluffs to what is now almost a ghost town. To the left stands an old house next to a boarded-up country store with an old-timey rusted gas pump. Up ahead to the left beyond a pasture, a vine-covered brick building looms hollow-eyed over on a lane leading to an old white church with a rounded metal cupola roof. No sign identifies it, and the church looks abandoned. Off to the right stand more sagging buildings, a large camphouse with a screened-in porch and barking dog—and the original Rodney Presbyterian Church.

> Chamberlain Hunt Academy at Port Gibson had a long tenure as a military boarding school with a reputation for academic excellence. Several famous alumni, including Louisiana governor John Parker and Olympic runner Donald Scott, matriculated at Chamberlain Hunt, as did a couple of notably infamous (by association) alumni—Lee Harvey Oswald's brother and stepbrother. After the JFK assassination, Chamberlain Hunt Academy made it abundantly clear in a public statement that Lee Oswald himself had never attended school there.

The brick building once faced the Mississippi River but now gazes sadly at shacks and willow thickets. Although the church is privately owned, it's on the National Register of Historic Places and the Windsor Battlefield Tour, and several markers around it tell the story. French explorers on the Mississippi River called the spot Petit Gulf, distinct from Grand Gulf a short distance to the north. It was settled in the late 1700s and incorporated as Rodney in 1828, after territorial judge Thomas Rodney. The Presbyterian church was built that same year. Located advantageously with a riverboat landing, the town grew to encompass thirty-five stores, a bank, a newspaper, and five hundred residents.

> In September 1863 during the Civil War, the Union gunboat USS *Rattler* anchored offshore, and the Presbyterian pastor invited its men to church. The captain and eighteen crew members attended. A local Confederate cavalry heard about the visit, rode in, and captured the men. When news reached the *Rattler*, the remaining crewmen began bombarding the town. The Rebels sent word they'd hang the prisoners if the shelling didn't stop, and the *Rattler* backed off. A cannonball remains lodged in the church's front wall to this day. Union troops got their revenge the following year by plundering Rodney, but that same winter the USS *Rattler* was driven aground in Grand Gulf by a strong wind and sank.

Cholera and yellow fever dealt Rodney serious blows in the 1850s, and then came the Civil War in the 1860s. In the aftermath of the war, a sandbar formed in the Mississippi River, diverting its course to the west. Things went downhill for Rodney from there. In 1869, fire swept through the town, destroying most of its buildings. When a railroad came through well to the east in the 1880s, Rodney lost all commercial appeal and was officially abolished in 1930. Now the main industries are farming and hunting, judging by the number of camps scattered around the area and the big farms farther on.

A gravel road continues south of town along the edge of the bluffs toward the Potkopinu Trail segment of the old sunken Natchez Trace. Potkopinu is a Natchez Indian word for "little valley." Off to the west of this severely rutted gravel road stretches a vast farm field that was once the bottom of the Mississippi River.

> North of Rodney and west of Port Gibson once lay Bruinsburg. Built in the 1700s by an Irish settler at the confluence of Bayou Pierre and the Mississippi River, little Bruinsburg would play a big role in the Civil War when General Grant crossed the Mississippi River there with twenty thousand Union soldiers to besiege the Gibraltar of the Confederacy at Vicksburg. Within two years of Grant's landing, the once prominent port town of Bruinsburg was abandoned. Now it lies on private land, and the only remaining reference to it is a historical marker on Church Street in Port Gibson that reads, "Bruinsburg: About fourteen miles west at the mouth of Bayou Pierre is the old river port settled by Peter Bryan Bruin in 1788. It was visited by Aaron Burr in 1807. Grant landed there in the Vicksburg Campaign of 1863."

OLD NATCHEZ

Like Vicksburg, Natchez stands on a towering bluff with only a narrow strip called Natchez Under-the-Hill situated by the water below the bluff. The downtown area and Natchez Under-the-Hill maintain a historic feel with carriage rides, antebellum homes, and other old buildings. Old Natchez is a lot like the New Orleans French Quarter but without the big-city feel. Founded by the French in 1716, Natchez is actually two years older than New Orleans—though of course Native Americans lived here long before there was a town.

> The original European-descended American settlement at what is now Natchez was known as Fort Rosalie, established in 1716 and renamed some fifteen years later. The name Natchez (pronounced NATCH-es) is derived from the name of the dominant Native American tribe that inhabited the area at the time of the Spanish and French explorers. An early gazetteer states that the name refers to "the sunset tribe," but that and other etymologies such as "to break off," or "running man," or "salty" are now considered unlikely.

In frontier days, Natchez-Under-the-Hill was a mile wide and bustling with commerce. Now the Mississippi River here has crept eastward—four hundred yards since 1800—leaving only a narrow strip of land with a couple of restaurants, a gift shop, a saloon, some old buildings, and a public boat ramp. A riverboat casino is usually docked here as well.

Up on the bluff, the town does a brilliant job of showcasing the river with the Natchez Trail along the bluff. The paved walkway along the top of the two-hundred-foot-tall bluff offers sweeping views of the river and the Louisiana lowlands. The walkway is lined with benches, historical markers, and beautiful old crepe myrtles. At each end, the trail drops down to a lower path at the base of the bluff so you can walk a loop. At the south end is a park on the bluff with benches, picnic tables, and live oak trees where people sit in the shade soaking in the river view and breeze. To the south stretches the Highway 84 bridge.

> Across the river from Natchez, Vidalia, Louisiana, has its own river walk closer to the water's edge. Vidalia was the setting for a notorious frontier fight when Jim Bowie killed Major Norris Wright in an 1827 sandbar duel that escalated into a brawl, leaving two men dead and two seriously wounded. Both Bowie and his knife gained nationwide fame from the incident.

DEEP HISTORY

Looking out from the bluffs above Natchez Under-the-Hill, it's possible to imagine how far floodwaters extended in pre-levee days, or even in post-levee days when the man-made banks couldn't hold back the waters, such as in the Great Flood of 1927.

One of the most gripping accounts of such conditions is in the appendix to Mark Twain's *Life on the Mississippi*, where he presents newspaper accounts of the flood of 1882 when waters extended from Natchez to Catahoula Lake, Louisiana, more than fifty miles away. A look at a map makes this understandable. The Red River flows southeast across Louisiana, absorbing the Black, which in turn has gathered the Ouachita, Tensas, and Little Rivers, among others. Whenever the Mississippi River would flood all these streams did the same, forming a sheet of brown water from the Mississippi bluffs all the way to the edge of the piney hills in central Louisiana.

Reading about the human tragedy resulting from such floods makes it easy to understand why society has tried to master the Mississippi River with levees, dredging, and other projects. Native Americans like the Natchez Indians made far smaller but nonetheless lasting changes to the landscape by building mounds.

The Natchez Indians first enter recorded history in the 1540s when they made Hernando de Soto's fearsome, gold-seeking Spanish explorers flee like scalded dogs. The Spaniards, so mighty on shore with their blunderbusses, armor, and war dogs, were out of their element on the water, where the Indians could harass their cumbersome boats with hundreds of swift dugout canoes. The Natchez chief, Quigualtam, left no doubt as to his tribe's military superiority when his navy chased the Spaniards downstream and out of Natchez territory, which then stretched from modern-day Greenville to Fort Adams.

In 1699, Pierre Le Moyne, Sieur d'Iberville, arrived and found the countryside settled by Native inhabitants, with fields, roads, and hamlets. By this time, the Natchez Indians were much diminished by the advent of European illnesses. By the end of the seventeenth century, some four thousand Natchez lived in about ten villages east of the modern-day town, ruled by the Great Sun, who lived in a 45-by-25-foot cabin on a 10-foot-high earth mound.

The French settled in the midst of them, farming and trading. By 1729, some four hundred Frenchmen and two hundred Africans were living around what is now the town of Natchez. The once-mighty Natchez Indians found themselves in a subservient position. That made for inevitable tensions, and when they arose, the French responded with an iron fist. In November 1729, the Natchez rose up and massacred the settlers. Their uprising encouraged the Yazoo Indians upriver to do the same on a smaller scale. These massacres were as shocking to the French as the September 11, 2001, terrorist attacks were to modern Americans, and the French reacted much as the Americans did after 9/11—by going on the attack.

From then on, as far as French military officials were concerned, the only good Natchez was a dead one. And because the French had numerous allies among other Indian tribes, such as the Choctaw and the Tunica, the Natchez were in dire peril. Knowing they were no longer safe in their home villages on the Mississippi River, they fled in various directions. A large contingent built a fort near Sicily Island, Louisiana, to await the inevitable reprisal by the French.

The French arrived in January 1731 in the midst of a cold, wet winter. Over the ensuing days, after many skirmishes and negotiations, some Natchez escaped while the rest surrendered. In the end, the French left with a few hundred prisoners. The remaining Natchez scattered across the South and ceased to exist as a distinct linguistic group. Their mounds still stand, along with a museum and replicas of their houses, at the Grand Village of the Natchez Indians off Highway 61 in Natchez.

A living link remains in the form of the popular powwows held at Grand Village every spring. These powwows are based on the customs of the southern Plains Indians, not southeastern tribes such as the Natchez, but most tribes do gather for various ceremonies, festivals, and dances.

WILD COUNTRY

South of Natchez lie St. Catherine Creek National Wildlife Refuge, the mouth of the Homochitto River, the flatlands around Lake Mary, and the mouth of the Buffalo River. The Buffalo used to spread out into a series of lakes east of Lake Mary, but somewhere along the line it turned north into the Old Homochitto River, which was the channel of the Homochitto River until the US Army Corps of Engineers rerouted it to the Mississippi in 1938. The Old Homochitto empties into Lake Mary, itself an old oxbow channel of the Mississippi.

Below the mouth of the Buffalo looms the majestic bluff where Fort Adams once stood. The bluff was visited by French explorer Robert de La Salle, who began his famous expedition down the Mississippi River in February 1682 from what is now Illinois. After forty-four days, he reached the mouth of the Red River, and on March 29 Father Zenobius Membré held Easter Mass on the high bluff on the east side of the Mississippi River—the first definite record of a Christian service in Mississippi. La Salle proceeded to the mouth of the river, and in 1698 Jesuit missionaries from Quebec arrived at Fort Adams to work among the Houma Indians, building a chapel on Blockhouse Hill, as the bluff was later called.

The church was abandoned in the early 1700s, but in 1706 Father Antoine Davion, a missionary among the Tunica Indians on the Yazoo River, moved to Fort Adams. He built a new chapel on the same spot as the first church and stayed until 1722, when the Capuchins, a French missionary legion, took over the work in the southern part of the Mississippi Valley. For years the bluff was referred to as La Roche a Davion (French for "the Rock of Davion") in honor of Father Davion. The high bluff also served as a military site—Forts Prudhomme and Assumption for the French, Fort Ferdinand for the Spanish, and Fort Adams for the United States. Fort Adams was the site of several treaties, negotiations, conspiracies, and battles.

In the Civil War, the Union stationed its gunboat USS *Chilicothe* on the river to defeat Confederate attempts to take the hill. After the war, the adjacent town thrived until the Mississippi River channel began swinging west. Now the fort is gone, the river is two miles away, and the village of Fort Adams, located on Highway 24 about twenty miles west of Woodville, barely exists.

STEAMBOAT QUEST

North of Fort Adams is a small lake marking the 1994 excavation site of a sunken steamboat. On May 8, 1837, the northbound vessel *Ben Sherrod* was engaged in a midnight race with another steamboat when it exploded and sank, killing an undetermined number of people. In addition to a cargo of cypress and cotton, records indicated a large number of coins was on board the vessel, as well as numerous items of historical interest.

Built in 1835—early in steamboating history—the 393-ton side-wheel steamboat measured 153 feet, 9 inches long, and 27 feet wide. While later steamboat models had lightweight hulls with flat bottoms and timbers well apart, the *Ben Sherrod* had curved sides and huge side timbers closely spaced, comparable to an oceangoing ship.

History buff James Moore of Woodville first heard about the *Ben Sherrod* as a fifteen-year-old boy, he told the McComb *Enterprise-Journal* in a 1994 interview. In 1980, he began a search for the site and eventually found it east of the Mississippi River, which had shifted course over the years and left the wreck buried under silt. Led by Moore and backed by the Penelore Corporation of Columbus, Mississippi, work got under way on the archaeological excavation in 1994.

To do the digging, a huge dragline crane with a six-cubic-yard bucket was shipped by barge to the riverbank below Fort Adams and "walked" overland to the site, which is over a mile from the Mississippi River. The excavation saw numerous setbacks, including frequent flooding of the site by shallow water tables in the Mississippi River floodplain.

In 2000, the vessel was found seventy feet deep in the mud, upside-down and exploded. Shortly after reaching the remains, Moore died of a heart attack while operating a backhoe at the work site. The excavation, which continued for years, uncovered a keg of nails, a couple boxes of augurs, wood drill bits, and some ceramics. The quest has since been abandoned. It remains unknown if the stash of coins was ever found.

> Across the river from Fort Adams stands a Corps of Engineers structure at Old River, Louisiana. The Red River, having absorbed all the water north Louisiana has to offer, joins the Atchafalaya River just seven miles from the Mississippi, linked by Old River. Since the Atchafalaya provides a shorter route to the sea, if left on its own it could become the main Mississippi River channel. So in 1963 the Corps built the Old River structure to control the Mississippi's flow into the Atchafalaya and provide an emergency outlet for floodwaters. During serious floods, a spillway at Morganza, Louisiana, can also be used to take pressure off the Mississippi. In 1987, the Corps added another structure near Vidalia, Louisiana. Even with all this, there is no guarantee the Mississippi River won't someday change course.

MISSISSIPPI WATERFALLS

Just downriver from Fort Adams, Clark Creek tumbles out of rugged hills known as the Devil's Backbone. The woods around the mouth of the creek are posted by a hunting club, but a short distance inland is Clark Creek Natural Area, which features waterfalls up to twenty feet tall, rugged hills and hollows, lush forest, abundant wildlife, clear streams, and bizarre clay formations. The state has built gravel walkways with wooden stairs and bridges, benches, and observation posts.

Clark Creek Natural Area has been through a lot of changes since the state purchased the property in the late 1970s. The natural area was established in 1978 as a joint effort of the Mississippi Wildlife Heritage Committee, the Nature Conservancy, the International Paper Company, the Bureau of Outdoor Recreation, David Bramlette, and the Wilkinson County Boards of Supervisors and Education. As use increased, erosion on the clay trails worsened and litter mounted, with a mini–garbage dump springing up near the entrance and beer cans left around waterfalls.

In the early 1980s, the Mississippi Department of Wildlife, Fisheries, and Parks took action. In 1982, the department posted regulations that banned camping, fires, rappelling, tree-cutting, off-road vehicles, off-trail hiking, and firearms outside hunting seasons. In 1983, volunteers from the University of

Southern Mississippi spread gravel on the trail, built wooden bridges, and installed wooden steps on steep slopes. Garbage cans were also placed in the parking area.

In 1996, the trail system was totally revamped, with fresh gravel, new bridges, stairs, observation posts, benches, even a swing at an overlook. The trail was extended; outhouses were added, and later a bathroom facility. There are even maps on stands along the path that show not only the layout but the location of waterfalls. According to the map, the seven-hundred-acre area has eleven waterfalls, though the wildlife department website claims there are fifty (it probably depends on the definition of "waterfall").

> Clark Creek Natural Area is home to at least three record trees—a world-record Mexican plum and bigleaf snowbell, and a state-record hop hornbeam.

The first waterfall on the trail is one of the best, tall and wide. Clark Creek itself is shallow, and in the summer people wade and play amid the echo of crashing water, the smell of wet clay, and the lush growth of ferns, moss, and other wet plants. It's tempting to follow the creek from here down, but that's not advisable due to the highly fragile nature of the soil. Instead, gravel trails lead over the hills with spurs down to the waterfalls. The main trail ends at a tributary to Clark Creek, where there's a cluster of waterfalls. A rarely used dirt path continues across the creek to form a four-mile loop.

Adventure on the River by Ernest Herndon

Joey Cargol's trip down the Mississippi illustrates the challenges the Big River poses to modern paddlers. In 2020, the forty-one-year-old Cargol of Gretna, Louisiana, floated the entire river in a wooden canoe.

A pilot on oceangoing ships in the Mississippi River, Cargol had already traveled the world, lived overseas, run with the bulls in Pamplona, and climbed the pyramids, among many other adventures. Since boyhood he had wanted to canoe the Mississippi. At age ten he had even drawn up a detailed itinerary of a trip.

He finally got his chance. Equipped with a seventy-three-year-old wooden canoe, Cargol launched in the headwaters at Lake Itasca, Minnesota, on May 31, 2020, following the plan he had drawn up as a boy, but things went bad from the get-go. The river was so low he had to drag the boat most of the first thirty miles, punching three holes in the hull the first day.

"It was the hardest thing I've ever done," Cargol said. "I've packed a moose up a vertical mile of mountain, blew out my guts, had to have surgery. That was nothing compared to pulling that canoe twenty-three and a half miles."

His plastic five-gallon jug also sprang a leak, leaving him without water.

"My kidneys shut down. I had to go to the emergency room," he said. "I passed out several times, fell into the water. I almost drowned. [I got] covered in leeches. After that, me and the Lord had a good coming together."

Cargol prayed for "water under my keel and water under my tongue." Almost instantly, a huge rainstorm struck. "I've said a million prayers in my life. I've never had a prayer answered within thirty seconds." He collected enough rainwater to keep on going, then found a farmhouse where he could replenish his water supplies. "I realized my path was laid out before me," he said. "Every day I had trials and tribulations. Every time there was a way through."

In hindsight, "God was preparing me for the trials and tribulations that would come ahead," Cargol said. Stretches that were supposed to be smooth churned with rapids because of low water. One night, wolves surrounded his tent, knocking into it as they sniffed around. Wake from recreational boats and towboats posed a constant hazard.

The old canoe sustained numerous cracks and punctures. Cargol patched them with epoxy, then stopped long enough to coat the vessel in fiberglass. It, too, wound up cracking. He portaged around ten dams, passed through twenty-seven locks, battled relentless headwinds, and negotiated rock weirs with raging currents.

"I came across one [weir] that was six feet wide, four feet deep, and it almost sucked me in," he said. "By the grace of God I didn't go down."

At one point he got trapped under the front of a barge, but the captain spotted him and backed up. Yet all along the way, Cargol was amazed at "how welcoming the people were up and down the Mississippi River. There's lots of river angels—people who help you out on the river."

Tropical Storm Cristobal slammed him with twelve days of twenty-knot winds. On one river lake, he was struggling to make progress in a windstorm when a trapper showed up and led him to a side canal. Another time, he had tied his canoe to a floating dock and camped on a bluff when a towboat wake swamped the canoe, strewing gear down the river. Cargol jumped in and gathered what he could.

He had envisioned paddling eight-hour days, making cozy camps, and recording his experiences in a journal. Instead he found himself paddling fourteen-hour days, often without a chance to eat. When he did eat, he sometimes dined on frogs, mussels, fish, snails, and bugs.

He carried two tents, a fifty-dollar pop-up and an expensive expedition model. The latter was destroyed in a storm, but the cheaper pop-up proved reliable and snug. By the latter part of the trip he simply lay down in the sand and slept without shelter or cover.

"I just got to that point, I was like a dog. I turned around three times and went to sleep," Cargol said.

He broke two paddles and developed arthritis in his hands but persevered until he reached the Gulf of Mexico on August 8.

"I made it. I survived it. I wouldn't change a thing," Cargol said.

THE DELTA

> The Mississippi Delta begins in the lobby of the Peabody Hotel
> in Memphis and ends on Catfish Row in Vicksburg.
>
> —DAVID L. COHN

What locals typically call the Mississippi Delta is not actually the river delta of the Mississippi River. Rather, it is the delta of the Yazoo River system, and—unlike the actual Mississippi River delta at the mouth in Louisiana—it lies within the bounds of the State of Mississippi. This alluvial floodplain is cut by a mind-boggling maze of tributaries, many of them navigable, including the Yazoo, Coldwater, Tallahatchie, Yocona, Yalobusha, and Sunflower Rivers as well as an uncountable profusion of smaller creeks, sloughs, and bayous.

Ever susceptible to spring flooding, most of these waterways have been channelized into long, straight ditches and canals, and an extensive system of levees, dams, weirs, and jetties have been constructed to try to keep the rivers and creeks in their place, tame, and out of homes and farmlands.

To the naked eye, the Delta appears flat as a pan, but it actually rises and falls gently as a result of countless years of meanderings of the Mississippi River. These rich, ridge-and-swale, Yazoo Delta soils were once covered with a lush hardwood forest, but most of these ancient trees were felled in the nineteenth century and the entire region turned into agricultural lands, first for King Cotton, and later for soybeans, corn, and sugarcane.

Navigable rivers of the Mississippi Delta

YAZOO RIVER

> [Vicksburg is] a delightful little city of emerald clad hills adorned with cedars, evergreens, and coniferous plants, where the yellow current of the Great River of Death mingles with that of the more powerful stream, the Mississippi, sweeping in arrogant beauty to the gulf.
>
> —W. C. BROWN

In its long and colorful history, the Yazoo River has accommodated everything from cypress dugouts to steamboats and from Civil War gunboats to modern barges. The Yazoo drains a vast area once covered with forests of equatorial proportion, of which there are still some formidable remnants.

The Yazoo begins at Greenwood with the confluence of the Tallahatchie and Yalobusha Rivers, and snakes southwest to the Mississippi River at Vicksburg. The

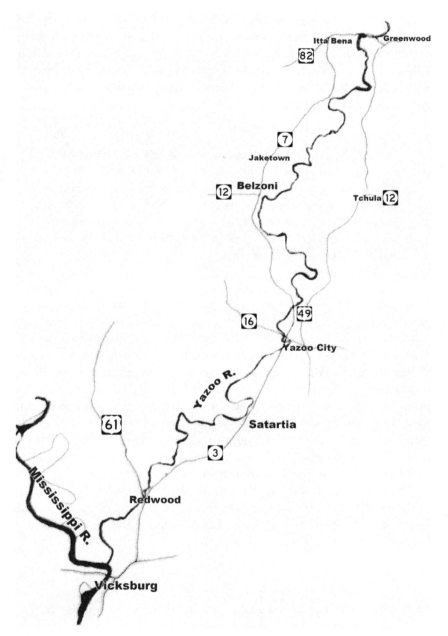

The Yazoo River

Yazoo itself stretches 169 miles long, but factoring in its longest tributaries—the Tallahatchie and Coldwater—it extends the length to nearly four hundred miles.

For the first hundred-plus miles, the Yazoo flows mainly through farmland. Below Satartia, however, portions of Delta National Forest and large hunting tracts appear, offering a hint of the mighty forests that once dominated this quintessential Delta waterway.

> The Yazoo River takes its name from the tribe that once occupied the lower reaches of the river near present-day Vicksburg. The Yazoo Indians were documented by French explorers in the early 1700s but were exterminated in war against the French and their Choctaw allies after the Natchez massacred French settlers in 1729. Nothing is known of the Yazoo language, so no one knows the original meaning of the name, but popular etymology equates "Yazoo" with "River of Death."

Barges travel the river all the way up to Greenwood, and Yazoo tributaries are navigable by smaller craft for great distances as well: 170 miles on the Big Sunflower, 60 on the Yalobusha, 40 on the Tallahatchie and its tributary the Coldwater, plus nearly 30 on the Little Tallahatchie. That doesn't take into account the upper reaches of those rivers or lesser streams such as the Yocona and Skuna.

Most of these waterways are a far cry from their original condition, having been channelized and otherwise refashioned to curtail floods, accommodate agriculture, and drain once malarial swamps. Several have been dammed to form reservoirs, whose spillways release their streams onto the flat floodplain of the Delta. On their way to the Yazoo, the rivers are thickened with a gumbo of silt seasoned with chemicals from farm fields and factories.

Given such factors, the Yazoo seems to offer little enticement for anyone but towboat pilots and catfishermen. Yet this is a river rich in history and lore—author Willie Morris and humorist Jerry Clower lived in Yazoo City, for instance—and with many attractions even yet.

> Geologists use the term "yazoo" to refer to any tributary that runs alongside a larger river for a long distance, as the Yazoo runs alongside the Mississippi. Because yazoo tributaries run parallel to a larger river, they prevent other tributaries from flowing into the larger river, just as the Yazoo River keeps the Tallahatchie, Coldwater, and Sunflower Rivers from reaching the Mississippi.

Yazoo Indians

The entire Mississippi River Valley is laced with Native American pathways and dotted with the remains and artifacts of Native American villages. Most of the waterways throughout Mississippi show evidence of habitation and activity by indigenous people, and the Yazoo is no exception. Its watershed has been the home and hunting grounds of numerous groups, including the eponymous Yazoo Indians, the Choctaw, and the Chickasaw, as well as smaller tribes.

A mound site that particularly intrigues archaeologists lies about two miles north of Belzoni right on the banks of an old channel of the Yazoo. This site, now known as Jaketown, consists of two large, wooded mounds. There were more, but the other nearby mounds were plowed for agriculture in the 1800s. The remaining Jaketown mounds are on private land and have not been excavated, but archaeologists say that Jaketown might be the oldest continuously inhabited site in Mississippi. Artifacts found near the mounds have been dated to as early as 1750 BC, making them nearly as old as the UNESCO World Heritage Site at Poverty Point, Louisiana, which is thought to have the oldest earthworks in the Western Hemisphere. Poverty Point is located across the Mississippi River from Jaketown.

The Yazoo River once had an international reputation as something of a Shangri-la. French explorers had scarcely arrived in the South before they began to realize the potential of the incredibly lush Delta soil. Speculators like John Law of France enticed settlers with claims of an agricultural paradise. Companies and government officials competed to get their hands on tracts of Yazoo farmland. Settlers discovered the land to be fabulously rich, sure enough, but also fraught with fevers and swamps—bolstering the significance of the name "River of Death."

The Dreaded Mosquito

No one is quite sure how the "River of Death" name came about, but one plausible theory is through disease—in particular, malaria and yellow fever. Since microbial and viral disease vectors leave no fossil record, researchers can't be sure whether these diseases existed in North America before Columbus. It is thought that they didn't, but certainly by the time the first European farmers cut trees and the first African slaves plowed ground, mosquito-borne illnesses were entrenched.

Malaria, which at one time spread across the United States under the colloquial name "ague," has since been relegated largely to the tropics thanks to public health campaigns against its carrier, the *Anopheles* mosquito. But as recently as the 1940s, catching malaria was the risk taken for traveling a river like the Yazoo. "Malaria," incidentally, means "bad air," due to the long-held theory that it was caused by humid nocturnal miasmas.

It wasn't the night air that caused it but the mosquitoes that rode that air, as researchers finally determined in the late 1800s. *Anopheles* mosquitoes inject their victims with malarial parasites, and *Aedes aegypti* mosquitoes spread the yellow fever virus, both of which cause illnesses characterized by chills and fever.

In the case of malaria, the parasites stay in the liver and can reemerge for years. Some strains are hard if not impossible to cure. Even prevention is problematic, as the parasites become resistant to medicines after a time. African American slaves used a concoction made from soaking red-oak bark in water to combat it, or making a tea from "yellow-top weeds." Peruvian Indians used a medicine from the bark of the tropical cinchona tree, and for centuries the essential ingredient, quinine, proved to be the most effective treatment, long before scientists knew what caused the disease.

> Mississippi physician Henry Perrine was a pioneer in the use of the wonder drug quinine. Numerous patent medicines contained it as well, and old-timers remember remedies like 666 and Grove's Chill Tonic. Quinine is a harsh drug, however, with a host of side effects including tinnitus, or ringing in the ears. Fortunately, safer alternatives were devised in the twentieth century.

In addition to treating these tropical mosquito-borne diseases, health officials mounted a huge campaign to eradicate them by draining standing water, promoting the use of screened windows and doors, and spraying the pesticide DDT to wipe out the mosquitoes.

> Although DDT was banned in the mid-1970s, the pesticide residue has a half-life of decades, which means that a tremendous amount of the overspray that washed into the Yazoo Basin over a half century ago could remain trapped in the mud at the bottom of the river and its tributaries. Environmentalists fear that maintenance dredging of rivers such as the Yazoo or Sunflower could release trapped DDT and create renewed havoc on downstream wildlife populations.

DDT turned out to have harmful side effects, especially when used in greater quantities by farmers to kill other insect pests. As it got into the food chain, DDT caused the eggshells of predatory birds such as bald eagles to break before hatching. The eagles dwindled from tens of thousands in the 1700s to fewer than 450 nesting pairs in the lower forty-eight states by the 1960s. Banning the chemical played a major role in the eagles' rebound. By 2021, they numbered more than three hundred thousand in the lower forty-eight states. The DDT ban also ended hopes—perhaps unrealistic anyway—of eradicating malaria worldwide, but not before it had disappeared from the United States.

Modern-Day Mosquitoes

Even without malaria, mosquitoes can still be hellish on the Yazoo in warm weather. Residents and visitors may get them in their mouths, ears, and nostrils, in their drinks and in their food. Even with repellents and thick clothes, human visitors may still get well chewed.

The wretchedness of this environment helps explain why people, from early settlers to modern farmers, were so eager to clear the land, drain the swamps, build levees, channelize rivers, spray chemicals—anything and everything to convert this jungle hell into habitable farmland.

"The best thing about the Yazoo, it actually makes you appreciate the [Army Corps of Engineers] for the first time in your life," said author W. Hodding Carter, who canoed the river in 2011. "There was a reason they wanted to do all those things."

At the same time, the Yazoo River has lots of charm, especially where it borders big woods. Delta National Forest and a vast adjoining tract of stockholder-owned private hunting land draw outdoorsmen galore, especially hunters seeking raccoons, wild hogs, deer, and squirrels.

Lack of access to the river itself keeps it relatively untraveled. Paddlers may see big alligators plus a host of waterfowl, especially wood ducks, herons, and egrets. Animal tracks from deer to bobcat pit the muck, while fresh-peeled beaver sticks litter the banks.

"If people want a real taste of what life was like here a couple hundred years ago, they should take this trip," Carter said. "The whole time you're on this river, you don't think you're in the Delta—the Delta as we know it. It does make you rethink what the Delta was like, what it could be like again."

Civil War on the Yazoo

The Yazoo River was the center of another sort of battle in the 1860s. As the Civil War raged across the South, Generals Ulysses S. Grant and William Tecumseh Sherman tried to use the Yazoo as a backdoor entrance to Vicksburg, because the city was thought to be impregnable from its perch atop the Mississippi

River bluffs. All of these Yazoo attempts were made in the dead of winter and early spring, when the temperature, mosquitoes, and vegetation would have been more favorable.

General Sherman made a first attempt to approach Vicksburg late in 1862. Known as the Battle of Chickasaw Bayou, this engagement ended disastrously for the Union. Steamboats dropped off more than thirty thousand Union soldiers twenty miles north of Vicksburg near Eagle Lake, where they made for the city by way of slow-moving tributaries. Although they outnumbered nearby Confederate defenders by more than two to one, Union troops became entangled in the vegetation and mired in the bayous, and wound up easy pickings for the Rebel defenders. Nearly two thousand Union soldiers were killed and more than five hundred captured or missing by the time the Union army returned to their boats.

> The Battle of Chickasaw Bayou was also known as the Battle of Walnut Hills. This area of northwest Vicksburg near the Yazoo River and Chickasaw Bayou was called "Nogales" by Spanish explorers in reference to the profusion of walnut trees. This was later anglicized to Walnut Hills, which became the Union name of the battle that the Confederates called Chickasaw Bayou.

In February 1863, Union troops blasted the Mississippi River levee at Montezuma Bend sixty miles south of Memphis and rode the water south and east across Moon Lake, Yazoo Pass, and Cassidy's Bayou to the Coldwater River, a high-water route used in the days before levees were built. This attempt to approach Vicksburg by way of the Coldwater was particularly nervy because of the sheer length and circuitousness of the route. But Union officers obviously thought that navigating an army along these paddleways was better than trying to attack Vicksburg from the Mississippi River. Confederate troops felled hundreds of trees across the tributaries, but Union soldiers painstakingly cleared them out and continued down the Coldwater and Tallahatchie toward Confederate Fort Pemberton near Greenwood. The Rebels finally had to sink a huge steamboat across the river as a barricade, and that, along with heavy fire, turned the Yankees back.

Simultaneously with the Coldwater approach, another Union contingent tried to take gunboats on a passage to the Yazoo via Steele Bayou, Deer Creek, and Rolling Fork, but they were turned back by impenetrable willow thickets and sniper fire. Union troops also made attempts to dig a canal through De

Soto Point across the Mississippi River from Vicksburg, where they could find shelter from Confederate fire while preparing to attack—another failure.

The Union was forced to try yet another, finally successful, strategy involving multiple distractions with small feints north of the city near Chickasaw Bayou and with Benjamin Grierson's 1,700 cavalry guerrillas tearing through central Mississippi disrupting supply and communication lines and creating havoc. Meanwhile, Grant marched an army southward along the Louisiana side of the Mississippi River past Vicksburg, then ferried his troops across the river to the port of Bruinsburg. From there, they made a looping approach to Vicksburg by way of Port Gibson, Raymond, Jackson, Champion Hill, and the Big Black River.

The citizens of Vicksburg, under daily artillery bombardment during the siege, found that the safest living arrangement was to dig bomb shelters under their basements or into the sides of the bluffs. Living in these caves in unsanitary conditions with nonexistent privacy, citizens and soldiers alike rapidly ran through all provisions and resorted to eating anything they could catch, be it mule, cat, rat, or songbird.

On July 2, 1863, an article in the Vicksburg *Daily Citizen* described the sweet taste of mule meat and exhorted citizens to think of mules as a premium source of food. An editorial in that same issue jibed, "[T]he great Ulysses—the Yankee Generalissimo, surnamed Grant—has expressed his intention of dining in Vicksburg on Saturday next, and celebrating the fourth of July by a grand dinner and so forth. When asked if he would invite Gen. Jo Johnston to join he said. 'No! for fear there will be a row at the table.' Ulysses must get into the city before he dines in it. The way to cook rabbit is 'first catch the rabbit.'" This issue of the paper was printed on salvaged wallpaper due to a wartime paper shortage.

> Earlier in 1863, Dr. N. B. Cloud of Savannah, Georgia, published in the periodical *Southern Field and Fireside* a description of his wife's search for a suitable wartime substitute for coffee. Union blockades had rendered coffee so expensive that southerners had tried roasting and brewing rye, ground peas, corn, and potatoes. They finally settled on roasted okra seeds as the best substitute for coffee. Can you imagine a wartime meal of mule, kitten, and okra-seed coffee?

Two days later, Confederate general John C. Pemberton surrendered Vicksburg, and the invading troops found the printing press of the *Daily Citizen* still set to print that editorial. In an unused column, the Union victors typeset their own response and had copies printed and circulated: "Two days bring about great changes, The banner of the Union floats over Vicksburg, Gen. Grant has 'caught the rabbit'; he has dined in Vicksburg, and he did bring his dinner with him. The 'Citizen' lives to see it. For the last time it appears on 'Wall-paper.' No more will it eulogize the luxury of mule-meat and fricasseed kitten—urge Southern warriors to such diet never-more."

Reworking the River

In 1876, the Mississippi River swung away from Vicksburg, leaving the waterfront stranded. The cutoff lake left in the old river channel was named Centennial, since it was formed a hundred years after the nation's founding. With the Vicksburg waterfront silting in, Congress authorized the Army Corps of Engineers to close off the natural mouth of the Yazoo and divert it through the city. The Yazoo Diversion Canal was completed in 1903—one of many man-made changes to the Yazoo and its tributaries.

From earliest settlements, landowners had built countless drainage canals and levees to ward off floods, eventually leading to the tatterdemalion landscape seen today. But it took the flood of 1927 to convert haphazard skirmishes into all-out war. In that disaster, the Mississippi River broke the levees and turned the Delta into a swirling brown sea, claiming an estimated one thousand lives in the Delta alone and costing the nation a billion dollars. One man reportedly rode a motorboat straight across from Sataria, Mississippi, to Monroe, Louisiana—a distance of more than seventy-five miles—in that flood.

Rather than bowing to the river's dominance, the government responded with ever grander schemes to thwart it. Because part of the problem was the tendency of Delta streams to flood in concert, between 1937 and 1954 the Corps of Engineers dammed the Coldwater River to form Arkabutla Lake, the Little Tallahatchie and its tributaries for Sardis Lake, the Yocona for Enid Lake, and the Skuna and Yalobusha for Grenada Lake, among other flood-control projects.

A Maze of Waterways

The fifty-three-mile Yazoo segment from Satartia to Vicksburg passes some good Delta woodlands. Access to the river is difficult at most places, including Satartia, because of steep mudbanks and a clipping current, more than might be expected from a Delta stream. Approaching barges add to the turbulence. Forest appears on the right bank eight miles below Satartia.

> On the Yazoo, bank fishermen catch flathead catfish ranging from a couple pounds to fifty or sixty. Commercial fishermen also catch buffalo fish in hoop nets. Wildlife abounds on the river, with beavers swimming about openly and coyotes yodeling at night. Mink and otter come ashore for moonlit walks, and muddy shores reveal the prints of deer, beaver, great blue heron, alligator, and wild turkey.

The old mouth of the Big Sunflower River enters from the north several miles below Satartia. A backwater levee has cut off its flow, leaving just a shallow remnant of the old river fed by other drainage canals. Across the Yazoo from the mouth of the Big Sunflower stand some wooded Indian mounds, one of which has a brick cistern on the top, apparently from an old house site. The old mouth of the Little Sunflower appears another eleven miles downriver on the right. Its shallow stretch of water is blocked off by steel gates. Another opening allows passage via the Little Sunflower into Delta National Forest, a scenic woodland route.

Haynes Bluff, once the site of the main Tunica Indian village, stands to the south some thirty-three miles below Satartia. In 1706, as tensions mounted among French, English, Chickasaws, and other tribes, the Tunicas abandoned their homes and moved to southwest Mississippi and adjoining Louisiana. A decade later, the French built a fort at Haynes Bluff. The town of Redwood grew up a couple miles south. Nowadays, heavy industries are the main feature, sucking river water out from huge pipes, pumping foul-smelling effluent back in via pipes that are often submerged and out of sight. Evidence of industrialization persists from here to Vicksburg.

Below Steele Bayou, a channel to the right shows the old route of the Yazoo before it was diverted to Vicksburg. Now it's silted in to a narrow creek connecting with a wider riverbed. At King's Point Ferry, five miles past Steele Bayou, ancient rusted barges litter the banks, reminiscent of the wrecked steamboats on the Congo River in Joseph Conrad's great river novel *Heart of Darkness*. The Yazoo is wide and slow by this point.

As the river approaches Vicksburg, the high bluff that almost thwarted Union forces looms into view. At the base, the Yazoo intersects a canal that leads from an industrial harbor on the left to the Mississippi River on the right, past rows of moored barges and a casino beside the landing at the foot of Clay Street. The River of Death swings sharply to the right into the canal, hooking past the northwest corner of Vicksburg National Military Park. From there, it is a couple of miles out to the Mississippi.

Snakes as Big as My Leg, by Patrick Parker

Anyone who hikes the trails at Vicksburg National Military Park learns that the terrain, vegetation, climate, and insects are formidable. A few years ago, members of Boy Scout Troop 124 of McComb wanted to attempt a springtime hike at the park. We picked a date at the end of March that was good with everyone's schedule, but by the time that date approached, half the Scouts had something else come up, so we put it off a week.

The next weekend it was raining, and inclement weather kept pushing the hike back week after week. The only remaining opportunity for the year, the absolute final date we would even consider walking the fourteen-mile trail, was the first weekend of June.

I called the park to verify our arrangements, and the ranger I spoke to said, "Ooh, child! You can't bring children walking out here this time of year. There's snakes as big around as my leg out there."

I asked her if the snakes were likely to be in the middle of the road, because that's where the Scouts were going to be, and she backpedaled. "Oh, I thought you were talking about the twelve-mile [Al Scheller] trail through the woods. No, a road hike should be fine." Some years later I attempted the Al Scheller Trail myself and totally agree with her that it would only be fit to hike in the uttermost dead of winter.

That first weekend of June, there was not a cloud in the sky, and the high temperature was projected to be ninety-eight degrees. We set out as soon after the crack of dawn as we could get there—a couple of adult assistants, eight Scouts, and me. That day we got a firsthand education about some of the hardships faced by soldiers in the Civil War.

We were hiking at about the same time of the year that the Siege of Vicksburg was fought, so conditions must have been similar to those of 1863—dragging men and supplies over stupendous terrain through the worst summer heat and humidity Vicksburg could offer, with greenbrier and blackberry brambles tearing at skin and clothes. At one point in the exhausting ordeal, one of our adult leaders, regardless of snakes and ticks, lay down in the grass under a shade tree near the National Cemetery and panted, "Y'all just pile dirt on me and bury me here."

We eventually got him up and moving again and made it to the halfway point—the USS Cairo Museum overlooking the Mississippi River. We had lunch, replenished our water, and soaked up some air conditioning, but that long break just made the following two-mile stretch to General

Grant's Circle at the northeast corner of the park all the more torturous. I think that was probably the longest two-mile walk of my life.

By the time we were nearing the end of the fourteen-mile trek, we had managed to stretch what should have been a seven- or eight-hour hike into eleven hours. Park rangers had started driving by every so often with worried looks on their faces, obviously wondering if we were going to be able to complete our adventure before they had to close the park gates for the night.

We did finish the hike, and the Scouts and adults stretched out in the deepening shade of the parking lot until one of the leaders said, "How about we drive around the corner to a restaurant and drink some sweet tea?" That revived every Scout instantly—the adults not so much.

As rough as this Scout troop had it, conditions were far worse for the Union soldiers who wore wool uniforms while maneuvering four hundred miles inside the enemies' homeland, breathing clouds of malarial mosquitoes and being shot at by expert marksmen. And they didn't even have the benefit of a raised parkway with mowed shoulders, so they would also have had to contend with those snakes as big around as a park ranger's leg.

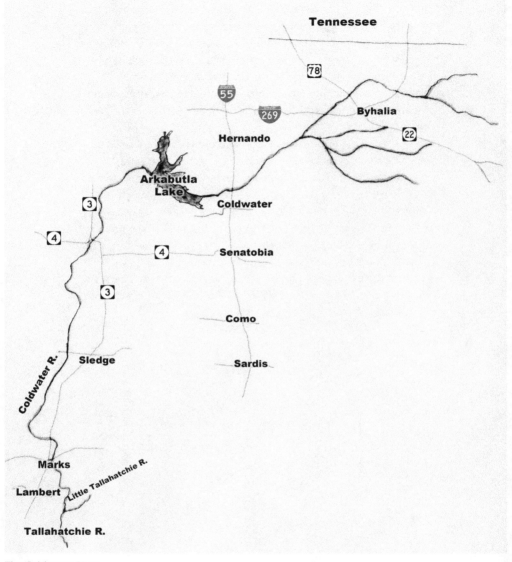

The Coldwater River

The muddy Coldwater River

COLDWATER RIVER

Men may dam it and say that they have made a lake, but it will still be a river. It will keep its nature and bide its time, like a caged animal alert for the slightest opening.

—WENDELL BERRY

It's not easy figuring out the maze of waterways that is the Mississippi Delta, but it all seems to start with the Coldwater River. At 132 miles, the Coldwater is the longest tributary of the Yazoo River, which is the Delta's defining waterway.

The Coldwater starts north of Holly Springs just ten miles south of the Tennessee state line. Drivers get a good glimpse of the Coldwater swamp from Interstate 55 near the town of the same name. For much of its length, the Coldwater River defines the sinuous, winding border between Tate and DeSoto Counties, and draws from numerous tributaries running through both.

Despite its appealing moniker, the muddy Coldwater River faces the usual Delta problems of channelization, erosion, and agriculture. Above Arkabutla Lake (Choctaw for "fine sandy bottom"), the Coldwater in places is a wide, channelized ditch; a twisty woodland creek; and a flooded deadwood swamp.

Below Arkabutla, it's a muddy, tree-lined, often channelized route through seemingly endless farmland.

Before the Mississippi River levees were built in the 1800s, during high water the river would overflow into Moon Lake, an oxbow north of Clarksdale. From there, water would flow through a bayou known as Yazoo Pass and empty into the Coldwater near the town of Rich. Yazoo Pass is a mere ten miles long but once formed an important high-water route.

After the Coldwater runs out of Arkabutla Lake, it joins the Little Tallahatchie just east of the community of Lambert to form the Tallahatchie River, which in turn joins the Yalobusha just north of Greenwood to form the Yazoo River. The Yazoo empties all these waters into the Mississippi River at Vicksburg.

A Visit to Arkabutla

Take Interstate 55 through north Mississippi and you'll pass near the four big Corps of Engineers reservoirs: Grenada, Enid, Sardis, and Arkabutla. Northernmost Arkabutla is the smallest of the four lakes at an average of eleven thousand acres.

The Corps created Arkabutla Lake by damming the Coldwater River in 1939–1943 in response to catastrophic Delta flooding. The town of Coldwater lay in the path of the reservoir, so the government moved the entire town and its seven hundred residents to its current location a mile to the south. The creation of the lake was humorously depicted in Joel and Ethan Coen's movie *O Brother, Where Art Thou?*, which was filmed in the vicinity.

Now Arkabutla Lake features excellent crappie fishing, sailing, birdwatching, RV camping, and hiking. Arkabutla is considered one of the top crappie lakes in the state, is a preferred destination for the Delta Sailing Association, and has 50-amp RV campsites, among other reasons to go.

Arkabutla Lake also offers hunting in designated areas, including a youth waterfowl hunt. There's a bird walk with a live exhibit of birds of prey. Guides lead birders along a five-mile nature trail, and hiking trails with loops of varying length near the dam wind through deep woods around the old Coldwater River bottoms.

Arkabutla Lake has hundreds of campsites, many with fine lake views. And though the lake is located thirty miles south of Memphis, it's big enough not to feel crowded.

Coldwater Road Trip, by Ernest Herndon

As my wife Angelyn and I drove back from Tennessee one springtime day, I tried to explain the maze of waterways in the Mississippi Delta in simple terms. After I ran through the routes involving the Coldwater, Arkabutla, Little Tallahatchie, Yocona, Enid, Yalobusha, Tallahatchie, and Yazoo, she said, "Would you repeat the first part?" I think she was more interested in the flowers in the towns we were driving through than in the waterways I was describing.

We detoured west of Interstate 55 so I could check out a couple of bridges for possible float trips. I had been pondering where exactly the Yazoo River heads up. That may not matter to most people, but it's the sort of thing that occupies my mind like a dog gnawing a bone.

We left the interstate at Batesville and approached the town of Marks on Highway 6 where the Coldwater passes by on the east side of town. We pulled over and I got out to take a look. The bridge offers no access to the river, but a road just south of it does.

We cruised south to the town of Lambert and turned east on Highway 322, where we entered what I think of as the true Delta—flat farm fields with only the occasional old house or barn to etch the emptiness. Always in the distance is brooding forest, reminiscent of the days when the Delta was a semiwild frontier.

An iron bridge crossed the Coldwater five miles east of Lambert, with a state boat ramp on the northwest side. Again I got out to take a look. Again, there wasn't much to see. Some crushed Budweiser cartons, woods, weeds, muddy water—the Delta.

The view was a little better from the bridge. There was no traffic, so we stopped to look. Downstream, the Coldwater ran fast and milky through a green tangle of willows. The river was high from rainwater released from Arkabutla Lake.

I looked upstream, hoping to see the mouth of the old Little Tallahatchie. My map indicated it should be in plain sight, but it wasn't. A man-made canal, the Panola Quitman Floodway, parallels the Little Tallahatchie several miles to the east, capturing most of its flow.

That's the thing about the Delta. The natural waterways are complicated enough, but the man-made changes make them infinitely more so.

We reached Highway 35 and drove south along the base of the hills at the edge of the Delta flatlands. At Charleston we climbed into the hills en route to the interstate. Angelyn marveled at the flowers, while I pondered the paddleways.

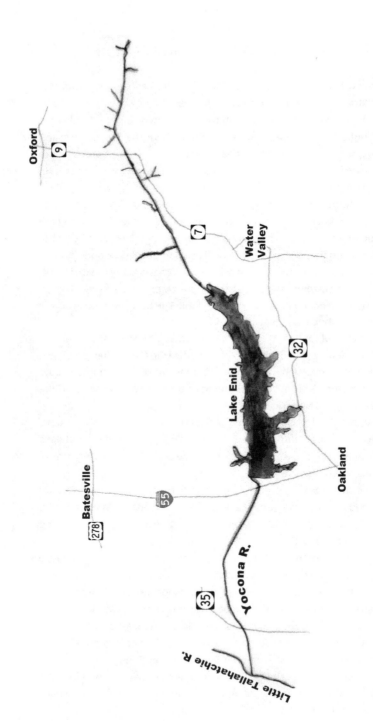

The Tallahatchie River from New Albany to Sardis Lake

TALLAHATCHIE RIVER

> You can't argue with a river, it is going to flow. You can dam it up, put it to useful purposes, deflect it, but you can't argue with it.
>
> —DEAN ACHESON

It's hard to think of the Tallahatchie River without remembering the day that Billie Joe McAllister jumped off the Tallahatchie Bridge, as Bobbie Gentry sang in her 1967 hit "Ode to Billie Joe." The song was deliberately vague about why Billie Joe jumped, though a later movie spelled out one theory. The song's plot, however, is as murky and confusing as the river itself, and that's saying a lot.

This tortured but still hauntingly beautiful Delta river, known as the Little Tallahatchie for much of its length, begins in northeast Mississippi with straight, channelized sections and runs west to Sardis Lake. Below Sardis it enjoys about twenty miles of freedom before channelization resumes with long ditches like the Panola Quitman Floodway.

> The name "Tallahatchie" comes from a Choctaw phrase that means "rocky river." Only when the Coldwater River joins it near Marks does the Little Tallahatchie become the Tallahatchie. It then connects with the Yalobusha River at Greenwood to form the Yazoo.

A Dark Past

An earlier Tallahatchie River bridge plays a central role in an infamous death that has haunted Mississippi and the nation as a whole for more than half a century—the kidnapping, torture, and killing of fourteen-year-old Emmett Till. Author Paul Hendrickson suggests in his book *Sons of Mississippi* that nearly all stories about Mississippi return eventually in some "spiritual, homing way" to Emmett Till and to the environment and circumstances of his murder—that is, to the Tallahatchie River of 1955.

That summer, young African American Emmett Till from Chicago was visiting relatives in the Delta community of Money when a twenty-one-year-old married white woman accused him of leering, whistling, or perhaps even propositioning her in the grocery store where she worked. Bystanders said they neither saw nor heard any untoward exchange between Till and the grocery

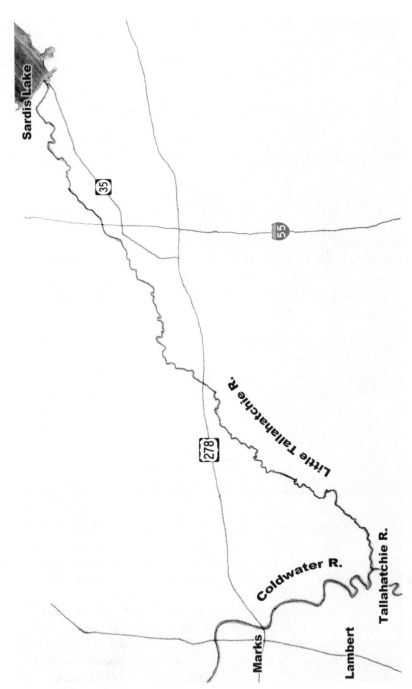

The Tallahatchie River from Sardis Lake to Marks

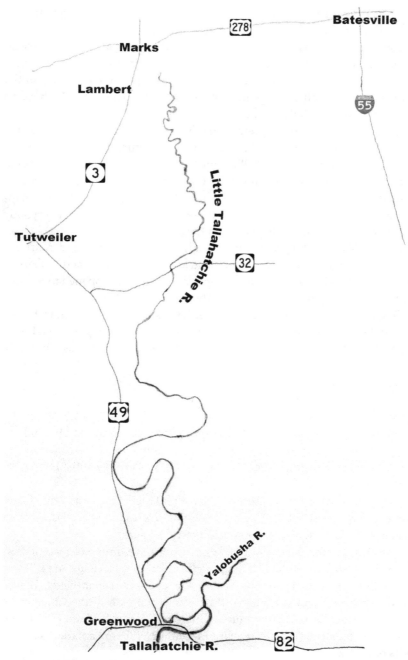

The Tallahatchie River from Marks to Greenwood

clerk. Years later she would admit in an interview that she'd exaggerated the incident when she first told her husband and his brother about it.

That night, the husband and his brother, along with a couple of African American hired hands, tracked down Till and took him from the home where he was visiting relatives. He was stripped and beaten, shot with a .45 in the head, and thrown off a bridge into Black Bayou at Glendora, just above its confluence with the Tallahatchie.

In trial, the two white men were promptly acquitted. The next year, protected by law from double jeopardy, they admitted to the murder in an interview.

Three days after the killing, Till's mutilated, waterlogged body was recovered from the Tallahatchie. When his body was returned to Chicago, his mother insisted on an open-casket funeral so the whole world could see what had happened to her son at that Tallahatchie River bridge. In her words, "Everybody needed to know what had happened to Emmett Till."

News of Till's lynching and murder catalyzed the simmering undercurrents of unrest throughout the United States and led to a much more active phase of the struggle for civil rights. "When people saw what had happened to my son, men stood up who had never stood up before," Mamie Till said.

Despite the high profile of the Till murder, his was not the first nor the last body to be disposed of in the languid waters of the Mississippi Delta. Looking back through newspaper archives, it almost seems like it was a monthly occurrence.

Little River, Big Lake

Like most Delta rivers, the Little Tallahatchie heads up in the blue hills of northeast Mississippi—near the town of Blue Mountain, in fact. Blue Mountain is home to the picturesque Blue Mountain College, a Baptist institution founded in 1873.

Tiny tributaries come together to form the Little Tallahatchie at New Albany, where canals carved out by the Corps of Engineers lead west until the stream regains some of its squiggles approaching Sardis Lake.

New Albany is home to the Tanglefoot Trail, a 43.6-mile rail-to-trail converted railroad bed in the Mississippi Hills National Heritage Area. "Here you will experience a bit of our history as you pass through fields, forests, meadows and wetlands while you travel down the path of the Chickasaws and Meriwether Lewis, or the railroad built by Colonel William C. Falkner, great-grandfather of Nobel Prize winning author William Faulkner," says the trail's official website.

The river passes through the Upper Sardis Wildlife Management Area before it reaches Sardis Lake, at 98,520 acres the largest of the four Corps of Engineers reservoirs in north Mississippi—and indeed, the largest lake in Mississippi, more than three times the size of Ross Barnett Reservoir at Jackson.

Sardis is home to several record fish, including a 27.25-pound silver carp; a 67.75-pound bighead carp; a 17.77-pound hybrid striped bass; and a 48-pound, 1-ounce longnose gar. The gar not only broke the state record of 40 pounds, it shattered the world unlimited line class record by 34 pounds.

Below the Dam

John Kyle State Park is located on the north shore of Sardis Lake near the dam. At Batesville, the river enters the true Delta flatland, where it becomes part of a maze of ditches, canals, bayous, and narrow oxbow lakes.

The Tallahatchie sports some gravel bars, which provide spawning grounds for bass. It also has some sandbars, and the water tends to be dingy rather than outright muddy. It would be clearer if landowners left more buffer zones of woods to prevent siltation. Unfortunately, there are miles of farm fields and cutovers clear to the bank, and the destructive effects are obvious to anybody on the river. Pull up under a bank and listen, and you'll likely hear the sound of dirt clods falling, since there are no tree roots to hold them intact. Even when there are trees, they're rarely more than a thin line, though there is a pine plantation or two.

Wildlife Aplenty

Considering how much the Tallahatchie has suffered from farming, logging, and Corps of Engineers projects, it's a wonder there's any wildlife at all. But, happily, its shores are typically packed with tracks. On one thin strip of mud and sand, backed by a willow thicket, you may see the parallel marks of deer, valentine-shaped hoofs of wild hogs along with their rootings, hand-like prints of raccoons, webbed hind paws of beaver, and coyote pugs and droppings. In the river, fish slap the surface. The deep, cloudy water is prime catfish habitat, while the gravel bars provide spawning grounds for bass.

At its junction with the Coldwater River just above Highway 332 near Marks, the Little Tallahatchie becomes the Tallahatchie, which goes on to join the Yalobusha River just above Greenwood to form the Yazoo. The Delta plays a mournful song at times, but who knows? Maybe even Billy Joe McAllister survived his plunge and is hiding out in the woods, biding his time, planning a comeback—just like the Tallahatchie River itself.

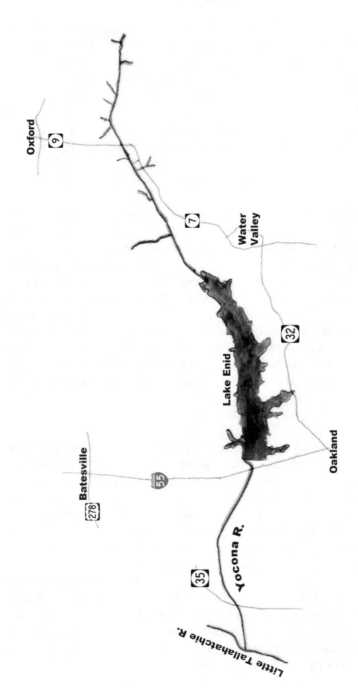

The Yocona River

YOCONA RIVER

> In the stream where you least expect it, there will be a fish.
>
> —OVID

The Yocona is a small river in an out-of-the-way part of the Mississippi Delta, but it is hardly inconsequential. The Yocona has oversized influence and issues—particularly downstream. This seventy-four-mile-long Tallahatchie tributary starts southeast of William Faulkner's hometown of Oxford and runs westward, joining the smaller Otoucalofa Creek at forty-four-thousand-acre Enid Lake. Above the lake, both the Yocona and the Otoucalofa have largely been channelized into long, straight eighty- to one-hundred-foot-wide canals for the lower fifteen or twenty miles.

> Yocona (locals pronounce it YOK-nee) is a contraction of the Chickasaw phrase *yockni catawpha hatcha*. It was the inspiration for William Faulkner's fictional setting of Yoknapatawpha County. Faulkner claimed that Yoknapatawpha translated as "water runs slow through flat land," but other sources suggest that it probably refers to "divided land" or "land torn apart," or perhaps even "plowed land." The Yocona's primary tributary, the Otoucalofa, may refer to a "chestnut tree stump" (perhaps a reference to beaver activity). One of the most evocative Indian placenames associated with the Yocona is the tiny crossroads community of Toccopola, which lies at its farthest headwaters. Etymologists think the name probably means "dismal prairie."

Enid Lake was completed in 1952 under the supervision of the Corps of Engineers. Their intent was to slow the passage of spring rains from the Yocona watershed into the Yazoo River downstream and thus help alleviate flooding. With a capacity of almost fifty-eight thousand acre-feet, the reservoir has helped to greatly diminish Delta flooding.

Enid Lake is ringed by George P. Cossar State Park, the North Mississippi Fish Hatchery, and no less than ten recreation areas. The hatchery, operated by the Mississippi Department of Wildlife, Fisheries, and Parks, raises fish to stock state lakes and other waterways. Species include magnolia crappie, Gulf Coast walleye, paddlefish, Florida and northern strain largemouth bass, triploid grass carp, and bluegill and redear bream. It's also home to a Visitor Education

Center with a ten-thousand-gallon aquarium, exhibits, art gallery, and conference room. There are ponds to raise fish and catch them.

> **The Old Bent Chief's Buried Treasure, by Patrick Parker**
>
> According to Alan Brown's book *Mississippi Legends and Lore*, in the 1830s the Yocona River was the boundary between a large, prosperous band of Chickasaw to the north and a smaller, less established tribe to the south. Apparently there was a drought one year, and the southern tribe, on the verge of starvation, sought permission from the northern chief, named Tobatubby, to hunt deer on his tribe's hunting grounds.
>
> Tobatubby, whose name means "Bent Old Chief," gave permission for them to kill fifty deer only. When the southerners crossed the Yocona, they found the hunting so rich that they accidentally killed fifty-three deer. To atone for their mistake, the southern tribe gave the three extra deer to the Bent Old Chief, and there were apparently no reprisals or repercussions.
>
> It is said that Tobatubby was also a significant figure in the world of white men. He was a wealthy planter, slave owner, and operator of a ferry across the Tallahatchie. Just before he died, he sold off several thousand acres of land and took payment in gold, which was supposedly buried with him in an Indian mound near his ferry.
>
> This buried treasure has been the subject of much speculation in Lafayette County for almost two hundred years now. One group of treasure hunters claiming to be descendants of the Bent Old Chief disappeared mysteriously one night during a dig, never to be seen again. Some say the treasure is still buried in that mound, but others say the actual site of the treasure mound was inundated by the waters of Sardis Lake.

YALOBUSHA RIVER

> There was an inevitability... which encouraged meandering...
> —ZADIE SMITH

The 128-mile Yalobusha River heads up in northeast Mississippi a short distance west of Tombigbee National Forest near the town of Houston. From its headwaters, the Yalobusha flows south for a ways before turning west, where it straightens out in channelized segments past the towns of Vardaman and Calhoun City, eventually merging with the Tallahatchie River at Greenwood to form the mighty Yazoo.

The Yalobusha and the smaller Skuna to its north come together at thirty-five-thousand-acre Grenada Lake east of Grenada. Hugh White State Park is located on the southwest shore of the Corps of Engineers reservoir, whose spillways produced the state record white bass at five pounds, six ounces.

> The Yalobusha, whose name means "tadpole place," is also home to some monster catfish. The name of the other river that feeds Grenada Lake, the Skuna, is a Choctaw word meaning "entrails" or "guts." The Skuna River heads up near the community of Algoma, another Native American word meaning "flower valley."

From the Grenada spillway, the waters of the Yalobusha gently meander right through the Lee Tartt Nature Preserve on the north side of town. Named in honor of slain narcotics agent James Lee Tartt, who was killed in a 2016 standoff near Iuka, the three-hundred-acre preserve includes critical wetland habitat in the Chakchiuma Swamp for migratory and nonmigratory birds as well as an urban forest and arboretum in Grenada.

> Holcomb, Mississippi, native Kristi Addis, on her way to winning the 1987 Miss Teen USA pageant, said that her favorite hobby was hand-grabbing catfish in the Yalobusha River. She had to explain that this meant catching fish with your hands. She expounded that the best way was to get an old bathtub to put in the river—presumably to sit in—"so that the snakes couldn't get you."

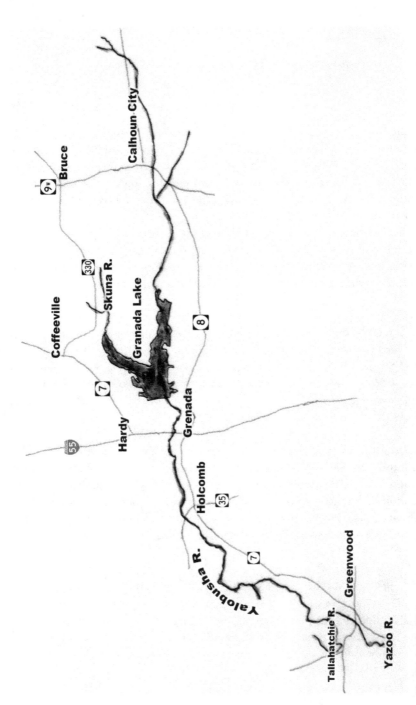

The Yalobusha River

From Grenada, the Yalobusha passes under Interstate 55 en route to Holcomb. Below Holcomb, the river enters the 9,483-acre Malmaison Wildlife Management Area, where the Yalobusha is at its prettiest.

In 1953, the Yalobusha was channelized from Grenada to its mouth at Greenwood, a distance of sixty-three miles. Over several decades the river regained its meanders, so it was dredged again, but this time only from Avalon down. That left nearly forty miles of good paddling from the dam to Avalon, including the stretch that runs through Malmaison.

Located in cotton country off Highway 7 southwest of Holcomb, the Malmaison WMA has big woods, primitive campsites, a three-mile trail, green-tree reservoirs (seasonally flooded bottomland hardwood forest), and wildlife galore. The hiking trail, created by the Greenwood Civic Club, goes uphill from the headquarters parking lot, where hills meet Delta flatland. The trail winds through land once owned by nineteenth-century mixed-blood Choctaw chief Greenwood LeFlore. Hunting is best for waterfowl, thanks to the green-tree reservoirs flooded in winter. But there are also raccoons, squirrels, wild turkeys, deer, rabbits—and coyotes, whose eerie howls echo through the woods at night.

Retired Mississippi State University fisheries professor and author Donald C. Jackson calls the Yalobusha "one of Mississippi's treasures." He should know. He has done research on all the Delta rivers as well as other state waterways. Indeed, Dr. Jackson has worked in wild places the world over, and he claims that the Delta tops them all—if people will just give it a chance.

The Malmaison Wildlife Management Area

If you float along the Yalobusha, particularly through Malmaison, it's easy to understand Dr. Jackson's enthusiasm. The banks are lined with forests of sycamore, the sun streaming through broad, green leaves on pale limbs. Birch, maple, and willow abound also. Beavers den in the banks and swim past, carrying bright, peeled sticks like kids sucking on candy canes. Overhead, red-tailed hawks, vultures, Mississippi kites, and great blue herons soar on thermal currents. In late winter, migratory waterfowl arrive like feathery tornadoes.

The Yalobusha has a good current and during low water passes some fine sandbars. Periodic releases from the reservoir partially submerge them but without muddying the water excessively. During late winter and spring, the river may get out of its banks, yet it's floatable at virtually any level. Even in flood the river is fairly docile after it tops the banks and spreads out.

Crappie school in those backwaters, while the river itself provides prime catfish habitat. The Yalobusha's Native name, meaning "tadpole place," suggests an abundance of prey for game fish. Flathead catfish—which Jackson calls "the old tiger of the murky depths"—eat only live prey, so trotline fishermen use bait such as minnows or sunfish. Blue cats and channel cats, on the other hand, eat nearly anything. All three catfish can easily top fifty pounds in size.

Several miles below Malmaison, the river has been channelized by the Corps of Engineers, and the banks form a straight levee topped by young willows. Channelization straightens out natural curves where water slows and fish thrive, cuts back on flooding that enhances crop production, and removes logs and brush where aquatic insects shelter and feed fish. Yet Delta rivers are resilient. Jackson has found that, even when channelized, they can cut new bends and regain fish populations within twenty-five years.

Paddling a Conservationist's Favorite River, by Ernest Herndon

It's easy for outdoorsmen to dismiss the Mississippi Delta. Its woods are mostly cleared, its rivers dammed and channelized. But to overlook it is a mistake, says former Mississippi Wildlife Federation Conservationist of the Year Dr. Don Jackson.

"[The Yalobusha] is one of Mississippi's treasures," Jackson says. "They just don't know it yet." Don's work takes him to wild places like Indonesia, Alaska, the Caribbean, and Latin America. But he's most passionate about the glories of his adopted state of Mississippi—particularly the Yalobusha, where he runs trotlines and hoop nets to monitor catfish populations.

I drove to the Malmaison Wildlife Management Area west of Grenada one November evening, pitched my tent in the frosty dark, and met Don the next morning over campfire coffee. He was coming back from a research project in his native state of Arkansas. He's always going somewhere, or "going crazy," as he puts it.

It didn't take long for me to understand his enthusiasm. We launched at the state boat ramp on Highway 8 just outside of Holcomb. The river flows out of Grenada Lake, and it was up, moving fast, and clearer than I expected. "When it's lower, it's lined with fine sandbars," Don said.

"These rivers are always young," he added, noting that they flood and meander so much that bankside trees don't usually survive to antiquity.

The forest was also impressive, especially after we entered the wildlife management area. Sycamores, birches, and willows predominated, their leaves singed with fall color. The Yalobusha really put on a show as we drifted. A red-tailed hawk, black vulture, and great blue heron circled in aerial aggregation. Beavers swam by with stripped sticks, diving when we got close.

We landed at the Malmaison ramp, and Don drove me down the river to see a recently channelized area. There, the bank formed a straight levee topped by grass and willow shoots. To Don, this part was a desert—but one with hope. Left alone, the river can recover. He has faith in the Delta.

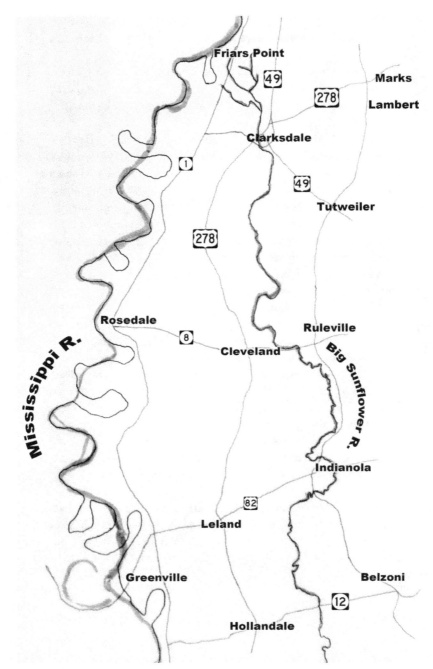

The Big Sunflower River from Friars Point to Indianola

BIG SUNFLOWER RIVER

I don't think there's anything on this planet that more trumpets life than the Sunflower.

—TIM FIRTH

The 221-mile-long Big Sunflower River is the longest of numerous waterways snaking across the Delta flats. Unlike most other Yazoo River tributaries, it doesn't start in the hills of northeast Mississippi but rather in the griddle-flat northwest corner of the state. The Big Sunflower is more of a distributary of the Mississippi River, running out of a small oxbow called Long Lake, Swan Lake, and bayous near Friars Point adjacent to the Mississippi.

The Sunflower meanders southward through the Delta past Clarksdale, Indianola, Anguilla, and Rolling Fork, where it enters Delta National Forest. It connects with the Little Sunflower River before it reaches a huge diversion canal, the Lower Auxiliary Channel, that parallels the Yazoo. Along the way, Sunflower tributaries include the Hushpuckena River (a Choctaw word for "sunflowers abound"), Quiver River, Bogue Phalia River (Choctaw for "long creek"), Silver River, Deer Creek, and Steele Bayou. It is said to be named for the fields of sunflowers that once decorated the Mississippi Delta.

> To get a feel for the Big Sunflower River, you might want to listen to some Delta blues songs such as "Moon Going Down" by Charley Patton or "Sunflower River Blues" by John Fahey. Fahey's song really captures the feel of the Sunflower with its slow rolling rhythm and its somber mood brightened by occasional sparkling notes. Listen to those songs and you'll be in the right frame of mind to contemplate the Big Sunflower River, which pulses through the heart of blues country.

Indians of the Sunflower

"The Delta has one of the richest concentrations of archaeological remains in the country," said Mississippi state archaeologist John Connaway in a 2004 *Enterprise-Journal* article detailing a dig he had recently completed near the Sunflower. Connaway and his students had unearthed a small Indian village near Clarksdale and were surprised to find that it had been a fortified site with a three-hundred-foot rectangular wooden palisade and bastions from which to defend the village.

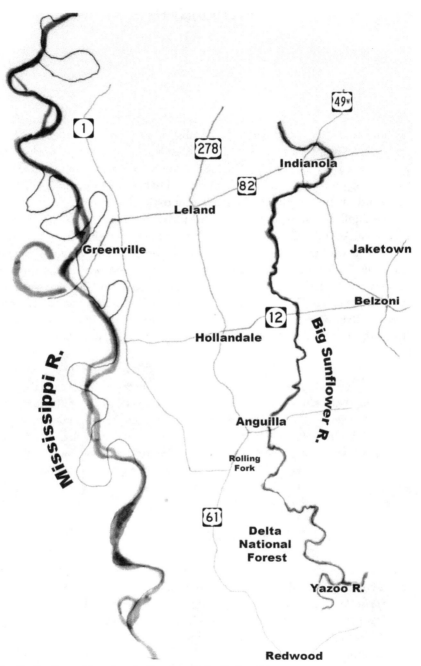

The Big Sunflower River from Indianola to Delta National Forest

Connaway said that palisades around Native American villages were rare, but this was the second they had found near Clarksdale. It was not clear whom the Indians of the Sunflower River were defending against, but Connaway hypothesized that whoever the invaders were, they would have coveted the ideal locations of these villages near the river with access to fish and other wildlife.

Despite the rarity of palisades in Native American villages of that period, the technology was not unknown. Clarksdale itself was built on the site of an ancient Mound Builder village that was protected by a short levee, or palisade.

Delta National Forest

When you drive through the Mississippi Delta along Highway 61, it's hard to imagine any forest at all amid the farm fields. Then you get a glimpse of Delta National Forest, like an island emerging from a calm sea.

Up close, the forest is a jungle of giant, vine-draped trees rising out of black muck, buzzing with mosquitoes, patrolled by cottonmouth snakes, alligators, and wild hogs. "It is one of the few hardwood forests remaining in the Mississippi Delta and the only bottomland hardwood national forest in the nation," reads a US Forest Service publication. One tree near a road measures four and a half feet in diameter, with a top high enough to demand a thirty-inch full-choke 12-gauge shotgun for knocking squirrels out. And there are bigger trees farther in.

> One of the highlights of this woodland is a stand of old-growth sweetgum, a rarity because sweetgum is an early colonizer that thrives when previously cleared lands are left fallow.

Here, the Big Sunflower is wide and currentless, punctuated by the occasional alligator. The channel forks, with Holly Bluff Cutoff recognizable by its unvarying straightness. Paddlers should take the old route of the Sunflower for a more aesthetic experience. Trees line much of the route, and there are places for picnicking and camping.

The river skirts the town of Holly Bluff and makes a sharp turn to the southwest. A few miles down, the national forest resumes on the right bank. This is catfish country, where hooks baited with shrimp are liable to bring in a mess of catfish. A nonmotorized boat is less than ideal on the lower Big Sunflower, which is wide and nearly stagnant, calling for continuous paddling. More fitting, perhaps, is a flat-bottom motorboat with equipment for catching catfish and white perch.

Paddlers looking for sandbars and clear water are simply out of luck. Instead, you should expect muddy banks and water like gravy. Stepping into the shallows beside a boat may involve sinking to your calves in mud. Knee-high rubber boots are recommended for all Delta river trips. The official name for the soil type in the Big Sunflower area is alligator dowling, better known as blue gumbo. "When it gets real soupy, real muddy, it is a blue color," a forest ranger said. Paddlers learn to lay logs down to get gear from boat to dry land. But the woods themselves are inspiring, with massive trees and abundant wildlife.

The lower portion of the Delta National Forest stretch is the finest the Big Sunflower has to offer. Here the river is narrower and has a discernible current. The Little Sunflower branches off to the north and leads into the heart of the national forest. Like many Delta waterways, it once ran clear as springwater. Although wide and blue on the map, here the Little Sunflower is a ditch, in places just a foot wide and an inch deep, conjuring visions of Humphrey Bogart towing his boat with Katharine Hepburn aboard in *The African Queen*. A better alternative is the long way around—following the Big Sunflower River in a meandering loop to the Six-Mile Cutoff, thence to the mouth of the Little Sunflower River and upstream into the national forest. Here, there are big woods with no roads or traffic. If there is any current at all, it leads upriver rather than down. The intimate-feeling stream winds five miles between oak bluffs to a Forest Service take-out.

Near the southern end of Delta National Forest, the Big Sunflower comes to a rather ignominious end. It once emptied into the Yazoo River eight miles below Satartia, but in the 1970s the Corps of Engineers completed the Yazoo Backwater Levee. The project blocked off the mouths of the Big Sunflower and Deer Creek, placed flood control structures at the Little Sunflower and Steele Bayou, and funneled all of those waters into the Lower Auxiliary Channel. The channel and levee, which roughly parallel the Yazoo to the north, aimed to protect the lower Delta from Mississippi River backwater flooding. As a result, the mouth of the Big Sunflower is silted in, shallow enough to wade. Across from the mouth of the Big Sunflower stand a pair of Indian mounds, covered in ragged forest, a haunting contrast with the miles of flat farm fields.

Home of the Blues

The Sunflower River is ground zero for the Mississippi Delta blues. After W. C. Handy "discovered" this unique music at the train stop in nearby Tutwiler, the Delta has become a sort of mecca for celebrity blues fans.

The Sunflower River Blues and Gospel Festival, which began in 1988, is held in August. Panny Mayfield—one of the founders of the festival and longtime lifestyle editor of the *Clarksdale Press Register*—writes, "In 1998 [Robert Plant] and fellow [Led] Zeppelin star Jimmy Page recorded 'Walking into Clarksdale' as a tribute to the city's music heritage as home base for early bluesmen Robert Johnson, Charley Patton, Muddy Waters, John Lee Hooker, Ike Turner, and others."

The next year, while on tour, Page and Plant returned to the Delta to visit historic blues sites including Tutwiler and Friars Point. In subsequent years, Plant often visited the Delta, seemingly on the spur of the moment, often popping into the Blues Museum unannounced. In 2009, Plant unveiled the Blues Trail Marker in Tutwiler.

One year at a festival in Drew, visitors included John Fogerty, formerly of Creedence Clearwater Revival. When it was his time to perform, he played a riff from one of his songs and compared it with Pops Staples's playing. "Now you know where I got it," Fogerty said with a grin.

Another visitor was Greenville blues harmonica player Willie Foster. "I was born on a cotton sack," he said. "My mother started having pains, and they told her to lie down on a cotton sack. But I'm still alive. Some people were born in a hospital and they didn't make it."

Reflecting on his lifetime of playing the blues, Foster said that the music became more up-tempo, easier to dance to. But it's still the blues. "I was born in the blues, I been in the blues, and I know the blues three times over—the young blues, the settle-age blues, and now I'm an old bluesman," Foster said.

> Robert Johnson's infamous "Crossroads" legend—he allegedly sold his soul to the Devil for mastery of the guitar—is centered around Dockery Plantation on the Sunflower River about thirty miles south of Clarksdale. There is much debate about the exact location of the actual crossroads, and every year visitors flock to the Delta to check out numerous widespread locales that are said to be the actual spot of the occult bargain.

Another celebrity to create a stir of excitement in the Delta was actor Morgan Freeman, who was born in Memphis and raised in nearby Charleston, Mississippi. In 2001, Freeman created a ripple of revitalization and gentrification in Clarksdale when he and his partner, Bill Luckett, opened a fine-dining restaurant named Madidi downtown. The restaurant operated for more than a decade, exposing people of the Delta to a different sort of culinary culture than they were accustomed to and serving as an anchor in Clarksdale's business district. In 2012, Madidi closed, and the building looking out over the corner of Delta

The banks of the Big Sunflower River in Clarksdale, Mississippi

and Second reopened as a posh hostel named the Auberge (think New Orleans comfort and Bohemian style but hostel prices).

When Madidi closed down, Freeman and Luckett opened a blues club a couple of blocks south on Delta Avenue next door to the Delta Blues Museum. Freeman's club was named Ground Zero as an homage to Clarksdale being traditionally considered the epicenter of the Delta blues.

The Quapaw Canoe Company—whose owner, John Ruskey, is also a blues guitarist—is also located on the bank of the Sunflower River in downtown Clarksdale.

> Morgan Freeman grew up in the Mississippi Delta around the same time as fellow Charleston native and blues legend Mose Allison. Allison's jazzy blues sound was influential in the development of musicians and bands from the Who to Jimi Hendrix, and from the Yardbirds to Jethro Tull. For a whimsical example of Allison's talent, listen to the song "Ever Since I Stole the Blues."

Most Delta juke joints aren't as fancy as the Auberge née Madidi or the Ground Zero Blues Club. In one joint, a dark, smoky room features a brightly

A dugout canoe being carved at the Quapaw Canoe Company in Clarksdale

lit pool table on one side and a blues band on the other. Customers, most of them Black, sit at tables with quart bottles of beer, bottles of whiskey in brown paper sacks, and red cans of Coca-Cola. A band belts out heavy-duty blues, interspersed with soul and rock numbers. Standby musicians replace players when they tire.

Cooled only by electric fans, the room feels ten degrees hotter than the air outside. The band begins a blues jam, slow and pulsing. The lead guitarist demonstrates his dexterity by holding the guitar behind his neck when he plays. A woman dances with arms raised. Drums sizzle, the bass throbs, and the lead guitar wails as the air fills with the sound of living blues.

Bear Hunters of Old, by Ernest Herndon

Delta National Forest and adjoining woodlands used to be renowned for its bears and its infamous bear hunters. Arguably the most influential bear hunter of all was Holt Collier (1848–1936), whose experience in treeing a bear with President Teddy Roosevelt led to the creation of "teddy bears." Collier, a former slave who fought with the Confederacy during the Civil War, shot his first bear at age ten and tallied over three thousand during the course of his lifetime.

As a hunting guide, he took Roosevelt on a bear hunt near Onward, Mississippi, in November 1902. Collier bayed a large male bear with his dogs and clubbed it with the stock of his shotgun when it mauled one of his hounds. He then roped the bear and tied it to a tree for Roosevelt to dispatch. When the president refused to shoot the defenseless animal, newspapers made much of his sporting spirit, with one writer incorrectly describing the bear as a cub. A New York store owner saw a cartoon depicting the hunt and created a stuffed animal he called a teddy bear. Collier served as Roosevelt's guide again in Louisiana in 1907. McComb author James McCafferty wrote two children's books about him: *Holt and the Teddy Bear* and *Holt and the Cowboys*. In 2004, the 1,400-acre Holt Collier National Wildlife Refuge was established on the Bogue Phalia, a Big Sunflower tributary. It is the first wildlife refuge ever to be named for an African American.

Another renowned bear hunter, Ben Lilly, was ranked with the likes of Kit Carson, Jim Bridger, and Davy Crockett. Lilly (1856–1936) was born in Alabama, raised in Mississippi, and did some farming in Louisiana before moving out west. He, too, achieved national renown after serving as a hunting guide for President Theodore Roosevelt. His story is told in the 1950 biography *The Ben Lilly Legend* by J. Frank Dobie. One of Lilly's haunts was the Sunflower River swamps, where he slew sixty-five bears. Among Lilly's many alleged feats, it is said that he could hoist a hundred-pound anvil in one hand, sling a five-hundred-pound bale of cotton over his back, execute a standing long jump surpassing the then–national record of almost twelve feet, and stand in a barrel and leap clear out without touching the sides. He was expert with rifle, knife, and cow whip, though he mainly took out his aggressions on beasts, not men, being reportedly of a "mild, Christianlike" temperament, as one observer put it.

Then there was Robert Eager Bobo (1847–1902). Bobo hunted on horseback with a pack of hounds. As McCafferty reported in his book *The Bear Hunter: The Life and Times of Robert Eager Bobo in the Canebrakes of the Old South*, Bobo claimed to have killed 304 bears, 47 wildcats, 21 deer, and 17 panthers in a single season. People traveled from far and wide to hunt Delta bears back then, and Bobo was a celebrity. Outdoor writers made him nationally famous in magazines of the day.

Those writers described oak trees five feet in diameter reaching sixty or seventy feet to the first limb. Some sycamores and cottonwoods were ten feet in diameter, and one yellow poplar measured twelve feet thick. Canebrakes stretched for miles. Wild animals of all sorts were incredibly abundant, and at the top of the food chain was the black bear. The bears, which weighed from 400 to 680 pounds, raided cornfields and hogs. For hunters intrepid enough to kill them, they provided an important source of meat and oil.

Bears are scarce in the Delta these days, but not nonexistent, thanks in large part to the Black Bear Conservation Program and its offshoot, the Mississippi Black Bear Program. Now there are enough that "bear crossing" signs are posted on Highway 61.

Navigable rivers of southwest Mississippi

SOUTHWEST MISSISSIPPI

Between every two pine trees is a doorway to a new world.

−JOHN MUIR

South of Vicksburg, the terrain of western Mississippi changes from gently rippling alluvial floodplain to tall loess bluffs, in places hundreds of feet high. This elevation makes the area perfect for the growth of tall, piney, highland woods, in addition to the hardwood bottoms of the Delta lowlands.

The rivers and creeks of southwest Mississippi are quite variable in their character. Bayou Pierre wallows its way through rocky hollows until it cuts through the loess bluffs into the southernmost reaches of the floodplain between Vicksburg and Natchez.

The Homochitto River, which drains the southwest corner of the state, usually trickles inches deep through sandy washes, but within hours it can become a raging flood with sucking, popping quicksand.

The Tangipahoa River, being more centrally located and somewhat insulated from the hydrological extremes of the Mississippi River, meanders around and through frequent logjams in the hardwood bottoms of southern Mississippi, gaining size in southeast Louisiana until it pours out into the Gulf of Mexico.

Also worth mentioning are the Amite and Tickfaw Rivers, which are logjammed creeks in Mississippi before opening up in Louisiana, and the Buffalo River, which heads up near Centreville and flows west into the Mississippi River near Lake Mary. None of these creeks are navigable in Mississippi.

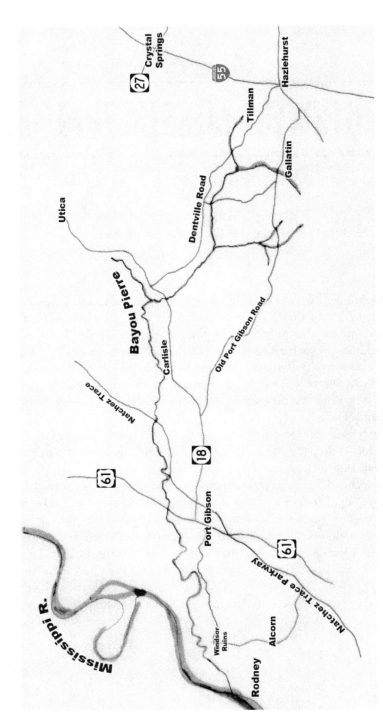

Bayou Pierre

BAYOU PIERRE

If it weren't for the rocks in its bed, the stream would have no song.

—CARL PERKINS

Just north of the uppermost reaches of the Homochitto River and its namesake national forest lie Copiah and Claiborne Counties, through which Bayou Pierre meanders.

Bayou Pierre rises from the high ground of Lincoln County and is joined by the outflows of four tiny recreational lakes in Copiah County—Lake Hazle, Calling Panther Lake, Lake Copiah, and Chautauqua Lake. It begins as a fast, clear creek but changes to a wide, muddy stream as it tumbles ninety-seven miles westward through piney ridges to the Mississippi River.

> Lake Chautauqua in Crystal Springs, one of the sources of Bayou Pierre, got its name indirectly from Lake Chautauqua in New York State. The New York lake's name may have been derived from a Mohawk (Iroquois) phrase meaning "place where one was lost," or it might have been a Seneca phrase referring to a "raised body." The lake in Crystal Springs was more directly named after the Chautauqua educational movement, sort of a combination of religious camp revival and Scout summer camp, which began in the late 1800s in New York and became so popular throughout the United States that President Theodore Roosevelt called it "the most American thing in America." The McComb *Enterprise-Journal* archives contain articles and advertisements for Chautauqua meetings that were held at Lake Chautauqua in Crystal Springs in the first two or three decades of the twentieth century.

Bayou Pierre was named not for some French trapper but for its rocky bed—*pierre* is French for stone and a bayou is a slow-moving river.

> The name of the county surrounding much of the headwaters of Bayou Pierre, Copiah County, comes from a Choctaw phrase meaning "calling panther," which also became the name of one of the lakes that give rise to Bayou Pierre. The stories surrounding the legend of the calling panther abound. According to one, during Choctaw days the low, swampy areas

around the head of the bayou were ruled by a fearsome wildcat. When the Choctaws surrendered the land to the US government, men began to try to build a railroad to transport the prized yellow pine timber that was being harvested in the region—but the railroad workers lived in terror of the shadowy cat that screamed at them from the swamp. Work came to a standstill until one staunch engineer named George Hazlehurst, unintimidated by the panther, walked right up to the edge of the swamp and returned the animal's blood-curdling scream. The workers rallied behind Hazlehurst, and when the panther saw that it had lost its power over the men, it faded into the forest, never to harass them again.

Unique Geology

Bayou Pierre looks like a typical southwest Mississippi stream—sandbars, bluffs, woods—but it has a secret history that ranges from ancient rocks to Civil War sites.

The late naturalist and wildlife photographer John Allen Smith of Meadville got glimpses of that history when he was researching endangered bayou darter fish. "While I was there I found a lot of petrified wood," said Smith, who also heard stories about General Ulysses S. Grant, whose army camped at Bayou Pierre before conquering Port Gibson in 1863.

"[Bayou Pierre is] a very nice example of places to go [rock] collecting," said Mississippi state geologist Mike Bograd. The river's gravel bars contain three-hundred-million-year-old clam-like fossils known as brachiopods and sea lily fossils called crinoids. They were probably washed into the area by meltwater from the north during an ice age a couple of million years ago. Then there's the clay.

"As you're walking through the stream and see interesting clays, some of these clays may be . . . deposited during the Miocene epoch, on the order of twenty million years old," Bograd said. "The interesting thing about Bayou Pierre and some of these other streams in southwest Mississippi is you do find rock layers where Miocene materials have solidified. That provides some of the little riffles or waterfalls that we might see in some parts of the state, because they're harder and don't erode. Those are very interesting and give a lot of character to the area."

Bayou Pierre's clays and clay rocks come in a variety of colors, including blue, green, orange, purple, gray, and brown. "The greens and blues are probably fresh exposures of the Miocene clays," Bograd said. "Upon exposure to the atmosphere and percolating waters and oxidation, these clays and their various constituents do weather. The reds, yellows, and browns are due to iron oxide, rusting if you will."

Other bayou features include petrified wood and geodes. On the upper reaches, "you can just stroll around and pick up pieces of petrified wood," Bograd said. "Much of it looks pretty much like a piece of wood—you can see a wood grain in it—but it feels like a piece of rock. That's because the mineral silica has replaced the organic material of the wood cell by cell."

Geologists aren't sure of the age of petrified wood, which could be anywhere from a few thousand to a few million years old. Bograd believes that Bayou Pierre's petrified wood is one or two million years old. The river's geodes are pretty, though not comparable to the huge, glittering specimens seen in rock shops. Geodes resulted from silica-rich fluids percolating through cavities in igneous rocks, leaving colorful bands of crystals. Bayou Pierre's geodes rarely exceed a few inches in diameter and tend to be cracked open. Rockhounds can best find such tidbits on the river's gravel bars. "Those are excellent places to collect because the materials have been deposited on these bars by natural processes," Bograd said. "It's been cleaned by water and by rainfall."

Native American Life

It was eons later that the Natchez Indians established their domain between the Yazoo and Homochitto Rivers, which included Bayou Pierre. "There hasn't been a lot of archaeology done along it, so not a lot is known about the area," said historian and author Jim Barnett, former director of the Grand Village of the Natchez Indians.

One thing that is known is that a new tribe, the Grigras, showed up in the late 1600s or early 1700s. "They were apparently a refugee group," Barnett said. "With the settlement of Europeans into the Southeast, a lot of tribes were being displaced very quickly. Many tribes, rather than trying to fight, would just pick up and move and form refugee groups. It was a pretty common thing for a settled, established tribe to adopt a refugee group."

That's what the Natchez did with the Grigras, who apparently established a village in the Bayou Pierre area. "They were part of the Natchez group that rebelled against the French in 1729," Barnett said. "The later war that drove the Natchez out also drove the Grigras out."

Later in the 1700s, Peter Bruin started the settlement of Bruinsburg at the mouth of Bayou Pierre. Andrew Jackson ran a store there and raced horses. Meanwhile, the town of Port Gibson flourished to the east. During the Civil War, General Grant crossed the Mississippi River from Louisiana and landed at Bruinsburg with twenty thousand troops. From there he took Port Gibson, which he called "too beautiful to burn"—and it still is. Grand Gulf Military State

Park has relics and information about local Civil War history. Point Lookout on Highway 552 west of Port Gibson overlooks Bayou Pierre and features a replica of the area's original Presbyterian log church.

Fish, Game, and Plants

The area surrounding Bayou Pierre is said to be the largest producer of southern yellow pine east of the Mississippi River and is home to a marvelous diversity of plant and animal life despite the ecological challenges the river faces. The Mississippi River keeps Bayou Pierre well stocked with fish, especially catfish. Local fishermen report blue cats and flatheads up to forty pounds on the lower bayou. Chicken liver makes a good trotline bait, and deer liver is said to be exceptional. Some anglers find the white perch fishing good in the bayou, too. Barfish, a type of bass, make their run in the spring, and though largemouth fishing is pretty sparse, anglers can pull a bass out from deep pockets.

> While plenty of people hunt and fish in the area, few take advantage of wild fruits, and even fewer gather medicinal plants, but it wasn't that way in the old days. B. A. Botkin's *A Treasury of Mississippi River Folklore* (American Legacy Press, 1955) describes numerous herbal remedies used by residents along Bayou Pierre. Saint John's wort is currently used for depression, but in earlier decades it was believed to protect people against lightning, ghosts, witches, and nightmares. It was also used to treat wounds, and dew collected from its leaves was thought to improve vision. Other Bayou Pierre folk cures include Sampson's snakeroot boiled as a tonic to enhance virility, ward off cramps, prevent snakes from biting, and improve one's skill at trading. A castor bean leaf poultice supposedly counteracted fevers, chills, headaches, and hot flashes. Devil's shoestring, a species of cross vine, was chewed and rubbed on the hands to give a man control over a woman and luck in gambling. The sensitive plant theoretically would make a person more willing to give up wicked behavior. Old-timers would chew heart leaves to soften the heart of the person they loved, or plant blue vervain, a member of the verbena family, to attract a potential sweetheart. Botkin enumerates other Bayou Pierre superstitions of interest to paddlers. Among them: Don't burn wood that pops, like sassafras, or someone may die. Don't burn wood from a tree struck by lightning. Stay away from trees that rub together in the wind and creak, as they may harbor spirits. And avoid a blooming redbud tree at night. Also called a Judas tree, it's supposedly the species Judas used to hang himself.

Biologists believe that white-tailed deer are at least as abundant now as they were when the first explorers arrived in the area. Deer played a major role in the exploration of Mississippi—and in the eventual downfall of its Native American tribes. In the 1600s, leather was used in all sorts of items, from shoes to clothes to furniture. The trade in deerskins started with a few bold explorers and adventurers swapping European goods for hides to the Indians. It ended with the Indians dependent on those goods, the deer depleted, and the land occupied by settlers. Deer, whose numbers were restored in the twentieth century, again fuel the economy as hunters spend huge amounts of money for everything from guns to four-wheel-drive vehicles to pursue them. Far from being threatened, their population has skyrocketed so much that state officials have encouraged hunters to shoot more does to deplete their numbers.

The Mighty Alligator

The American alligator is another species that was almost hunted to extinction in the early 1900s but that has, with the protection of people, rebounded successfully in recent decades. In fact, alligator numbers, too, have skyrocketed.

> Alligators abound on lower Bayou Pierre, producing a state record in 2017 when the hunting party of Tiffany Wienke of Vicksburg caught one that measured 13 feet, 7/8 inches, beating the previous record by an eighth of an inch. The alligator weighed 686 pounds and had a belly girth of 59 inches and a tail girth of 43 inches. The hunting party bagged the critter in the bayou near the Mississippi River.

Gators aren't as aggressive as their saltwater cousins the crocodiles, but they shouldn't be treated cavalierly. Indeed, crocs, gators, and caimans are among the most accomplished hunters on the planet. They rely on silence, speed, and surprise. The typical hunting strategy consists of spotting prey from a camouflaged position, ducking soundlessly underwater to approach closely, then lunging, biting, dragging the victim into the water, and spinning violently. That final lunge can span three times the reptile's body length. And once those jaws are clamped down, virtually nothing can open them.

In Africa and throughout parts of Southeast Asia and the South Pacific, humans constitute a part of crocodiles' diet. Although gators don't normally attack humans, as the two species come into contact, the odds of violence mounts. Biologists predict that as the federally protected gators live longer and hence get larger, they'll be more likely to attack.

> Alligators can reach nineteen feet in length; two-thirds that size is pretty common these days. But paddlers should be grateful they don't have any crocodilians like those that reigned eighty million years ago. *Deinosuchus*, or "Terror Crocodile," grew to thirty feet in length and weighed ten thousand pounds, according to archaeological finds in North Carolina, Texas, and Montana. The giant croc was a watery counterpart to the terrestrial T-rex, inhabiting the shallow tropical sea that covered much of North America and dining on dinosaurs like modern gators do on deer. Their era ended about sixty-five million years ago—fairly recent compared to some of the rocks along Bayou Pierre.

Texas Red and Oklahoma Kid

A 1930s outlaw called Texas Red (aka Levi George, Red Williams, or Ed Flowers) met his end at a place called Franklin Spur near Bayou Pierre. Texas Red and one of his cronies called Oklahoma Kid were staying at Red's house in Amite County. Burglaries had ensued throughout the community, and on New Year's Eve of 1939 a wild party with gunfire erupted at Red's place.

Doris Whittington Adams of Amite County was a little girl at the time. "I lived less than a mile from where this guy stayed," she said. "I passed there. I saw him a lot of times. I rode horses down there. Daddy saw him all the time. They [Texas Red and Oklahoma Kid] would be out." She said that Texas Red was a tall man, while Oklahoma Kid was short and always wore a black hat.

"Daddy was suspicious of Red. There was a lot of breaking-in going on," Adams said.

Adams remembers when a lawman, Phillip Shell, showed up at her house trying to recruit for a posse: "Phillip wanted my brother Gene to go down there and arrest Red. But Daddy said, 'Phillip, that's a dangerous man. You'd better wait till you get some law.'"

The lawman recruited Hillard Hall, and Adams's brother Gene led them to Red's house but didn't go farther.

> Don Simonton's book *Let the Devil Out* was turned into a 2021 feature movie titled *Texas Red* starring Mississippi blues musician and actor Cedric Burnside—grandson of famed Mississippi Delta blues guitarist R. L. Burnside.

"Phillip said, 'Come out with your hands up.' Well, he came out shooting, and that's how he killed the Hall boy. We heard the gunshots from our house," said Adams, who picked up other details from folks in the community later.

After the shootout, the posse found women's jewelry and clothing in the house, which were reportedly stolen from Johnny Mizell's store in Roxie. It wasn't clear whether Texas Red or Oklahoma Kid had killed Hillard Hall. Either way, the killing turned a local posse into a massive manhunt with some two hundred officers, two National Guard companies, and a team of FBI agents involved.

As the search went on over the ensuing weeks, the searchers would meet at Doris Adams's father's house. "They would gather . . . to decide where everybody was going to search. . . . Mama would make coffee. One day the men were getting ready to leave when one of their guns went off, blasting a hole in the floor. There were some scary times back then," Adams said.

Newly elected sheriff Cliff Herring offered a one-hundred-dollar reward, and reports of the fugitives started coming in from all over the state. At one point the sheriff's son, deputy Graham Herring, got a shot at Red and found blood, but later realized it might have come from Red's bare, raw feet.

Adams said Red had run out of his house without his shoes on. "That's why his feet were in such bad shape." She was referring to photos of Red's mangled feet after he was killed.

"It was an unusually cold winter with highs seldom above freezing and lows averaging eight degrees," Simonton explained in an interview. "Red's feet deteriorated and became bloody and mutilated."

On January 9, 1940, Red and Oklahoma split up at Natchez, with the Kid going west across the Mississippi River and Red heading northeast. The Mississippi River bridge was then under construction, so it's not clear how the Kid got across, possibly in disguise on a ferry. He was never heard from again, though some say he settled in Monterey, Louisiana, as a schoolteacher.

Red continued north through Harriston, Red Lick, Pattison, and Hermanville, eluding lawmen all month long—an incredible feat with hundreds in pursuit amid bitter winter weather. A story arose that he had magical powers as a shapeshifter and could turn into an animal when he needed to. In Jefferson County, he sneaked into a barn, lighted a fire to get warm, and burned the structure down. When the landowners came out to see what was happening, Red fired shots at them as he fled.

Eventually, lawmen brought in a federal marshal with bloodhounds—Forrest "Coochie" Massa from Hazlehurst. On February 3, Massa struck Red's trail and spotted him climbing out of a ravine by a railroad at Carlisle, where an old railroad bridge crossed Bayou Pierre. Massa shot Texas Red with a .351 caliber

Winchester semiautomatic rifle, mortally wounding him. Red supposedly refused to say a word before he died a short time later.

"Daddy never talked too much about it," said Massa's son in a 2017 interview. He confirmed that his dad had been a federal marshal—"he and my grandfather were involved in the pursuit of Bonnie and Clyde at one time"—but said he had gotten out of law enforcement. The younger Massa still has the rifle his father used to shoot Texas Red.

The body was taken to Fayette for identification and laid out on the town square for public viewing, "as they used to do in the old west," Simonton said. From there he was taken to Meadville. Retired Meadville dentist Dr. Coley Ratcliff said that he, his brother, and a friend went to see the body. "They had him down in the basement of the courthouse. The only thing I remember was his feet were wrapped in gunny sacks."

Mamie Halford said, "I was a little girl with big ears, and I remember sitting around listening to the older folks talk about it. When we heard he was killed, my dad brought me to the courthouse. We went up to see him. He was lying there on that cot, covered up except for his head and feet. He was a big fellow." She added, "I always heard them say they thought Oklahoma Kid was the one that killed that man. Maybe they shouldn't ought to have been chasing Texas Red."

A woman from Brookhaven who claimed to be Red's sister came to claim the body and said his real name was Ed Flowers.

Historian Simonton said it's a matter of debate whether Red was a "criminal, outlaw, terrorist, and killer," an "antihero" of the likes of Butch Cassidy and the Sundance Kid—or if he was even guilty of the crimes he was accused of. "This is not a question I can answer," Simonton concluded.

Paddling and Portaging Bayou Pierre, by Patrick Parker

My wife Elise and I had planned to double-team the river. She would drop me off at the put-in on Carter Hill Road with a kayak and drive around to the take-out at Highway 18, about eleven miles downstream, where she would spend the day fishing and secure us a mess of fish to eat for supper by the time I arrived.

We'd done our homework before we ever got to Bayou Pierre. We'd read guides and articles and talked to old-timers who grew up in that area—but as a ranger once told me, "You never know until you go."

First of all, as I stood on the Carter Hill Bridge gazing out at the river, it looked nothing like the photos from Google Street View. The camera car must have passed over that bridge during a flood, as there was no sand to be seen in the photos, just tea-colored water flowing unobstructed through dense jungle on both sides. When we actually got there and stood on top of the bridge looking down that late-summer morning, the river was a winding trickle with wide sandbars on both sides.

We walked across the sparsely trafficked bridge a couple of times searching for the best route down to the river. Two of the corners of the bridge were blocked with impenetrable jungle, and the other two, while technically passable, were positively eaten up with pepper vine. Even though pepper vine is nonirritating, it mimics poison ivy closely enough to give even an expert pause, and, like Virginia creeper, it tends to coexist with poison ivy.

While I was working up my courage to drag my kayak through the pepper vine, Elise spotted a concrete storm drain leading like a children's playground slide from one corner of the bridge down to the bayou. I decided this was the best way to get down from the bridge, so I spent a few minutes dragging the kayak through the greenbrier and blackberry thickets growing over the drain. Eventually I got to the river, put my kayak in, and got everything situated and in order. I waved my paddle in a triumphant farewell like an explorer as Elise took photos from atop the bridge, but before I got around the bend and out of sight I was dragging the boat across the sandy bottom of the inches-deep creek.

Throughout the day I alternated paddling happily and dragging the kayak through knee-deep quicksand. Trumpet vine was in full bloom, and, as the breeze tickled the trees, it dropped blossoms into the river to float along with me. In some areas the sandbars stretched into the distance. Yellow Sand Creek joined from the south and Choctaw Creek from the north, but neither deepened the flow—they just widened it.

I got to the Foster Creek confluence, having passed a large Boy Scout reservation about five miles south of the bridge. Foster parallels Bayou Pierre for a couple hundred yards before plunging in. The creek was actually flowing better than Bayou Pierre, so I dragged my kayak across a sandbar and put in there just to have some water under my keel—but it didn't last.

I've heard it said that if anyone ever tells you they actually enjoyed a portage, they're lying.

Bald eagles and great blue herons watched as I alternately paddled and portaged. Head-cutting erosion became more evident, with sandy walls flopping off into the creek as I slipped past. High on a bluff I saw construction equipment and remembered hearing that much of the adjoining land had been purchased by a conservation agency working on both protecting the bayou and improving access for paddlecraft.

I floated on through the morning and into the afternoon. At one point I glided past a sandbar with massive petrified logs—much too large to carry in the kayak or drag with me.

Eventually, I came around the bend and saw the Highway 18 bridge, but no sign of Elise. As I drew closer, I "woo-hooed" two times, then three. Finally she popped up from under the bridge where she'd been snoozing in the sun. No fish had been biting, and it had taken me longer than expected because of all the portaging. So we did as all great fishermen and explorers do after an adventure—we ate fish at a restaurant.

All in all, I enjoyed exploring this eleven-mile stretch of Bayou Pierre—even the eight miles of portaging.

HOMOCHITTO RIVER

> Stop shallow water from running, it will rage.
>
> —ROBERT GREENE

Homochitto is Choctaw for "big red" (*homo*: red, *chitto*: big). Starting in Copiah County south of Hazlehurst, the Homochitto River wanders west through sparsely populated Franklin, Wilkinson, and south Adams Counties, including the 190,000-acre Homochitto National Forest, en route to the Mississippi River just south of St. Catherine Creek National Wildlife Refuge.

The Homochitto used to flow into Lake Mary, an oxbow lake off the Mississippi west of Woodville, but the Corps of Engineers routed the river directly into the Mississippi in 1938 in a project called the Abernathy Channel. The long-term result has been violent floods, quicksands, and collapsing banks.

Fortunately, the Homochitto is not usually so violent. But it is wild in other ways—home to alligators, bears, deer, snakes, catfish, and gar. In addition to the usual cottonmouths along the river and in the swamps, Homochitto National Forest is renowned for its massive timber rattlers, which can reach five or more feet in length. The river harbors some big fish, too, including catfish upward of thirty pounds.

Okhissa Lake

Most of the fishing takes place not in the river but in 1,100-acre Okhissa (oh-KISS-ah) Lake, located on tributary Porter Creek in Homochitto National Forest near Bude. The 97.1-foot earthen dam, tallest in the state, was completed in 2005, and the lake opened to the public in 2007.

> The name Okhissa was chosen among 108 entries in a contest. It's a Choctaw word for "porter," fitting since the lake was built on Porter Creek and the name was the brainchild of Franklin County librarian Jo Porter. Porter grew up in the Berrytown community several miles from Porter Creek and said she wasn't sure if it was named for her ancestors. "I thought since the Choctaws were so heavily populated at one time in here, this would be a neat way to say thank you to them," she explained. "This was their land before we came in here."

The Homochitto River

Green woods and brown water of the Old Homochitto River

While Okhissa is a popular place to fish, it's also a great spot simply to paddle and sightsee. On a map, the lake resembles a lightning bolt, wide at the north end, pointed at the south, with sharp coves forking off all over. Paddlers can explore one cove after another. They're likely to see iridescent dragonflies plus a variety of birds, notably redwing blackbirds, great egrets, great blue herons, little blue herons, green herons, even ospreys and bald eagles, which nest at the lake. On the wooded shores they may spot a doe drinking at the water's edge. If the air is still they may hear the rustle of leaves, the purr of a squirrel, the thunk of a distant boat. Part of the appeal of this spread-out lake is that, even when the parking lot is nearly full, paddlers will rarely see more than a couple of boats at any given time.

Indian Weirs and Canoes

The Indian tribes that lived along the Homochitto River didn't have motorboats or rods and reels, let alone a man-made lake. To catch fish, they used a more primitive method of fishing: weirs. They cut pine saplings with stone tools, trimmed them into poles, and sharpened the ends. Using wooden mallets, they drove the posts about two and a half feet apart in the riverbed in a V-shaped enclosure, mouth facing upstream. They wove leafy saplings and branches or cane mats among the posts to serve as walls. Fish were channeled to the tip of the V, where they would swim into a small, enclosed area. The Indians would net or club them, no bait needed.

In 1975, Thomas Sturdivant of Rosetta found some posts in the Homochitto sticking up after a bank collapsed. Archaeologists dated the Sturdivant weir to AD 1465. In 1991, Lydell Rand of the Bunkley community found another one dating to 1350. Archaeologists took sample posts from both weirs to Jackson and chemically preserved them.

Indian canoes have also turned up in the Homochitto. One discovered in the early 1970s measured twelve or thirteen feet long and dated to 1465. It had squared-off ends with a platform at each end. A hole was bored into one of the platforms, presumably for a mooring pole or rope. Weirs dating to the 1800s have also been found. The presence of nails and boards indicates that they were used by settlers. Such finds are extremely fragile and usually decompose rapidly after being unearthed.

Indian Mounds

A pair of Indian mounds south and east of Lake Mary provides evidence that these waters have been fished for thousands of years.

"In some ways things haven't changed all that much," said Dr. Megan Kassabaum of the University of Pennsylvania, who has led digs at the Lessley and Smith Creek Indian mounds. She cites a "focus on fishing, deer hunting, people living widespread around the area coming together for important events—that was true for Wilkinson County people then and it's true now."

The two mound sites are located along Highway 24 West and are part of the Mississippi Mound Trail, which roughly parallels the Mississippi River. Each site has a historical marker, though the mounds themselves are on private land.

The Lessley Mound was built around AD 1300 and was used as recently as the late seventeenth century. Farther west, between Lake Mary and Fort Adams, is the Smith Mound complex, three mounds surrounding a plaza dating to around AD 750, though items found at the site date as far back as 250 BC.

Kassabaum, author of *A History of Platform Mound Ceremonialism* (University of Florida Press, 2021), believes that the inhabitants were ancestors of the Natchez tribe, which was virtually wiped out in battles with the French in the early 1700s. When the mounds were built, the Mississippi River channel was probably at Lake Mary. Since the mounds aren't far from natural bluffs, their function was less practical than social, Kassabaum said. Instead of serving as a refuge from floods or as high ground for visibility, they were central gathering places for a dispersed population, where people would come together for funerals, feasts, and such. In time, the sites became villages.

Frontier Fighter

Native Americans ultimately came into conflict with white settlers, and one such settler, Lewis Wetzel, was reportedly buried beside the Homochitto River. The infamous Indian fighter from the Ohio Valley occasionally visited his cousin Phillip Sycks (also spelled Sikes, Sykes, and Six) at Sycks's farm on the Homochitto at Havard's Ferry, now Rosetta. Born in 1763, Wetzel was "by far the greatest Indian fighter this nation has known," said researcher Robert Hand of Newtown Square, Pennsylvania.

Wetzel apparently developed his hatred for Native Americans while growing up in the Ohio Valley after being captured and brutalized as a boy before making a daring escape. After that, he vowed to kill every Indian who crossed his path, and he meant it, whether peacetime or not. He grew his black hair to knee length, learned to reload a muzzle-loading rifle on the run, and disappeared alone into hostile territory across the Ohio River, returning with strings of scalps. His single-handed attacks on bands of Indians in their own territory showed utter fearlessness. His expertise in guerrilla warfare was unsurpassed.

There has been a tendency to lionize him for his Olympian strength, speed, and bravery. Zane Grey did just that in novels like *Spirit of the Border* and *The Last Trail*. But Grey and some historians glossed over Wetzel's brutality, such as the cold-blooded murder of peaceful Indians—he is reported to have shot two Choctaw canoers from the front porch of his cabin on the lower Big Black River for no reason except that they were Native Americans.

In Mississippi, Wetzel allegedly ran a horse-stealing ring, rustling horses from settlers and selling them up north. He was arrested in Natchez and imprisoned in New Orleans on charges of counterfeiting. Imprisonment aged the frontiersman, reportedly turning his hair white before he reached fifty. Despite Wetzel's dark deeds, it was a cruel era, and he saved many lives, rescuing people captured by Indians and warning settlers of impending attacks.

Opinions about where and when he died are divided. Robert Hand and some others, including Allan W. Eckert in his book *That Dark and Bloody River* (Bantam, 1995), opine that Wetzel died in the mid-1800s in Texas after many more adventures. Earlier researchers believed he died of yellow fever in 1808 at Havard's Ferry and was buried on the south bank of the Homochitto near what is now Rosetta. Dr. Albert Bowser dug up the supposed remains in 1942 and transported them to West Virginia for a monument. An eyewitness of the exhumation, the late Marie T. Logan, wrote: "Parts of the rifle and the beads of a bullet pouch forming the letter 'W' were beside the bones. Shortly after the air hit it the bones crumpled to dust, but beneath the body were the marks of wavy hair in the hard clay—marks that reached from the head to the knee."

The Story of Free Woods

Around the time Wetzel may have been buried on the south bank of the Homochitto, a white settler named John W. Miller gave ten thousand acres across the river to his half-Choctaw daughter, Clorie Miller. Later, another white man in the area, John Wilson, married an African American woman known as "Black Mary." The families linked up through marriage, producing progeny that combined three races. The owners of the Miller tract decreed that there would be no enslavement of their offspring. Thus began Free Woods, one of the most unusual communities in the South, an area where slavery was abolished and races intermingled before the Civil War.

Free Woods lies in deep, hilly forest north of the Homochitto River in southwest Franklin County. The last point of reference before embarking down Free Woods Road is a little burg by the name of Knoxville, just north of a slightly larger village called Garden City. At Knoxville, turn east off Highway 33, cross the railroad tracks, and then turn right on an even smaller road, which wends southeast into the forested darkness of Free Woods—or what was once Free Woods.

Harry Gibson is one of several hundred modern-day offspring whose origins lie in Free Woods. The Detroit attorney was born in 1937 in a log cabin in the community, and the first five years of his life there—before moving to Houston, Texas—left him with glimpsed memories of sugarcane and pine trees. "Seven or eight families intermingled over the years, so there's a lot of cousins who are married on both the mothers' and the fathers' side," said Gibson, who along with his cousin, the late Marshal Miller of Coles, researched the history of Free Woods.

Ghosts of Nebo Lake

Across the river to the south of Free Woods is the now defunct Nebo Lake Recreation Area in Homochitto National Forest. According to legend, a couple from Virginia moved here in the early 1800s and brought two pear trees with them. Only one survived, and it's still here—six feet, seven and a half inches in circumference. The trunk is hollow and nearly dead; there are no pears to be found. A small, sturdy trunk grows from one side of the old one, but whether it can survive in the dense forest is questionable.

Virgil Sturdivant remembers eating the fruit as a kid. "They were a soft pear like the old eating pears, we'd call it. The tree had a big canopy and branches came down to the ground."

"The story has it that the pear seeds were brought to Amite County by the Lusk clan, planted on their place," said genealogist Neal Randall, whose great-grandfather was Davis Lusk.

Lusk Cemetery is still there as well, or what's left of it. Sturdivant said some folks from Natchez held a seance there and made off with a bunch of tombstones. Depressions in the ground indicate plenty of graves hereabouts, but there are only a few markers among the head-high weeds. "Samuel Lusk, Pvt. NC Militia, Revolutionary War, April 9, 1750; April 14, 1825." Also, Reuben Cassels, died 1841 (no birth date listed); J. W. Ewell, 1843–1888; and John H. Lusk, 1785–1852. "There were probably forty headstones in here, maybe more," Sturdivant said.

> There are ghost stories like that of Old Man Wilson, who ran Wilson's Ferry on the Homochitto River in the 1800s. Wilson supposedly hanged slaves from a chain attached to a red oak tree. He allegedly buried a chest of gold in the swamp and raised a bunch of cats. "My daddy said he's been out at night and heard cats meowing," Sturdivant said. "My grandpa would be out fishing at night and somebody tapped him on his shoulder and there's nobody there. . . . I've had my hair raised up several times over here at night. They said you could say his name three times—'Wilson, Wilson, Wilson'—and he'd show you things." Sturdivant took advantage of that tale by playing pranks on the gullible. "We'd bring city kids down here and make varmint calls," he said. Sturdivant also recalled a man up the road telling him about hearing hoofbeats at night and seeing a headless horseman ride by his house.

The Forest Service closed Nebo Lake Recreation Area years ago after vandals destroyed the picnic tables and other amenities. Then the Homochitto River claimed the lake, so now there's nothing but woods. Sturdivant recalled drownings there and elsewhere on the river.

A Rock and a Hard Place

The Homochitto Valley shelters mysteries much older than Free Woods. One of those is Hattiesburg quartzite, found in parts of Franklin County. It's unusual to find large rocks and boulders of any sort in this part of the world—not sandstone, not soft clay rock, but hard gray boulders. This particular stone has a glassy, smooth face.

Gloster resident Wayne Havard, a flintknapper by hobby, found it to be excellent for making arrowheads, yet he has never run across any Native American artifacts made of the stuff. "None of them [experts] have an answer why," said Havard, who has chunks of the quartzite at his home. "The best explanation I've had is they [Native Americans] traded it. I've walked these creeks I don't know how many miles looking for materials to flintknap, and [artifacts] are scarce as hen's teeth."

North of the river on Highway 33, Havard points out a vein of white chalk that is part of the formation and extends into Wilkinson County. He finds big chunks of gray rock beside backroads that lead south into Free Woods where tall longleaf pines—once the dominant tree species here—overshadow the road. Throughout the area, boulders litter the slopes, not a common site in most of southwest Mississippi. Havard recalls speaking with now retired Forest Service archaeologist Sam Brooks, who told him that Natchez Indians and early settlers used slabs of Hattiesburg quartzite as building foundations. It's also been used for burial vaults and tombstones. But if they turned it into arrowheads, there are few to be found.

Archaeologists are puzzled as well. "The question of why was this material 'avoided' still begs to be answered today," according to a report by Frank Gagne, Homochitto Ranger District archaeologist. "Was the outcrop considered sacred and something to be avoided or was there a taboo for one or another reason? Was it only traded? The list of questions goes on and on, but the answers are yet to be answered."

Memories of Mastodons

The area offers other evidence of prehistory in the form of fossils—such as *Gomphotherium*, a mastodon-like creature that roamed these woods. Wayne Havard ran across fossilized remains in 2014, to the delight of scientists. "It looks like we're dealing with something that we've never encountered before in Mississippi," said George Phillips, paleontology curator for the Mississippi Museum of Natural Science. "Wayne is the only one who has found a pre–Ice Age *Gomphotherium*."

The Ice Age, or Pleistocene epoch, lasted from about 2.6 million to 11,700 years ago. The Pliocene epoch was earlier, dating back 5.3 million years. Before that was the Miocene, which goes back 23 million years.

"Wayne's is the oldest *Gomphotherium* found yet," Phillips said. Havard, whose main stomping ground is the Homochitto River Valley, found a complete set of molars and good portions of the tusks. Citing the landowner's wishes, he would only say the site is in Amite County. Havard invited Phillips and state geologist James Starnes to his house to take a look in 2017. Phillips consulted with Richard Hulbert of the University of Florida, who said the fossils appeared to come from a *Gomphotherium simplicidens*.

"The *Gomphotherium* had four tusks," Havard said. "It had an extended lower jaw, with two shovel-like tusks and two upper tusks similar to elephants. It lived in a swamp and marsh environment. The lower tusks scooped up vegetation from the marshes and swamps." This particular *Gomphotherium* was one of the smaller varieties, standing about six feet tall. Larger ones reached nine feet in height.

Phillips said that southwest Mississippi is part of a "broad, ancient coastal plain younger than ninety million years. It's very fossil-rich." *Gomphotherium* and the mastodon are two of three prehistoric elephant-like creatures, the third being the mammoth. "Neither one is a true elephant, whereas mammoths are true elephants," Phillips said. "Mastodons are Ice Age—Pleistocene epoch."

Starnes points out that Amite County would have been a coastal swamp in the Pliocene epoch, with palm trees instead of pines and oaks. *Gomphotherium* and its kin were right at home in that environment. "They're really, really funny-looking animals," Starnes said. "They've got shovel-shaped tusks on the top and bottom. They were more browsers, like a deer." Mastodons, too, were browsers, while mammoths were grazers, Starnes said.

The Answer at River's End, by Ernest Herndon

As I woke in the predawn darkness to go to Lake Mary, I had to wonder: why in the world do people make the trip to this end-of-the-world backwater—not just now and then, but regularly? It's a long drive from anywhere, and any way you slice it, it's going to cost money: boat, fishing tackle, bait, food, fuel, maybe a camp. Why bother? That's what the Mayor and the Judge were aiming to show me.

Aubrey Rimes was Pike County Southern District justice court judge and Osyka municipal judge. Jamie Harrell served two terms as Osyka mayor. Both men have fished at Lake Mary off and on since childhood.

We met early that morning at an old fishing camp and climbed into a fifteen-foot green aluminum fishing boat. Rimes cranked the motor, I untied us, and we puttered up the Old Homochitto River. The water had dropped five feet during the previous week. You could see the pale mud ring around tree trunks. We passed open fields on our left and a smattering of camps on the right, then entered the forest.

"It's nothing but woods from here to Natchez," the Judge said.

The morning air was mild and green-sweet as we rounded bend after bend, spooking small flocks of white egrets and random herons. A pair of fallen-in camps lent a desolate air. An alligator swirled the water and went under. Gar splashed around us as the boat moved forward. The soft air, the smells, the woods, the water all make up a major part of the lure of Lake Mary.

The river, which had been angling north, gradually narrowed until it split into west and east prongs. We turned left up the west and meandered through tall forest until we saw a sprawling hunting lodge on the right. "That's Buck Island Hunting Camp," Rimes said. "Not many eyes have seen that."

Around the next bend, a fallen tree blocked our way.

We returned to the forks and headed up the east prong, passing under a primitive bridge leading to Buck Island. As the river narrowed, the trees got bigger, especially cypress with their giant flaring buttresses, but also lowland oaks, sycamore, hog pecan, and locust. The ground was swept clean from floods and aglow with short, green growth that would flourish until the next high water. Fine sawdust ringed the trunk of a locust tree. I looked it up later and discovered that something called a locust borer may have been responsible. We only saw one tree like that.

Back on the river, we passed under another, even more primitive bridge. Rimes was hoping to reach an old sunken steam engine, but getting there is always dicey. If the river is too low, logs block the way. If too high, the engine is submerged.

We crept on upriver, toward the elusive sunken engine, like Marlow seeking the mysterious Colonel Kurtz in Joseph Conrad's quintessential river novel Heart of Darkness. I half expected arrows to come flying out of the woodland gloom.

In high water, the Judge said, you could make it all the way to the main Homochitto River. However, there was another bridge and a giant logjam between here and there. We came to a fallen tree that completely blocked the river. Without a saw, there was no getting through. Exploring time was over. The Judge turned the boat around as we headed downstream to check the trotlines. We had a new quest now—catfish.

We were especially hoping to catch yellow cats, which the Judge said is the best eating catfish of them all. As we ran lines, we kept hauling in blue cats and yellow cats, and tossing out gar. Then we caught a small,

The Mayor, left, and the Judge with catfish

mottled, blackish catfish that the Judge called a Homochitto River yellow cat, as opposed to the Mississippi River yellow cat, which is golden.

Back at camp, the Judge tossed the fish onto the dock. He then loaded them into five-gallon buckets to carry up to his cleaning deck. Finally, all the fish were piled on the skinning deck, which had a large stainless steel sink, weighing scales, and skinning hooks. When he finished his skinning, the tally was twelve blue cats weighing a total of 108.5 pounds, and seven yellow cats at 68 pounds—in all, nineteen catfish weighing 176.5 pounds. The biggest blue cat was 22.5 pounds, the biggest yellow 17. Not bad for a morning run.

The Mayor and the Judge had answered my question. The allure of Lake Mary is in its lush symphony of land and trees, water and wildlife, fishing and friendly people.

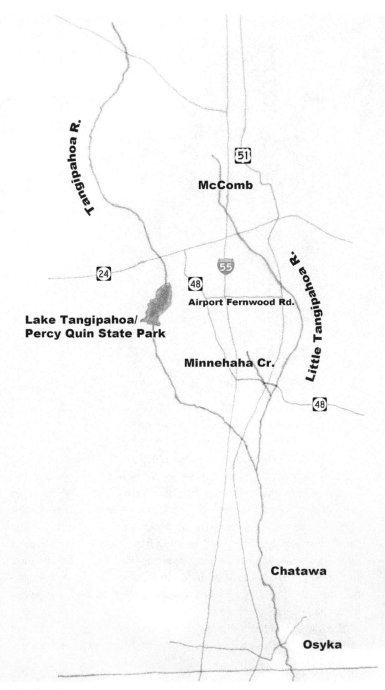

The Tangipahoa River

TANGIPAHOA RIVER

> Extremes beget limitations, even as a river by its own
> swiftness creates obstructions for itself.
>
> —ROBERT INGERSOLL

The Tangipahoa River—like the Amite and Tickfaw—begins as a logjammed creek in Mississippi, only to become navigable in Louisiana. Though deucedly hard to paddle in Mississippi, the Tangipahoa is rich in history and other items of interest.

The stream arises in the northwest corner of Pike County near Highway 98 west of the town of Summit in southwest Mississippi. From there, it snakes southward back and forth across the Amite County line, mostly unseen behind wooded fence lines and in the interstices between agricultural fields. The Tangipahoa only really peeks out of the greenbrier and muscadine-tangled woods at larger crossings like Highway 98, Muddy Springs Road, and Highway 51. At those bridges, this river can look temptingly navigable, but for the most part, it is not.

> The word Tangipahoa is a Native American phrase referring to "cornstalk gatherers," apparently a subgroup or nickname for the Choctaw Natives of the area. The Tangipahoa passes near the communities of Chatawa, an Indian word meaning "Choctaw hunting grounds," and Osyka, apparently named for a Choctaw hero or chieftain nicknamed "Eagle Man." Tributary Minnehaha Creek means "Laughing Waters," and Tangipahoa's southernmost Mississippi tributary, the Bala Chitto, is a Choctaw name referring to a "big thicket."

Percy Quin State Park

Along its route through the west side of Pike County, the Tangipahoa subsumes the waters of Haymans Creek, Peavine Creek, and Cobb Branch before gathering at five-hundred-acre Lake Tangipahoa at Percy Quin State Park.

Percy Quin was built in the late 1930s on 1,400 acres of land donated by the estate of local schoolteacher and congressman Percy E. Quin. Quin's homeplace, which now has a historical marker, still stands just northwest of the park on Mississippi Highway 48, and there are Quins buried in the 1700s-era DeKane Cemetery within the bounds of the park.

Percy Quin is one of the first state parks built in Mississippi. At that time there was no state park commission, so the park plan was overseen by a national commission. Advance planning started in August 1935, and construction work began in December 1935 with initial plans calling for a lake of greater than five hundred acres.

Percy Quin State Park was a Civilian Conservation Corps project that mostly employed World War I veterans and young men who had been brought up during the Great Depression. The workers, called "enrollees," lived in military-style camps and were led in their work by Navy Seabee engineers as well as local professional engineers.

This project to place a new state park on the banks of the Tangipahoa River was by no means a sure thing. Local newspaper articles and editorials throughout the 1930s detail the ups and downs of the park plans. When the administrative ardor in Washington began to stall in early 1936, the plan was championed by then-mayor of McComb, X. A. Kramer, and local newspaperman J. Oliver Emmerich.

Kramer entertained visiting dignitaries, of whom there seemed to be an unending stream, by taking them on tours of the proposed park site and wining and dining them at his private palatial retreat on a bluff overlooking the Tangipahoa River downstream at Chatawa. Kramer's support was more than just cheerleading, though, as he led the McComb city board to purchase 212 acres of adjoining land to the west of the proposed lake. This land was donated to the park for the purpose of building "the finest group camp site in the State." Kramer's donation swelled the parklands to their current near-1,700-acre size. There was even some passing talk in the newspapers of the time of naming the impoundment Kramer Lake.

> J. Oliver Emmerich would continue his newspaper career throughout the 1960s and into the 1970s, during which time he would receive a Pulitzer Prize for his coverage of the civil rights movement in southwest Mississippi. Despite having a cross burned in his yard and an unlit Molotov cocktail lobbed into the home of his editor, Charles Dunagin, Emmerich continued to call on readers to "develop and actively promote a new sense of community responsibility," hoping that one day they could say, "We met a crisis with maturity. We did not panic. We exercised restraint." Each year since his death in the late 1970s, the Mississippi Press Association has awarded the J. Oliver Emmerich Award for Editorial Excellence.

Throughout the late 1930s, Emmerich wrote passionate and fiery editorials describing the benefits of the new park plan and the challenges the project was undergoing. In one editorial, he described politicians in Washington, DC, as "a clique who know as much about park development as a plumber does surgery" and accused them of "dilly-dallying."

In response to friend-making by Kramer and editorial pressure from Emmerich, both received telegrams from Washington assuring them and their constituents and readers that the Percy Quin Park project would soon be back on track, and the very next week it was. Construction began immediately on the two-thousand-foot-long Tangipahoa dam.

Completed in 1940, the Lake Tangipahoa dam has had a troubled history. In fact, almost immediately after the dam was completed and the lake filled and stocked with fish, the dam failed in 1942, flooding the downstream countryside. The dam was repaired by 1945 but failed again in 1983 after a record-breaking spring flood. This time the failure was due to a faulty valve in the spillway that could only be repaired by draining the lake. Then, in 2012, heavy rains from Hurricane Isaac caused the downstream slope of the earthen dam to slough off. Emergency repairs prevented the dam from completely failing, but officials were already preparing for a mass evacuation of downstream residents in case the dam collapsed. Later, the lake was drained and the dam rebuilt.

A Difficult Passage

Southward from the park, the Tangipahoa River crosses Interstate 55 and Highway 51 as it journeys to Chatawa, then roughly parallels Highway 51 en route to its outlet at Louisiana's Lake Pontchartrain. Roughly half of the river's 122 miles passes through each state. Mississippi's portion is a pleasant creek but rife with logjams, while in Louisiana it widens out and becomes shallow and sandy before narrowing and deepening again as it approaches Pontchartrain beneath the shadows of cypress trees and Spanish moss.

> Even locals run into problems trying to navigate near the source of the Tangipahoa. In July 2001, a pair of college lads, both in their early twenties, set off to canoe from Highway 51 to Chatawa, about six to seven miles. Frequent logjams forced them to portage through the woods. With night falling, they tried paddling back to a railroad track but wound up on a side slough. They called one of their mothers, who got in touch with a wildlife conservation officer. It took a few hours for the

> officer and a civil defense director to drive their trucks along a service road by the railroad track. On the fading phone, the officer advised the young men to leave the canoe, keep the moon to their backs, and walk toward the tracks. Using the dim light of a cell phone as a flashlight, they banged their way through the woods and waded through the swamp and across the neck-deep river. They finally reached the rescuers, but one of the trucks got stuck on the muddy railroad service road, and then the headlight of a train appeared. The officials got on the phone to try to stop the train, but it barreled past less than ten feet away. They got in touch with railroad officials and told them to stop train traffic between New Orleans and Jackson. They winched the truck out and finally made it to Chatawa in the wee hours.

The Tangipahoa River's main two tributaries, Minnehaha Creek and the Little Tangipahoa River, pass right through downtown Magnolia. Indeed, Magnolia was largely built between the arms of the two streams. Local octogenarian Hal Pezant says that when he was a small child, old-timers used to reminisce about a lake in Magnolia that had been formed by damming the Minnehaha. The lake was said to be large enough to put boats into and pretty enough to be an attraction. It must have been a private lake because Pezant said its demise came when the dam was dynamited and destroyed by some ornery fellow with a grudge against the landowner. The ruined dam is still visible in the woods. The concrete dam is old enough that it is completely covered in bright green moss and has huge oak trees growing through it, breaking and displacing parts of it.

> Generations of locals have cooled off in the waters of the Tangipahoa and Minnehaha. Retired South Pike School teacher Betsy Harrell tells of learning to swim in a couple of the deeper holes behind the Lee Street neighborhood in Magnolia. Hal Pezant recalls that the local kids had all the swimming holes in the Minnehaha mapped out and had even given the best swimming spots evocative names like "Rocky Bottom" and "Peter Deep."

Relics of the Past

That ruined Minnehaha dam is not the only remnant of bygone days to be found in the Tangipahoa and its tributaries. Other local residents have found artifacts they claim date back as far as seven thousand to eight thousand years.

"A lot of these sites were occupied," said the late Dr. David Snow, who owned a camp farther downstream at Chatawa. "Nobody knows the names of the tribes. Some people will say Choctaw. Nobody knows who was here seven thousand years ago."

Snow had a couple of small, elevated sites on his property that he believed were foundations for Native American structures. "You can see it's perfectly round, and you can see the remains of a fire in the middle of it," he said. "The location of this bluff, you had a sweeping view all around. And I imagine they liked the elevation to get away from mosquitoes."

On Bala Chitto Creek, another history buff found evidence that Native Americans traded far and wide for their artifacts. Pike County Historical Society president Malcolm Allen of McComb noticed that most of the rocks he picked up on his ancestor's farm over the years had a chip missing on one end. The reason for the chip, Allen believes, was to display the interior of the stone and prove to a customer that it was flint.

Flint, unlike local rock, was valuable for tools because it flakes. Allen figures that Natchez was the nearest trading center. Industrious Indians might have made the trek to buy chunks of stone wholesale, so to speak, and bring them back to sell retail. "The Indians here didn't have a lot to trade," Allen said, noting they probably used commodities like baskets and dried meat, beans, and corn.

Local history buff and Magnolia alderman Joe Cornacchione has found antique bottles, tiles, arrowheads, and other old artifacts on Minnehaha Creek property just northwest of the bridge on Highway 51. Cornacchione's most dramatic discovery was a largely intact foundation of an old mill in the creek bed behind his home. He spotted the mill foundation after stormwaters shifted the gravel and sand around in the creek bed. The foundation deck spans the twenty-five-foot creek and is about fifteen feet wide. It features mossy, hand-hewn boards and a circle four feet across in the center where a mill wheel must have been. In the 1800s, water mills were common on streams throughout southwest Mississippi. "In olden times the rivers afforded waterpower for water mills for grinding corn, ginning cotton, and sawmills," as written in "WPA Source Material for Mississippi History: Pike County," compiled in the 1930s. Creeks like Minnehaha powered mills, using not the huge paddlewheels found farther north but smaller iron "tub wheels."

Religious Retreat

Farther downstream at Chatawa, Saint Mary of the Pines was a beautiful Catholic retreat with attractive red brick buildings, towering pines, and rustling palm trees. It got its start in 1868 when Redemptorist fathers in New Orleans wanted a country retreat. They bought eighty acres at Chatawa, eventually expanding to three hundred. They constructed a frame chapel and a three-story brick building. In the 1870s, the School Sisters of Notre Dame began operating a Catholic school there and soon bought the whole thing from the Redemptorists for nine thousand dollars. More buildings went up as enrollment grew. Girls made up the majority, and in 1954 the school quit taking boys. In the 1960s, some old buildings came down and new ones went up, including a 160-bed dormitory. By 1974, though, enrollment had dropped off and, about one hundred years after it opened, the school shut down. It served as a home for retired nuns until it closed in 2020. In 2021 it was sold to Chatawa Retreat Center LLC for a nominal ten dollars and opened as Our Lady of Hope Catholic Retreat Center.

> In December 1941, film icon Maureen O'Hara married local film director Will Houston Price at Saint Mary of the Pines. According to members of the Magnolia Garden Club, the chapel was decorated with ferns imported from O'Hara's home in Ireland, and those ferns were later transplanted near the home where the couple had their wedding reception right on the banks of the Minnehaha. The descendants of those Maureen O'Hara ferns still populate the banks of the Minnehaha, predominantly southward from Magnolia, but also in the gardens of the ladies of the Magnolia Garden Club.

Chatawa Mysteries

Not far away from Saint Mary, on a high bluff overlooking the Tangipahoa, stands the privately owned Kramer Lodge, a massive, rustic house that once served as a retreat for former Louisiana governor Huey Long and his cronies. The former mayor of McComb, X. A. Kramer, built both the lodge and the log cabin.

The deep woods of Chatawa have also given rise to monster legends, like the Chatawa Monster, long rumored to be a Mississippi version of Bigfoot. In the 1930s, old-timers say, a circus truck overturned on Highway 51, and two

The Tangipahoa River bridge at Chatawa

panthers escaped. Although circus officials claimed they recaptured the animals, people reported seeing a panther later.

Weird animal sightings continued to occur at Chatawa. In the late 1990s, a local woman said she saw a monkey swing out of a tree, land in the road, stand up, and eat something. When she slowed her car, it ran off. The woman insisted it was not a squirrel, raccoon, or other creature. She described it as two and a half feet tall with a long tail. Kramer Lodge had various exotic pets including monkeys in the 1930s, but a wildlife biologist said he doubted that a population of monkeys could have survived in the wild there that long, especially without having been reported.

Chatawa Infrastructure

The Chatawa flow well on the CN Railroad right of way, used for decades by citizens as a free source of water, was closed in 2012 by order of the railroad after litter, especially plastic jugs, accumulated to horrific proportions in the damp woods below the well. That same year, the Chatawa post office closed its doors. Located across the railway from the Chatawa well, the post office had been a hub of activity for the southern Pike County community since the

1930s. Operations had been indefinitely suspended because of structural damage it received from flooding from Hurricane Isaac in 2005. The twenty-nine customers who received their mail at post office boxes in Chatawa then had to go to Osyka to get their mail, and Chatawa mail was delivered out of Osyka,

Strange Fishes

The Tangipahoa and its tributaries provide good fishing for catfish, bream, and bass, but fishermen occasionally tie into some more unusual species as well. In 2018, three young men were fishing in the river at Highway 24 west of McComb when they caught something they'd never seen before. The fish, caught on a rubber lizard, resembled a gar but turned out to be a chain pickerel—also known as a green pike, duck-billed pike, black pike, or jackfish. Chain pickerel have also been caught and photographed upstream in Lake Tangipahoa.

According to a publication of the Mississippi Department of Wildlife, Fisheries, and Parks, "Freshwater Fishes Common to Mississippi," "These fish are long and slender with a long mouth and well-developed teeth. The lower jaw is longer than the snout. Chain pickerel have dark brown or green chainlike marks on the sides with a dark back. The snout is dark, and fins have a dusky coloring to them. Chain pickerel can weigh two to ten pounds and can reach lengths up to 31 inches." The state record is 6.25 pounds, caught in Bay Springs Lake. Pickerel are edible but very bony.

The late Charles Ray Pigott, one of Pike County's most original thinkers, suggested a great new Mississippi outdoor tourist event: the running of the eels. Pigott explained that freshwater eels, even those found in ponds, are actually born in the Sargasso Sea. If you know when to watch, he said, you may witness huge masses of baby eels migrating up area paddleways like the Tangipahoa River.

Paddling Lake Tangipahoa, by Patrick Parker

In Ernest Herndon's classic 2001 travelogue/guidebook *Canoeing Mississippi*, he describes the north end of Lake Tangipahoa as "a curvaceous avenue into the heart of a swamp . . . not plagued by issues of landowners, liability, or access." Of course, reading such an auspicious account of such a convenient adventure made me want to experience that lake anew. Fortunately, Lake Tangipahoa is only a few miles from my house, so I threw my eight-foot sit-in kayak into the truck and headed out.

Usually when I go hiking or paddling I try to have something that I'm looking for—some purpose to my expedition. I'll try to find a plant I can't identify or look for animal tracks on the banks. This time I just wanted to experience the lake that Ernest describes in that book.

It was a cool and breezy early-summer morning when I put in at the marina, and I immediately set out clockwise around the lake past the dam and emergency spillway. The bottom of the spillway is usually a good spot to see a fish-kill sample of the occupants of the lake, and it's not uncommon to spy an osprey or bald eagle hanging out eyeballing the fish. This time there were no fish hawks and no fish kills.

Beyond the spillway, the first thing that caught my eye was a profusion of wild hibiscus (also called rose mallow) in full bloom dotting the banks with large pink and white blossoms. This southwestern corner of the lake shore is the overflow for the park's primitive camping area. I think I recall some old-timers calling this wooded part of the lakefront "Coon Holler." The inlet next to it is Coon Cove. I have camped here since I was a child. I even remember doing our wilderness survival campout here when I was in the Scouts. It's not very wilderness-y, but I suppose it is remote enough for an eleven-year-old to get a taste of the wild. Even as an adult, it is still my favorite camping spot at Percy Quin State Park.

The next thing I noticed was that the water plants were also in full bloom. The first of these that I saw was the spatterdock, or yellow pond lily. The blossoms erupt out of bulbs that float along with the distinctively shaped leaves. The west side of the lake is also positively eaten up with the glossy round leaves and lavender blossoms of water hyacinth, occasionally piling up several feet high along the banks. It is a beautiful plant but overly prolific. Water hyacinth can easily become a nuisance to boaters.

Gliding past wild azalea and Chinese tallow trees hanging out over the water, I noticed a glut of low-hanging muscadine vines with fully ripe fruits. It was pretty early for ripe muscadines—they are an end-of-summer fruit—but I guess these vines have a super-abundance of both water and sunlight, so they were producing early.

As I crossed the inlet between Coon Holler and the group camp (alternately named Camp Beaver or Camp Sunshine), I spotted white egrets and blue herons balanced on logs, fishing. I was very calm as I slowly and silently glided toward them, hoping for a good photo or two, but there is only so much that herons will put up with before they flap their way to another fishing spot. I never got within fifty yards of these.

Another common denizen of lakes like Tangipahoa is the magnificent bryozoan (*Pectinatella magnifica*). These colonies of microscopic organisms float along in clumps of translucent gel, and if you look closely you will see that the gel is speckled inside with dark stars or asterisks. Whenever we come across colonies of magnificent bryozoan, my sons call them "snot monsters" (as did I when I was their age), and my daughters call them "Juicy Lucys."

Toward the north end of the lake, far beyond the domain of the skiers, I discovered a water bird that I'd never seen, or at least if I have seen it before I've never put a name to it. The common gallinule (*Gallinula galeata*) is the American subspecies of the Old World moorhen (*Gallinula chloropus*)—also known as swamp chickens. Their distinctive features include a red shield over the forehead and beak, and nonwebbed feet. These juveniles lacked the red shields.

I had intended to follow the channel of the river upstream from the northern end of the lake, as Ernest describes in his book, but that end of the lake was still matted with the spatterdock, hyacinth, and marsh grasses that overtook the lake during the dam repairs after Hurricane Isaac in 2012—so much so that I did not feel like dragging my way through it fighting for every foot of advance. So I turned east and came to the bank near the lodge. Perhaps an airboat would unlock the north end of the lake and the creek channel for me next time.

The east side of the lake is wholly different from the west side. It is the difference that human development makes. Whereas the west side is wild with water plants clambering onto the banks and thick undergrowth reaching down to dip branches into the water, the developed east side is characterized by high red clay banks eroded from wave action and runoff and held together by the roots of grass. Large trees occasionally lean out over the water, producing deep patches of cool, delicious shade.

As I paddled my way back toward the marina, pausing in each patch of shade, I saw a third species of water plant in full bloom—American white water lily with its large distinctive flowers. I spent a few minutes photographing it, and when I looked up at the bank I saw yet another old friend in bloom—elderberry.

I've been camping and fishing and hiking and paddling around Lake Tangipahoa for the past forty-five years or so, and I don't think I've ever been there without seeing a new-to-me plant or creature. Every trip there is a luxurious nature education. That's why it has become my favorite place to hike and one of my favorite places for a paddle.

DOWN THE MIDDLE

> You can't be unhappy in the middle of a big, beautiful river.
>
> —JIM HARRISON

A vertical stripe down the center of the State of Mississippi is characterized by rolling hills of red clay with areas of deeper topsoil or mixed clay and organic soil, which make good growing conditions for a little bit of everything from hardwood to pine to prairie. Likewise, the paddleways flowing through the center of the state illustrate a little bit of everything.

The Big Black River flows diagonally southwestward, dividing the alluvial Delta from the piney southwest. The Pearl River runs almost directly southward, alternately taking the form of swampy bayou, winding creek, bubbling riffles, tannin-stained oaky stream, wide river, swamp, marsh, and estuary. Its major tributaries include the Strong River, which enters from the east after tumbling over rocky rapids, and the Bogue Chitto River, which enters from the west in Louisiana's Honey Island Swamp.

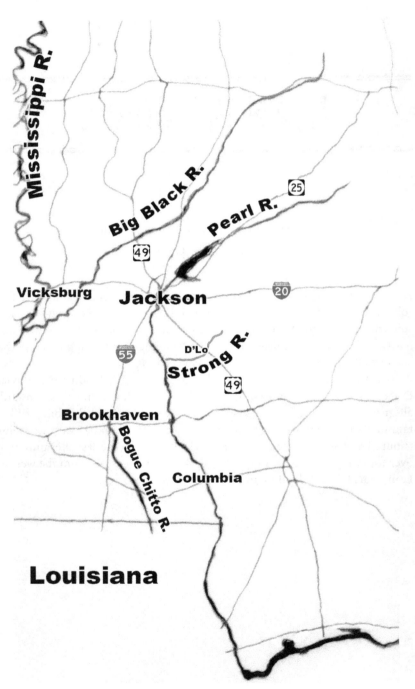

Navigable rivers of the middle region of Mississippi

PEARL RIVER

The world is your oyster. It is up to you to find the Pearl.

—CHRIS GARDNER

The Pearl River is one of the largest of the river systems that flows into the Gulf of Mexico. According to Joseph Lang's 1972 "Geohydrologic Summary of the Pearl River Basin," this watershed stores about three billion acre-feet of good-quality fresh groundwater in shallow aquifers. Lang describes the groundwater as soft with sodium bicarbonate but otherwise low to moderate in dissolved solids. This same report states that the Pearl River Basin and the surrounding Gulf coastal plain "has more potential for ground-water development than any other region of comparable size in the nation."

The Pearl vies with the Yazoo River in being the dominant river system within the State of Mississippi. The Pearl stretches 444 miles (incidentally, the same length as the Natchez Trace) from northeast Mississippi down the center of the state to the coast, draining an area of about 8,700 square miles. The Yazoo is only 188 miles long, but its widespread tentacles of meandering tributaries drain an area exceeding 13,000 square miles.

> The Pearl River got its first European name, La Rivière des Perles, from French explorers who discovered pearls near the mouth of the river and who simply translated the Acolapissa Indian name, Taleatcha. A mother-of-pearl industry sprang up as mussel fishermen went out on the river in flat-bottom boats and caught their prey with long-handled scoops such as those used on the coast for oystering. They'd bring their catch to shore and boil the mussels to remove the meat, which would be used for fish bait, while the shiny inner shells were sold to companies that converted them into buttons. This industry along the Pearl River continued into the early twentieth century but has faded in this modern era of mainly plastic buttons.

Described as flowing "from Nanih Waiya to NASA," the Pearl River starts as a trickle beneath the shade of cypress and tupelo gum trees near the legendary homeland of the Choctaw nation, twenty-some-odd miles northeast of Philadelphia, Mississippi, and passes through the state capital, where it is impounded at thirty-three-thousand-acre Ross Barnett Reservoir. Fifteen miles southwest across the lake, the river spills over a dam, foaming white into

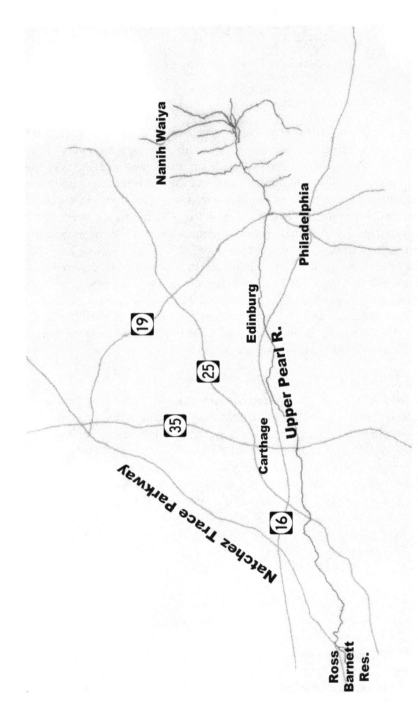

The Pearl River from Nanih Waiya to Ross Barnett Reservoir

The Pearl River begins in the cypress swamps of Nanih Waiya.

Rankin County, and cuts straight through the city and on down to the Mississippi Gulf Coast near the Stennis Space Center. Prior to emptying into the Gulf of Mexico at Lake Borgne, the Pearl River defines more than sixty miles of the border between Mississippi and Louisiana.

The Pearl begins as a cypress swamp, progresses to a logjammed creek, then slows to slack water as it approaches Ross Barnett. Below the reservoir are long stretches of big river with infrequent access, then some of the most impressive swamps in the southeast United States as the river nears the coast. All in all, the Pearl provides paddlers and sportsmen with a real sense of isolation, despite passing directly through metropolitan Jackson and eventually pouring into the Gulf of Mexico less than ten miles from the Gulf Coast's metropolitan areas. The Pearl is home to an abundance of wildlife rarely encountered on more accessible waters.

> The fact that the Pearl arises in Indian territory is apparent from the prevalence of Choctaw place-names along the river, especially north of Jackson. Nanih Waiya, considered the homeplace of the Choctaw, refers to a legendary shaman's "leaning stick." The Bogue Chitto, or "Big Creek," is actually the name of two Pearl River tributaries within Mississippi. Another tributary, the Yockanookany, refers to a "land of rivers." Pushepatapa is a "sandy-bottomed" creek. Pelahatchie means "hurricane creek," and Bogalusa means "dark water."

Indians of the Pearl

One version of the Choctaw origin story tells of nomadic ancestors from far beyond the great river to the west traveling for forty-two years before coming to rest at an old site made by an earlier mound-building culture near the confluence of several large creeks. They named the mound that they found Nanih Waiya, or "leaning stick," in reference to a divining rod their shaman planted in the hill, indicating that this was to be their new home.

Other versions of this oral history agree that proto-Choctaws settled near the confluence of several large creeks, but suggest that they constructed the Nanih Waiya mound themselves to inter the bones of their ancestors, which they had been toting around for forty-two years.

> "If the creek don't rise" is a common phrase used to express uncertainty about future plans. A couple of etymologies have been proposed for the origin of the phrase. One obvious explanation is that if the waterways in the area were to flood, that might make travel impossible. Alternatively and more probably, the expression is attributed to Benjamin Hawkins, a Revolutionary War companion of George Washington and later Georgia state representative. Hawkins was a prolific author on the topic of southeastern Indian nations, including the Creek. At one point in the late 1700s, upon receiving a summons to report to Washington, he supposedly responded in writing that he would comply with the summons, "God Willing and the Creek don't rise," apparently referring to the bellicose Creek nation.

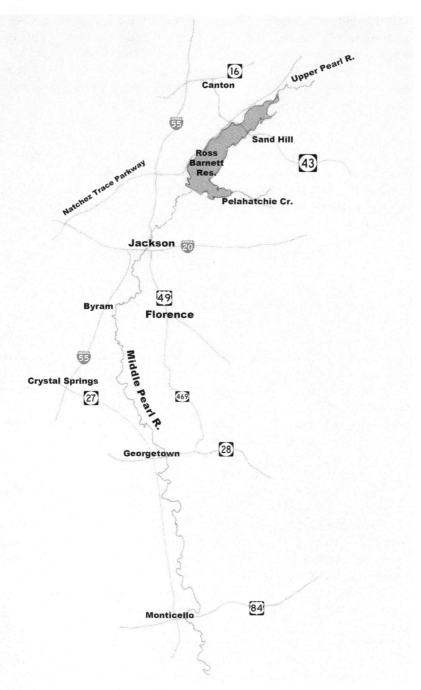

The Pearl River from Ross Barnett Reservoir to Monticello

It is hard to tell exactly which large streams these Choctaw legends are referring to. Within just a handful of miles of Nanih Waiya are numerous candidates, including Big Slough, Old Creek, Fox Branch, and Bogue Chitto Creek of central Mississippi (not to be confused with the Bogue Chitto River that feeds the Pearl far downstream). In any case, all of these creeks and others come together near Nanih Waiya to form the Pearl River.

Still another origin story has it that the Choctaw, Chickasaw, and Creek nations were all born inside the earth and emerged from the mouth of a cave in a large, wooded hill about a mile east of the Nanih Waiya mound site. The Chickasaws moved northward and eastward to occupy the Appalachian foothills near the Tennessee River, the Choctaws spread southward, and the Creek nation migrated eastward to territory that would become eastern Alabama and Georgia.

Europeans and Natives Collide at the Pearl

Since the Pearl River cuts such a prominent swath down the center of Mississippi, it is understandable that its course would intersect with ecological, cultural, economic, and political crosscurrents of the state. Indeed, the Pearl is a river of intersections and collisions.

Just as the Natchez Trace and the Pearl River meet north of the state capital of Jackson, the uppermost reaches of the Pearl River mark the collision of European-descended Americans and Native Americans in the eighteenth and nineteenth centuries.

In the eighteenth century, Spanish, French, and Anglo-American navigation and economic interests connected at the Pearl River. In the summer of 1732, French explorers mapped the Pearl from its mouth to its source. They found the area largely unpopulated, either due to seventeenth-century Choctaw-Chickasaw wars or perhaps due to European diseases spread two hundred years earlier by Hernando de Soto's expedition.

These explorers thought the Pearl was a promising paddleway that could provide access to the interior of the continent, except they found it choked with driftwood and downed trees. Sixty years later, just before the Mississippi Territory was formed, US surveyors found the Pearl in the same logjammed condition.

In the summer of 1813, "[t]he Creek Indians, in the newly formed Mississippi Territory, attacked Fort Mims in what is now Alabama (between Pensacola and Mobile on the Old Federal Road), and slaughtered and scalped over 500 people including militia men, civilian men, women and children," Pike County Historical Society president Malcolm Allen wrote in a history of the War of 1812. The Creek Indians had allied with the British under the influence of Tecumseh.

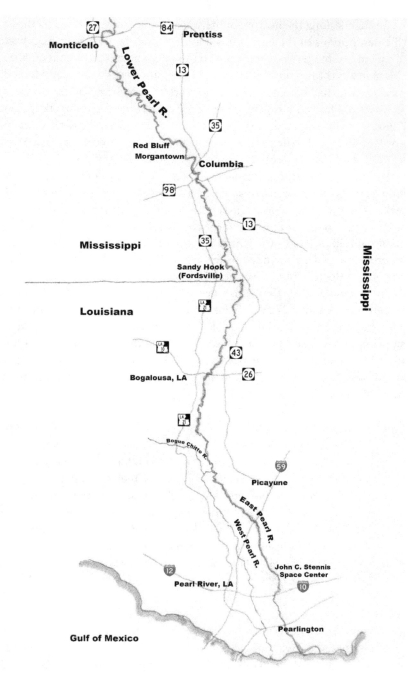

The Pearl River from Monticello to Pearlington

Residents along the nearby southern Pearl River were alarmed by the horrific descriptions of the Fort Mims massacre, and the uprising was expected to spread, so able-bodied men grabbed their guns and mustered for combat. A stockade was thrown up around the house of John Ford, an itinerant Methodist preacher who had homesteaded on the Pearl River at Sandy Hook, Mississippi.

Local militias were organized by county. After brief training, they joined Andrew Jackson's men as they set out to attack the Creek Indians to the east. The Creeks were defeated and eventually forcibly relocated west of the Mississippi River, but the War of 1812 had reached south Mississippi.

Following the campaign against the Creeks, Jackson set out for New Orleans after learning that a large British fleet was approaching in the Gulf of Mexico. Jackson's army crossed Black Creek near Brooklyn, Mississippi, and encamped at Reverend John Ford's newly fortified homestead. Part of the Black Creek National Hiking Trail near Janice Landing is named for Jackson. There are records of a soldier, wounded in this campaign, being buried at Love Creek just off the Bogue Chitto River near Holmesville, Mississippi.

In November 1814, the British fleet appeared off the coast of Louisiana, intending to capture New Orleans, control access to the Mississippi River, and seize the Louisiana Purchase. Jackson arrived, along with many Mississippians, and defeated the British on January 8, 1815. (That spawned a fiddle tune, "Eighth of January," the melody of which was later used for the song "The Battle of New Orleans" written by Jimmy Driftwood and popularized in 1959 by Bobby Horton.)

> Because the Choctaws were amenable to alliance and treaty, the European Americans designated them as one of the "Five Civilized Tribes" along with the Chickasaw, Cherokee, Seminole, and Creek. Their status as "civilized" would not, however, prevent the removal of these tribes along the Trail of Tears. A local legend has it that everywhere along the Trail of Tears that Cherokee women's tears struck the ground, white and gold *Rosa laevigata* (Cherokee rose) flowers sprang up. Actually, *Rosa laevigata* is native to East and Southeast Asia and was introduced into the United States in the late 1700s.

In 1820, the US government, represented by Andrew Jackson and Thomas Hinds, signed the Treaty of Doak's Stand with the Choctaw, who had allied with Jackson against the Red Stick Creeks during the War of 1812. The parties met, conferred, and signed the treaty near the confluence of the Pearl River and the Natchez Trace north of Jackson, Mississippi. The Treaty of Doak's Stand ceded approximately half of the Choctaw lands in Mississippi to the United States and set the stage for a removal of most of the Choctaw to lands west of the Mississippi River. This Choctaw removal began in earnest in 1830 with the Treaty of Dancing Rabbit Creek, which was signed near Macon, Mississippi, on the banks of Dancing River Creek, a tributary of the Noxubee River, which in turn flows into the Tombigbee River in Alabama

Despite the fact that the Choctaw removal to Arkansas and Oklahoma was accomplished largely bloodlessly via treaty, it was a forcible relocation and such a long, hard trek that the Choctaws described it as a "trail of tears and death." French philosopher Alexis de Tocqueville actually witnessed part of this phase of the Trail of Tears and describes it in his book *Democracy in America* as "ruin and destruction . . . a final and irrevocable adieu."

Heyday of Steamboats on the Pearl

The Pearl River's shallow and logjammed nature historically made it largely nonnavigable, leading to numerous improvement projects. Soon after the War of 1812, the Pearl was made navigable by steamboat as far north as Sandy Hook, or Fordsville as it was known then. Between the mid-1800s and the early 1900s, channels were cleared, dredged, and periodically maintained in both the West Pearl River (Louisiana side) and the East Pearl River (Mississippi side). For about a century, steamboats and commercial ships navigated the Pearl as far north as Edinburg northeast of Jackson, but nowadays you would be hard pressed even to put a kayak into the Pearl fifty river miles downstream of there. Somewhere around Carthage is now the functional highest point of navigation for any sort of paddlecraft.

Civil War Comes to the Pearl

In the 1860s, the intersection of the Pearl River and the Natchez Trace at the young state capital would be the scene of the collision between Union and Confederate forces just prior to the siege of Vicksburg.

After an unsuccessful attempt in the winter of 1862 by Union general William Tecumseh Sherman to approach Vicksburg via the Yazoo River, 563 Union soldiers were listed as captured or missing. Around 400 of those captured soldiers were moved to Jackson and imprisoned inside an old covered railway bridge that had been partially burned. That makeshift Pearl River Bridge POW camp burned completely sometime later, but a detailed sketch done by Forty-Seventh Missouri Infantry colonel Thomas Clement Fletcher survives in the Museum of Fine Arts in Boston, Massachusetts. Fletcher himself also survived to take part in the Battle of Chattanooga and the Atlanta campaign the next year. He would eventually become the first postwar governor of Missouri.

Fletcher's sketch of the Pearl River Bridge POW camp suggests that the remaining portion of the bridge over the Pearl was perhaps a quarter of the width of the river—perhaps sixty feet long and twenty feet wide. That comes out to just two or three feet of floor space for each of the four hundred prisoners.

Accounts of the makeshift prison describe deplorable conditions similar to the more famous POW camp in Andersonville, Georgia, only smaller, colder, and more cramped. There was no heat and no beds. Multiple prisoners died each day, and Fletcher's sketch shows bodies left by the front door to freeze as prisoners were dying faster than they could be interred.

Four months later at the end of April 1863, Grant crossed the Mississippi at Petit Gulf (aka Bruinsburg) at the confluence of the Mississippi River and Bayou Pierre. From there his army attacked Jackson, rescuing the prisoners who had survived the Pearl River Bridge POW camp and securing his flank in preparation to besiege Vicksburg.

> To protect their livestock from the approaching Union soldiers, some Jackson-area residents drove their animals into a swampy bend of the Pearl River and cut a canal across the bend to divert the river, confining the animals to a man-made island. The legend does not tell us how well this plan worked, but the area is now a small oxbow lake named Mule Jail right in the middle of Jackson about a mile below the reservoir outlet. Although Mule Jail Lake is privately owned, there are public walking trails around it that are accessible from Spillway Road.

Ross Barnett Reservoir

While parts of the upper Pearl may be floatable during high water, during normal conditions the highest seminavigable point is at Battle Bluff Road about halfway between Carthage and Edinburg. From there to Highway 35 south of Carthage is still likely to be rife with logjams and sandy shoals. The Pearl widens and slows at the mouth of Tuscolameta Creek just upstream from Highway 25, where dwindling current turns into slack water on down to Leake County Water Park and a low-head dam. Motorboats travel this stretch of the Pearl, but not as many as on the river below the low-head dam, which is wide open all the way to Ross Barnett Reservoir.

The reservoir is certainly the biggest development project on the Pearl. It was planned as a three-and-a-half-mile-long dam that would contain a 30,000-acre lake with a 120-mile shoreline. The reservoir was expected to swell seasonally to as much as 47,000 acres. The Corps of Engineers had considered the plan as early as 1938 and deemed it "impractical." Montgomery Watson Engineering (now MWH Global) did the construction under the direction of the Pearl River Valley Water Supply District. At the time (the early 1960s), it was the largest public project ever undertaken in Mississippi, at $25 million, and was funded by the surrounding five counties and the city of Jackson.

At 134 square miles, Ross Barnett is an intimidatingly large body of water. Factor in speedboats, sailboats, and subdivisions, and it might seem like just another giant lake. But the reservoir contains many hidden treasures in the form of coves and creeks that provide peaceful and intimate exploration. Bicyclists, hikers, and joggers enjoy the scenic roads around the reservoir as well. The banks are dotted with small parks where kids and dogs wander. Houses range from cottages to mansions, but most are attractive, in part due to local building codes. Many have docks and boathouses. Even so, there is plenty of nature in the form of cypress, pines, and marsh.

The Mill Creek cove is a good example of the numerous tributaries to the reservoir. As you enter the cove from the main lake, the channel gradually narrows past houses and docks and under a low-hanging bridge. Beyond that stands a library on the right bank—yes, residents can paddle right up to their local library. A little farther upstream, Mill Creek crosses Lakeland Drive near the Northwest Rankin schools.

The buildings thin out along the muddy creek bordered by tall, lush forest. You're liable to see a large alligator sink up ahead, leaving a ripple. There are also great blue herons, white egrets, red-winged blackbirds, and many other birds. Huge trees tower all around—hickory, oak, ash, elm—with a lush understory. Farther up, the creek flows over a metal barrier just inches under the surface. A canoe or kayak may make it unscathed, but a larger boat would likely get scratched. Next up are rocky shoals that become too shallow even for a canoe or kayak, and the creek comes to an end. Back downstream to the bay, you can explore channels and islands, a lovely mix of nature and suburbia, with lots of trees and flowering plants. Mill Creek is one of countless creeks and backwaters to explore, as a map of the reservoir testifies.

A more insidious threat—to the environment if not to humans—is something called giant salvinia. In 2019, Ross Barnett officials had to lower the water level and lay a yellow boom at the mouth of Pelahatchie Bay to curtail the invasive plant, which is native to Brazil and is affecting waterways around the state. Plants like salvinia can cling to boat trailers, propellers, and hulls and spread from one lake to another. Giant salvinia is one of many invasive aquatic species infesting state waters. Others include coontail, water milfoil, hydrilla, bladderwort, duckweed, water hyacinth, water shield, alligator weed, parrot feather, torpedo grass, eelgrass, lily pads, American lotus, and more.

> Gators are an all-too-common sight on the reservoir. In 2019, Dwain Brister of Pike County and Angie Walsh Bateman of Liberty teamed up with Chris and Amiee Campbell of Brandon to bring home a 12-foot, 5¼-inch gator in the Ross Barnett Zone north of Highway 43 in the Pearl River. They were hunting around daylight when they tied into the big one, having already caught and released numerous other good ones. "We got him hooked and he fooled around for probably forty-five minutes on the hook," Brister said, referring to treble hooks cast from rod and reel. "We got him beside the boat and knew he was a good one." They discovered that the gator had been tagged by the Mississippi Department of Wildlife, Fisheries, and Parks, which keeps up with some of the big ones, especially in Ross Barnett Reservoir. When the hunters got it to the boat, they snared it and secured it with hand lines before dispatching it with a shotgun blast to the center of the head. Brister was pretty sure this was the same gator they had hooked and lost the morning before. "He pulled 150 yards of line off the reel. We couldn't stop him, we couldn't turn him. He got in the lily pads," Brister said, noting that the gator snapped the line and escaped. The next day, though, "we got a chance to get on him, and we made it happen this time." The gator weighed 461.5 pounds. It was longer but lighter than the 11-foot, 5-inch, 540-pounder they'd caught the prior year in the upper Pearl.

Giant salvinia appears to be in a class by itself due to the rate at which it multiplies. "This particularly nasty plant can form mats several feet thick," as is written in the government publication *Managing Mississippi Ponds and Small Lakes: A Landowner's Guide*. The publication further describes the plant as a "nonnative aquatic fern that floats on the surface of the water. Leaves are in whorls of three, with two opposite leaves with distinct midrib, and a third submersed leaf that resembles roots." There are ways to treat it, but they are expensive. Efforts at Ross Barnett have included lowering the reservoir's water level and blasting the plant with flamethrowers. There are chemical applications as well, even a salvinia-eating beetle. But salvinia has a way of persisting—and spreading.

Ross Barnett is popular with fishermen, but perhaps nowhere more so than the area right below the spillway. Fishermen often stand along the shore, taking advantage of the churning waters. Great blue herons gather in unusual numbers to catch fish as well. Water gushing from open gates in the spillway provides a good current. White perch, bass, and catfish aren't the only fish in the water. Federally threatened Gulf sturgeon sometimes manage to make their way upstream from the Gulf to spawn. Another big fish occasionally spotted rolling the water is the paddlefish, sometimes called spoonbill catfish. From here, the river meanders through surprisingly wild-looking country despite being in the middle of Jackson. This is also a stretch where one or more lakes have been proposed—unsuccessfully so far—to reduce flooding and spur development.

Below the Reservoir

The stretch of river below the Ross Barnett spillway includes ten miles to a boat ramp at LeFleur's Bluff State Park's Mayes Lake day-use area off Lakeland Drive. Around a bend headed downstream from the spillway, the river narrows, flanked by white sandbars and big woods. Massive trees tower along the banks, reminiscent of tropical rivers. A tributary leads to an enclosure of green shadow and songbird silence. A hawk screams as it soars above the cypress trees. Sandy circles visible underwater mark the beds of fish like coppernosed bream. White flecks floating on the still water are the husks of midges, tiny insects that feed the fish. Back on the river, barn swallows flit around nest holes in the bank. Dirt paths show where beaver, deer, and wild hog slide down to the water's edge. There are no camps and surprisingly little litter. About the only evidence of humanity is a distant hum of traffic.

At LeFleur's Bluff State Park on the west bank, hiking trails lead from the river to the Mississippi Museum of Natural Science, which features fantastic exhibits representing natural habitats found throughout the state.

> As fine as the reservoir-to-Mayes-Lake stretch is, most people in the Jackson area have probably never seen this stretch of the Pearl. Indeed, a Jackson canoe vendor and outfitter said he'd never floated that stretch and only knew of two people who had.

The distances between access points below Jackson are impressive, more than fifty miles in places. Boat ramps are far apart on the lower Pearl, public lands minimal. This situation is not uncommon with a sizeable river like the Pearl, with steep banks flanked by oxbow lakes, sloughs, and swamps. Down here, the river is wider than most paddlers are used to. With few exceptions, paddlers stay on smaller streams, while fishermen prefer lakes.

One advantage to a big river is the broad vistas of clouds. It's worth bringing along a guide to cloud formations just to learn to identify them. Floaters are likely to see bald eagles soaring overhead, their fanned white tails backlit and white heads snowy in the sunshine. Then there are the herons, hawks, vultures, kingfishers, wild turkeys, songbirds, and ducks galore.

Threats to the Lower Pearl

At the southern edge of LeFleur's Bluff State Park, a low-head dam at the Jackson Water Works pumping station blocks boat traffic. Dams, canals, levees, and water control structures are known to have highly negative effects on wetlands and the ecological services they provide. Rock weirs and low-head dams impede Gulf sturgeon and other migratory species from accessing upstream areas. Increasingly, these artificial structures are being removed to allow natural river activities to resume.

> The Pascagoula River system is one of the few remaining southern waterways with natural water regimes, and is a potential model for restoring the Pearl River floodplain.

Another problem for many landowners along the Pearl, especially downstream of the reservoir, is erosion. When the outflow gates at Ross Barnett shut after a flood, water levels in the Pearl can plummet as much as twenty feet in three days. The saturated, suddenly exposed banks collapse, dropping trees and tons of soil into the river, a huge problem for landowners. Reservoir officials note that after a late-spring flood the reservoir must retain enough water to supply the Jackson area through the summer, and that may require shutting the floodgates and causing a fast drop downriver. They also point out that fallen trees and caving banks occur above the reservoir as well, which suggests the problem may be partly natural. Release of water can also cause unexpected rises downriver that can affect paddlers and campers, who may discover the water level rising for no apparent reason.

Threats to the Pearl Basin are not confined to the reservoir and lower river. The conservation group Wildlife Mississippi purchased 4,600 acres adjacent to the uppermost Pearl to serve as a protected area for threatened species and as a buffer between urban development and the drainage that provides most of Jackson's drinking water. The area was later named the Fannye Cook Natural Area after the Crystal Springs native who championed efforts to create the Mississippi Game and Fish Commission and the natural science museum.

Pearl Riverkeepers and the One Lake Project

In response to ecological challenges, the Pearl River Basin has another group of champions. Formed in 2017, the Pearl Riverkeepers is a large group of volunteers who take on big issues, including pollution, water testing, and development.

The Pearl Riverkeepers organization was founded by retired navy helicopter pilot and flight instructor Abby Braman. Because of the obvious need for a group of volunteers to help protect the Pearl River Basin, the group's ranks were rapidly swelled by naturalists, Scouts, and other conservation-minded residents of Mississippi and Louisiana up and down the river.

Projects of the Pearl Riverkeepers, in conjunction with other government and conservation organizations, include organizing river cleanup days, training citizen scientists, monitoring bacteria in Ross Barnett Reservoir, developing recreational access to the river south of the reservoir, and monitoring sediment pollution.

The fledgling environmental group's biggest early battle was to oppose the so-called One Lake Project, a proposed flood control reservoir that would involve dredging and straightening the Pearl below Jackson in addition to damming the river to impound a 1,500-acre lake just below the outlet of the reservoir. Numerous public meetings were held, but opponents, including the Pearl Riverkeepers, claimed that public response was stifled. After a flurry of press releases by lake opponents, including the Pearl Riverkeepers and Sierra Club, officials from counties, cities, and parishes up and down the river passed resolutions opposing the One Lake Project. Hinds County supervisors weighed in in favor of the project, as did Rankin officials, but on a vastly reduced scale.

As it stands, the freshwater pouring out of the Pearl moderates the salinity of the Gulf, making that area a haven for oysters and other wildlife. Oysters are still big business even though the mother-of-pearl trade died off in the first half of the 1900s. In fact, it may have been the oystermen of the mouth of the Pearl, fearing for their livelihood, who put the final nail in the coffin of the One Lake Project hundreds of miles upstream.

Tributaries Navigable by Paddlecraft

The Pearl has few tributaries navigable even by paddlecraft. The main ones are all south of the reservoir and include the Strong River, which comes in from the east near Georgetown, and the Bogue Chitto River, which winds through southwest Mississippi before entering the Pearl just below Bogalusa, Louisiana.

The Pearl is, however, fed by many creeks that are enjoyed by local folks willing to deal with logjams and shallows for some good fishing or outdoor adventure. For example, the Yockanookany (Yock-a-NOOK-a-nee), which enters from the north above Ross Barnett Reservoir between Highway 25 and Leake County Water Park, is a fine fishing creek, but you'll need to pack a chainsaw with your tackle box. An easier way to see the Yockanookany is to paddle upstream from the Pearl, where you can experience a half-mile or more of quiet water and deep woods before coming to fallen trees. Much the same can be said for more tributaries downstream, like the Fair River, Silver Creek, and White Sand Creek in the Monticello vicinity, Louisiana's Pushepatapa (push-pa-TAP) Creek near Bogalusa, and Hobolochitto Creek (Ho-bo-lo-CHIT-to, locally known as "the Boley") near Picayune, among others. These are lovely little streams but can make for difficult paddling.

> A comedian struck a note with his middle-aged audience when he commented, "I really thought as a kid that quicksand would be a bigger problem in the world than it is." Indeed, it seems like back in the day, every other superhero or Western TV series eventually got around to having a protagonist trapped in quicksand and barely escaping. Quicksand is not uncommon on southwest Mississippi streams. If you wade the sandy shallows of the Pearl or Homochitto Rivers, you just might plunge up to your knees in quicksand, a soupy mix of sand and icy water. It's good to hang onto your canoe or at least carry a paddle when wading such places, to help get yourself out. Quicksand is caused by water percolating up from underneath, turning solid sand into the consistency of wet cement. Fortunately it is rarely more than a few feet deep and has little in common with the man-eating suction pits of old movies.

The Strong River enters from the east a couple miles downstream from Georgetown. The Lower Rockport Road bridge is next. On an unnamed tributary, clear green water forms a demarcation line where it enters the Pearl. Vanilla Water Park is a good take-out north of Monticello.

The fifty-mile stretch of Pearl River between Monticello and Columbia was split in 2010 with the construction of a bridge six miles north of Columbia. The $20.5 million project was the first phase of a three-phase plan to extend Highway 44 east from Jayess to Goss—Phase One connected Highway 587 near White Bluff on the west side of the river to Highway 13 near Goss on the east, a distance of six miles.

It's still a fine stretch of river, even with the bridge. You can launch at Atwood Water Park at Monticello into the wide, muddy Pearl, where walls of woods lean on either side. In the summertime, a mockingbird may make a high, lonesome sound over the low sizzle of cicadas. A large alligator swims across the river. An anhinga shoots past like a black tube with wings. In three miles, Silver Creek flows in from the left—wide, willowy, and shallow. A couple miles farther on, a bayou-like creek enters from the right. A bright yellow oriole perches on a limb, where it evidently has a nest. Farther downriver are a couple of buzzard roosts where dozens perch in a tree or squat on a small gravel island at a stretch of swift water.

A sandbar on the east side of the river provides shelter from the harsh evening sun by a screen of small willows. Deerflies hover about amid the surge of cicadas. At night mosquitoes emerge, while crowds of mayflies cluster around a lantern or flashlight. Summer nights are hot, but at 3:30 a.m. a cool breeze stirs the trees, and at 4:00 a train blasts down the tracks on the west side of the river, igniting a pack of coyotes, who yarble in response.

Daylight comes with a spell of brief morning cool. White Sand Creek enters from the east, shallow, swift, and quicksandy. In the woods, white elderberry flowers stand out against the jungle greenery. A towhee whistles. A fish crow says "ah-ah," an American crow "caw, caw." Anhingas, kingfishers, kildeer, great blue herons, little blue herons, egrets, hawks, alligators, dragonflies, deer, turtles all make appearances. A diamondback water snake crosses the river in a fast line, in a hurry to avoid alligators. By noon on a summer day, the sandbars are so scorching it's hard to walk barefoot.

In sharp contrast is the water at the mouth of Tilton Creek. The clear, swift, spring-fed stream runs through a cypress canyon and spills over a shallow sand shelf into the deep, dark Pearl—an oasis. At the Goss bridge, which has a boat at a ramp on the northeast side, weekend visitors might include four-wheeler riders, swimmers, and beer drinkers. This being Mississippi, they're likely to greet strangers politely and conclude with, "Y'all have a safe trip."

Mississippi's "Little Grand Canyon"

About ten miles north of Columbia Water Park near Morgantown lies a geological wonder—a remarkable semicircular canyon opening toward the Pearl

Red Bluff on the Pearl River above Morgantown

River to the east that some have called "Mississippi's Little Grand Canyon." Though it's named Red Bluff for the predominance of red clay, you can also see streaks of purples and tans.

Local residents say it's always been there. Geologists say it was formed by an ancient river flowing across the area thousands of years ago depositing silt across south Louisiana, Mississippi, and the Florida panhandle. More recently the canyon has been expanded by erosion from rainfall as well as springs that flow through the bottom of the canyon feeding the Pearl. At times, the top edges have crumbled and sloughed off, widening the canyon and forcing the rerouting of nearby State Highway 587.

Below Ross Barnett Reservoir, the Pearl River widens into open water.

A Trip Downriver

Back on the river, you can't see the Grand Canyon–like geology far above on the west bank. The air smells fresh where a creek enters, with scents of lemon and rose. A flock of white birds rockets overhead so fast that at first you might think you're hearing some sort of aircraft. In a sharp bend, springwater spouts from mossy clay banks—nature's faucets.

Motorboaters wave as they pass, going to and from the Morgantown boat ramp downriver. As with the folks at the Goss bridge, people on rivers are nearly always friendly and hospitable. After dusk, a boat cruises along the bank, shining a spotlight into the trees. After a while, though, the night turns quiet and cool.

In the cool, gray morning, the river is smooth as a lake, and deer come down to graze at the water's edge. The wilderness spell is interrupted a bit at Morgantown by camphouses, tethered motorboats, and the smell of woodsmoke. The river stays wide and sluggish as it passes Holiday Creek and Harpers Creek and approaches the pavilion and boat ramp of Columbia Water Park.

From Columbia to Bogalusa is another fifty-mile stretch. There are boat ramps both at Columbia Water Park and Highway 98 at Columbia. The stretch begins with the sounds of traffic and industry, and a discharge pipe with a gush of green water. Shortly farther on, though, this distasteful scene is mitigated by the sight of bald eagles soaring overhead and alligators cruising silently. Traffic sounds give way to running water, rustling leaves, and birdsong, including the chittering of kingfishers zipping back and forth.

At dusk, swifts flap overhead, diving for bugs. If it's springtime, you may hear turkeys gobble as they prepare to roost. A heron croaks as it flies to a tree. Dawn birdsong is raucous. More turkeys gobble—you may even see a gobbler as it struts, turns, and spreads its fan, slipping in and out of the fog like a shadow. An osprey swoops down, screaming threateningly if you come near its high-tree nest. Mississippi kites wheel and dive, never flapping their wings. Quails whistle, doves call, owls hoot, crows cackle, songbirds trill. An alligator adds a bass note with a grunt.

Sandbars show tracks of bobcat, deer, fox, possum, raccoon, hog, coyote, nutria, and beaver, plus slide marks where gators and turtles have crawled out of the water and laid their eggs. People are the scarcest species out here, just a rare fisherman in a boat now and then. A sandy island about a quarter mile long and twenty feet wide topped with willows harbors gator tracks the size of a man's hand and a belly indentation where it lay under the willows watching. Farther down the Pearl is Hunt Bluff, which looks to be a hundred feet tall—a clay sculpture topped by pine trees. The Pearl reaches the Louisiana line northeast of the village of Angie, a short distance upstream from Hunt Bluff. From here south it forms the boundary between Mississippi on the east and Louisiana on the west.

The Atomic Era Comes to the Pearl

The only two times that atomic bombs have been tested on American soil east of the Mississippi River was when both were detonated within twenty miles of downtown Hattiesburg. Between Foxworth and Sandy Hook, Lower Little Creek enters the Pearl from the east. About twenty miles up Lower Little Creek toward Hattiesburg, near the confluence of Grantham and Half Moon Creeks, lies the Tatum Dome nuclear test site.

In October 1964, as part of Operation Whetstone, a 5.3-kiloton atomic device (about one-third the strength of the weapon that was dropped on Hiroshima) was detonated inside the Tatum salt dome more than half a mile below the surface of southeast Mississippi. This detonation, dubbed the Salmon Event, was part of a project by the Atomic Energy Commission and the Department of Defense to improve their ability to detect underground atomic testing by other nations.

Scientists had estimated that the explosion would probably displace the surface by less than one-eighth of an inch, but residents were evacuated from the area as a precaution. In actuality, observers at the site estimated the blast wave at approximately an inch. At ground zero, sweetgum trees and pines swayed in the ripple from the blast, while almost twenty miles away the *Hattiesburg American* newspaper building was buffeted as if by an earthquake for five or six seconds; 835 damage reports were filed from the Hattiesburg area—mostly broken windows.

Two years later, the next test, named the Sterling Event, involved the detonation of a 380-ton atomic device in the cavity that had been formed by the previous test. There were subsequent nonatomic tests performed at the Salmon site, and later there was an ill-fated proposal to store nuclear waste there.

After the site was closed, it was monitored for many years to make sure radiation did not escape. As expected, nothing but clean water and minnows have ever flowed down Half Moon and Grantham Creeks into the Pearl River. At one point, the federal government even offered to take journalists on a tour down into the dome to demonstrate that the radiation was contained. No journalists took them up on the offer.

Now the Salmon site has been turned over to the State of Mississippi, and it lies within the bounds of a national forest nursery. There are historical markers at the site but otherwise not much to see.

Honey Island Swamp

Starting at the community of Sandy Hook, the Pearl forms the Mississippi-Louisiana border, with Louisiana to the west and Mississippi to the east. Sandy Hook was named for a nearby creek whose bed was so sandy that several teams of horses had to be hooked together to pull a wagon through.

Below Bogalusa, the Pearl becomes complicated by man-made canals, low-head dams, and a rock weir. Even more complex is the labyrinth of cypress swamp and marsh within contiguous public lands reaching to the coast—Mississippi's 13,000-acre Old River Wildlife Management Area, the 36,000-acre Bogue Chitto National Wildlife Refuge, and Louisiana's 34,000-acre Pearl River WMA. By the time the Pearl reaches Highway 90 near the coast, it has divided into five distinct channels. Altogether, that's 250 square miles of swamp, and a paddlecraft is the best way to explore it.

At Pool's Bluff, about ten miles below Bogalusa, an old barge canal splits off to the southwest and runs due south along the west side of the basin. Also at Pool's Bluff, a sill, or low-head dam, crosses the Pearl. Several miles below Pool's Bluff the Pearl splits, with the river going east and Wilson Slough going west. In the past, most of the water went down Wilson Slough, but the Corps of Engineers built a weir across it to slow it down. A canoer died in 1998 while repeatedly running the weir's fast water, and the Corps reconfigured it to make it safer, but portaging is always advised for boats at man-made structures, which produce potentially deadly hydraulics.

The east branch of the Pearl goes southeast past Walkiah Bluff Water Park. It once continued south to Pearlington, but a huge logjam in the 1800s blocked the flow and sent the water west down Holmes Bayou, which joins Wilson Slough, which by that point is the West Pearl. The West Pearl meets the old barge canal just past what used to be the southernmost of three locks. Below Interstate 59, several bayous branch off, and below Interstate 10 the river itself splits. By the time it reaches Highway 90 it has five large channels. The East Pearl is the largest at that point but is more of an estuary. As you go upriver on the East Pearl from Pearlington, it gets small and logjammed by around I-59. The West Pearl contains the main current. The other three middle Pearls are more like big bayous.

This entire confusing region goes by the name of Honey Island Swamp. The town of Pearl River, Louisiana, claims to be the home of Honey Island Swamp, but it's hard to say exactly what that really is. There is an actual Honey Island—a patch of marsh south of Highway 90, east of the Middle Pearl River and north of Black Bayou—named for its population of wild honeybees. So you could argue that the real Honey Island Swamp is the marsh south of Highway 90. But the town of Pearl River is ten miles north of Highway 90. It's also at the northern end of the Pearl River WMA, so you could say that Honey Island Swamp and the Pearl River WMA are one and the same. Then again, the swamp really begins even farther north where the Pearl River splits into two channels some five miles south of Bogalusa, which is also where the Bogue Chitto National Wildlife Refuge begins. Or, you can extend the boundaries of Honey Island Swamp all the way north to Bogalusa by including the Old River WMA. No matter how you define it, public lands encompass a 250-square-mile wilderness along the lower Pearl River—an impressive wetland on a par with the Everglades, Okefenokee, Mobile-Tensaw, Pascagoula, Atchafalaya, and Big Thicket.

Honey Island Swamp is such a wilderness that US Special Forces use it for training. The Naval Small Craft Instruction and Technical Training School is based at the 128,000-acre Stennis Space Center on the east side of the river. Field training takes place in a 3,800-acre area a navy website calls "some of the finest riverine and littoral training areas in the world." Stennis is a world-class technological center, yet the remarkable thing is that, from the perspective of a paddler on the river, there's little evidence it even exists. Even today, despite all the changes, the Pearl River swamps seem more stone age than space age.

One way to explore this vast and mysterious swamp is to enter it from the Bogue Chitto River, which flows into it from the west. The Bogue Chitto crosses the West Pearl and meanders over a low-head dam into deep, dark forest.

Cypress-kneed streams course past an occasional, tiny, shaded sandbar. Small sloughs branch off here and there, and if you really want to see the inner swamp, take off down one. You may wind up on a swift, curving stream under huge trees that look like something in a Tarzan movie. Fallen logs make navigation even dicier. At last you emerge on a wide river—wide enough for headwinds from the south to whip the river into swells and whitecaps. Fortunately, sandbars are available for refuge.

If the big river seems too much, take off down another side branch. But expect it to divide again, with branches angling off to the north and east, continuing to split until it's narrow and swift. The ground in the palmetto jungle is rooted up by wild hogs with hooves that look the size of an African buffalo's. Bayous branch and branch again, spreading into wide channels through marsh country. Eventually, though, they will emerge at signs of civilization at Highway 90, the last road before the Gulf.

For a more modest excursion, you can check out the upper East Pearl from Walkiah Bluff Water Park near Picayune. Going upstream against a negligible current, you pass camps and houses on the right through zones of faint odors—wood smoke, sewage, laundry detergent, dead animal, hound pens. Dogs bark to the right, herons croak on the left. It's not far to the Wilson Slough diversion canal, the noisy whitewater chute built by the Corps of Engineers.

Or simply drive to the Pearl River WMA at the town of Pearl River. To reach the WMA, cross over the wide, swirling West Pearl River into a wooded realm of cypress swamp and hardwood forest. You may find the place surprisingly busy, especially on a weekend. There's a shooting range, nature trails, and deer-hunting food plots. A road ends at a missing bridge over the East Pearl River, which here is little more than a narrow, muddy slough, a far cry from the wide waterway it becomes at Highway 90 near the coast.

Perhaps the simplest way to explore this region is by boat from Highway 90, which has launches on the East, West, and Middle Pearl Rivers. From any of these, a boater can travel north into cypress swamp or south into the marsh. Whichever route you choose, a map, compass, and GPS are advisable.

On the broad East Pearl, which flows south from Pearlington, motorboats aren't uncommon, as skiers, fishermen, and joy riders enjoy the outdoors. Fortunately, the river is wide enough that their wakes shouldn't pose a problem. Four miles south of Pearlington is a sandbar on the far side of a channel, where you may be surprised by the massive hulk of an oceangoing ship passing to or from Port Bienville Industrial Park a mile and a half to the east. The sandbar was dredged from the bottom to keep the shipping channel open. The ground is mottled with the tracks of familiar swamp species like nutria, coyote, hog, and raccoon. A high bank provides an elevation from which to look out across the marsh to distant piney woods, billowing smokestacks, bridges, a train moving along a trestle, and open water. To the south, the Pearl empties into Little Lake, a bay that gives way to Lake Borgne, a much larger bay in the Gulf of Mexico. To the southwest, out of sight, sprawls New Orleans, and to the southeast the Chandeleur Islands.

The Space Age Comes to the Pearl

When newspaperman J. Oliver Emmerich commented that the Pearl River runs "from Nanih Waiya to NASA," he was referring to the legendary homeland of the Choctaw Indians at the headwaters and the space-age rocket testing facility at the mouth.

Originally named (noncreatively) the Mississippi Test Facility, the NASA installation on the banks of the Pearl River was built in 1961 as part of the Apollo space program. The main function at the facility was to test rocket engines, but for a while it also manufactured 155 mm shells, among other military equipment, for the army and marines. In 1988, the Mississippi Test Facility was renamed Stennis Space Center by President Ronald Reagan in honor of retiring Senator John Stennis.

The location on the banks of the Pearl near the intracoastal waterway allowed NASA to deliver engines and boosters by water. This water access, conveniently located between the NASA Michoud Assembly Facility in New Orleans and the Huntsville Space and Rocket Center in Alabama, made the Stennis Center one of two leading sites proposed to build and refuel shuttle solid boosters. The other was at the abandoned Yellow Creek nuclear site in northeast Mississippi near the Tenn-Tom Waterway.

The Swamp Dimension, by Ernest Herndon

I was planning a canoe trip through Honey Island Swamp when I read an article in a newspaper, "Missing Hunter Survives a Week on Worms, Snails." The story told of a turkey hunter who got lost in Honey Island Swamp near the mouth of the Bogue Chitto River and couldn't get out for a week. Hmmm.

Meanwhile, I asked around about the big wetland and discovered that quite a few people have gotten turned around there, though perhaps not quite so dramatically. As it turned out, my canoeing pal Scott Williams and I got lost in Honey Island Swamp also. We not only wound up on the wrong river, we wound up in the wrong state. You might say that we had entered another dimension—the Swamp Dimension.

Scott (a long-distance sea kayaker and sailor) and I (an any-distance canoer) had long been itching to explore Honey Island Swamp, ranked as one of the wildest areas along the Gulf Coast. The 250 square miles of woods and marsh lie along the lower Pearl River, which forms a border between Mississippi and Louisiana.

But the lower Pearl is not just one river. It includes the East Pearl, the West Pearl, the Middle Pearl, the West Middle Pearl, and countless other bayous, sloughs, creeks, channels, and alligator runs.

Armed with inadequate maps (this was before the era of portable GPS), our plan was simple—just canoe the Bogue Chitto River, cross the West Pearl, and take a right on the East Pearl. Then we'd drift downstream till we reached Scott's truck parked at Pearlington, near the coast.

We followed the slow, muddy Bogue Chitto through deep, dark forest. We made camp in the woods where a cypress-kneed stream coursed past a small, shaded sandbar.

When Scott and I make camp, one of our first chores was to sling our hammocks. He had a green military hammock he'd bought from a Miskito Indian in Nicaragua; mine was a huge red, yellow, and blue one given me by a Honduran farmer near the Salvadoran border. After we hung them and gave them a thorough comfort test, we pitched our tent, rounded up firewood, and cooked supper. It was all timed so we could stretch out in the hammocks by the campfire as night fell and the swamp came alive with noises.

We didn't get lost until the next day. That's when we turned off the main Bogue Chitto, following a mysterious wooden sign with an emblem of a canoe.

"Must be some sort of canoe trail," Scott said.

"That's funny," I said as we turned onto the cypress slough. "When I called the Pearl River Basin Development District for a map, nobody mentioned any canoe trails."

We soon passed more odd canoe signs bearing numbers with no apparent significance. Eventually we wound up on a swift, narrow stream under huge trees. My red fiberglass Old Town canoe slammed into fallen logs as we struggled to keep from turning over. There were no more canoe signs, and we had no idea where we were. I kept an eye on my compass, which pointed east, north, south, and occasionally west.

At last we emerged onto a wide river. Scott and I nodded as though we had planned it this way.

"This must be the East Pearl," I said.

"Must be," he said. (Only it wasn't.)

Now all we had to do was drift down to Pearlington over the next few days to get to his truck parked at Highway 90. But we quickly began noticing that our maps were wrong. They said we should soon pass Walkiah Bluff Water Park on the east bank of the Pearl River. There would be a boat ramp and water faucets. But the miles slid past, and no Walkiah Bluff.

We were also supposed to encounter Holmes Bayou branching off to the west. It, too, did not appear.

"These stupid maps!" I declared.

"I guess we should have gotten quad maps," Scott suggested.

"Maybe they closed that water park."

Not only were our maps lying, the very river itself was behaving suspiciously. Streams were flowing east out of the river when they should have been flowing west. Where could they be going? There could be just one answer—we were in the Swamp Dimension. Outdoorsmen familiar with swamps may know what I mean. They have a way of doing away with normal laws of physics. That's what I call the Swamp Dimension—sort of like the Twilight Zone but wetter.

Meanwhile, a brutal south wind whipped the wide river into swells and whitecaps, battering our canoe and taxing our strength. We took refuge on a sandbar and made camp.

As the wind died we heard highway noises nearby. That made no sense. According to our calculations, we were miles from the nearest road.

Next day, though, we passed under Interstate 59, evidently having paddled farther south than we thought. But we still felt certain we must be on the East Pearl.

Then a large branch of the river split off to our left.

"Hey, this must be Mike's River," I said, studying my map. "It angles off to the east for about ten miles and runs back into the East Pearl."

"Want to take it?" Scott said.

"Sure. It'll get us out of this wind."

We turned down the muddy river. It promptly divided again, with branches angling off to the north and east. Strange. What's more, we saw signs saying Louisiana Wildlife Management Area—yet by our reckonings we had to be in Mississippi. Was the very government itself in error?

Our stream continued to split until it was narrow and swift. Overhanging trees gave us a rainforest feeling. After a quick lunch of sardines and squashed mosquitoes, we resumed paddling.

"As long as we keep going downstream we'll be all right," I said.

The river ran into a wide, sluggish bayou with no current.

"As long as we keep headed south we'll be all right," I said.

The bayou angled northeast.

"Wonder where we are?" I said.

As shadows lengthened, Scott and I found a small strip of high ground in the jungle, right next to an area rooted up by wild hogs. We slung our hammocks, ate supper, and fell asleep in the tent listening to the death screams of small creatures in the night.

In the morning, dodging a cottonmouth snake, we loaded the canoe and paddled onto the bayou, expecting soon to reenter the East Pearl. But the bayou continued to fork, spreading into wide channels through marsh country. The Pearl River had utterly disappeared. We had to face facts: we were flat-out lost.

We tried to discern currents by the angle of lily pad stems and the pattern of the waves. Then we noticed surer signs—a utility pole, and a small bridge that had no business being there. At the bridge I asked an old-timer what road this was.

"Highway 90," he said.

Why, Scott's truck was parked on Highway 90!

"What river is this?" I asked.

"The Middle Pearl."

Scott and I stared at each other in bewilderment. Wrong river, wrong state. We had thought we were on the East Pearl in Mississippi but in fact were on the Middle Pearl in Louisiana.

I won't bore you with theories of how we wound up so drastically off course. Actually, I still haven't figured it out. I just chalk it up to being caught in the Swamp Dimension.

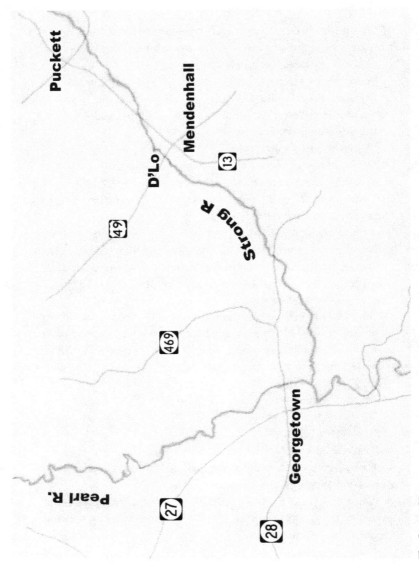

The Strong River

STRONG RIVER

*Life is like the river, sometimes it sweeps you gently along
and sometimes the rapids come out of nowhere.*

—EMMA SMITH

Bryan Batson nearly lost his life in the Strong River around 1960. He was with a group of boys canoeing the stream thirty miles south of Jackson when his canoe flipped and he went under. When he tried to surface, he found himself blocked by branches. Batson was about to run out of air when his buddy, Bill Lauderdale, reached down and grabbed him by the collar, hoisting him to safety.

> The Strong River (Choctaw *bogue homi*, or "bitter creek") is named for its strong, bitter taste. The reddish-brown tint that makes some of Mississippi's creeks look like tea comes from dissolved tannin washed out of decaying oak leaves and acorns. The bitter water also gave the town of D'Lo (pronounced DEE-lo) its name when early French explorers noted on a map that this place had "de l'eau non potable," or undrinkable water. The tannin-stained color of some southern creeks is so characteristic that it has influenced their names, such as Black and Red Creeks in Mississippi.

The Strong, though sluggish for most of its length, still poses some daunting challenges. Thirty years after Batson's near-death experience, he and Lauderdale arrived at D'Lo Water Park to float the river again—and indications were that this trip would be every bit as dangerous. The river was up, and the park manager warned they shouldn't attempt to float it.

This time Lauderdale and Batson had brought their young sons and three other friends. They had two canoes with them and had hoped to rent a third at the park, but the manager refused because, he said, the river was too dangerous. There was no way they could get down it without capsizing, he maintained. In the past, he said, teams had to rescue everybody from canoeing instructors to Corps of Engineers experts, all of them skillful but unable to handle the raging Strong River.

Unable to persuade the manager to rent them a canoe, the seven paddlers returned to the river for a closer look. They weren't reckless thrill seekers, but they had driven from many parts of the state to be here and weren't going to give up easily. Rapids thundered just above the boat launch, but otherwise the river looked OK, the level about six inches above normal.

That left the problem of getting five adults and two kids downriver in two seventeen-foot canoes. They held an impromptu discussion and decided to try it. But first they took precautions—getting a rescue rope ready, putting on life vests, tying gear in place, and preparing mentally to be hurled into a cauldron of icy whitewater. A cold front was moving in on the bright November day, so a capsize would be miserable—or worse.

The roar of the nearby rapids didn't soothe their nerves. Judging from the park manager's warnings, this river would be on a scale with, say, the Nantahala or Ocoee, both famous whitewater rivers in the Appalachians. A tad anxious, their canoes tippy with the loads, they pushed away from shore and wondered how long they had before the first capsize.

While drifting downstream and waiting for the whitewater, they admired the big cypress woods, swimming beavers, sunning turtles, gliding cranes. Wind gusted from the west, making paddling difficult on slow stretches. Finally they heard it—a crashing roar downstream around a bend. It sounded big.

Rounding the bend, they saw the whole river drop down over rocks. The lead paddler stood up to survey the rapids. He sat back down as the boat was drawn into the current.

In mid-rapid the canoe stopped and pivoted 180 degrees, caught on shoals. For an instant it looked like capsize time was here. But somehow it remained steady as they pushed off backward through the rapids.

Noting their near disaster, the second group paddled to the bank and got out to take a look. There was no easy course through the rapids, but they thought they saw a way to the left, providing the water wasn't too shallow. For all the talk of high water, the main danger on this kind of rapid was shallows, where a boat could lodge on rocks like the first one had done.

The second group paddled back upriver and turned around, drifting toward the rapids, backpaddling to slow their approach. As they neared, however, they noticed the first group onshore below vigorously motioning for them to go right.

The second group opted for the center and slid right into the heart of the rapids, into the crest of foamy white. The canoe went through as if on a cloud. The paddlers arrived at the shore to a round of applause.

Somehow they had survived. Sure, the rapids were only a few inches deep, and the bridge was a short distance downstream, but they figured they were real whitewater heroes. They didn't have to be rescued after all.

That experience pretty much summed up the Strong—beautiful, sometimes dramatic, but overall benign.

West to the Pearl

The Strong River begins in Bienville National Forest near Morton and flows southwest past Puckett and Mendenhall before reaching the Pearl River. Only about a third of its ninety-two-mile length is floatable, the twenty-five miles or so from D'Lo Water Park near Mendenhall down to the Pearl, and even the upper parts of that are too shallow at times. But those who have heard the thunder of its rapids will agree that the Strong is well named, even if the name actually refers to the taste of the water.

In February 1990, flash flooding on a tributary forced several hundred Mendenhall residents to flee their homes, taking shelter in a National Guard armory and a church. The tributary, which empties into the Strong about half a mile from town, rose about two feet in seven minutes, piling into the flooded Strong and flowing backward.

Lest you conclude this is a raging river, however, bear in mind that most of the time it's placid, more so than many state streams. There are long stretches with virtually no current at all, and only occasional shoals and falls for brief excitement.

The river is usually floatable at D'Lo Water Park, located off Highway 49 northwest of Mendenhall. The park—known locally as "the rock"—has a campground and provides canoe rental and shuttle service. From the park boat ramp to Chapel Bridge near Pinola is eleven miles. (Merit Bridge, a historic iron bridge, crosses five miles below the park but offers no public access.) In the dry season, this stretch of river may be shallow and require a good bit of towing. Otherwise it's just slow, coasting between walls of immense hardwood forest with few sandbars, inhabited by shy beavers, sunning turtles, and gliding cranes.

Just before Chapel Bridge is the abovementioned river-wide rapid, which can be exciting and fun provided there's enough water to get over it. The roar sounds intimidating, especially if the level is up a bit, but—as the paddlers above discovered—the main hazard is getting stuck on the rocks and having to wade a boat through.

Strong River Camp and Farm for boys and girls is located at Highway 28. The nine-mile run from Highway 28 to Bridgeport Road starts with a long rapid, then subsides into more quiet, leisurely water, perfect for silent contemplation. Sandbars, nearly nonexistent on the upper river, become noticeable at last. Scenic bluffs tower over the south bank about five miles below Highway 28. From Bridgeport Road, it's just three or four miles to the Pearl River. After that it is twenty-five miles down the Pearl to Wanilla Water Park.

The Strong's slow, often shallow nature makes casual fishing hit-or-miss. Hand-grabbers occasionally pull out some big catfish around D'Lo Water Park and elsewhere, and trotliners and bass fishermen report some success, but experienced fishermen sometimes come away empty-handed after a hard day's angling. To many, the Strong is best for daydreaming. Its big, quiet woods and generally unobstructed paddling make it perfect for thoughtful conversation and plans for future trips.

Grierson's First Raid

The Strong empties into the Pearl about fifteen miles east-southeast of Hazlehurst, one stop in a guerrilla campaign that Union general William T. Sherman referred to as "the most brilliant expedition of the Civil War."

In the early spring of 1863, General Ulysses S. Grant was preparing to attack Vicksburg and needed a distraction to draw Confederate defenses away from the bluff city. An idea was proposed to send a cavalry raid southward from Memphis through central Mississippi to sever rail and communications lines, sow disinformation, destroy supplies, and create general mayhem in hopes of drawing both attention and Confederate cavalry units away from Vicksburg.

The officers first offered the command declined because they preferred to participate in more glorious engagements, so leadership devolved to Benjamin Grierson, a music teacher from Illinois who had signed on as aide-de-camp to General Benjamin Prentiss. Prentiss's division had been decimated at the Hornet's Nest in Shiloh the year before, and Grierson had rapidly risen through the ranks. But he seemed an unlikely fit for commander of this raiding party as he was said to be deathly afraid of horses, having been kicked nearly to death by a horse as a child. Nonetheless, he was given command of 1,700 carefully selected horse troopers and ordered to rip southward through Mississippi.

Rip he did! Moving almost impossibly fast and living off the land and captured supplies, he evaded detection until he destroyed the rail station at Newton. From there he led pursuers on a confusing chase through southwest Mississippi, ending at Baton Rouge. An unexpected benefit of Grierson's brazen eighty-thousand-mile raid through the heart of the Confederacy was the intense damage it dealt to Confederate morale.

It is said that one stormy night Grierson's troopers were camped at the Strong River near Hazlehurst and came up with an idea for a different sort of offensive. The next day, two of Grierson's soldiers, posing as Confederate messengers, strode right into Hazlehurst and straight into the telegraph office, where they sent a disinformation telegraph to Confederate general John Pemberton at Vicksburg. Not satisfied with their daring infiltration, the Union spies stayed in town for a nice meal at a hotel. It was there that someone caught onto their ruse, and they had to shoot their way out of town to rejoin Grierson.

Strong River, Strong Man, by Ernest Herndon

As we approached the first rapid on Strong River below Highway 28, Phillip King of Brookhaven and I felt not the slightest concern. The water bubbled and frothed downstream and disappeared over a ledge with a roar. We should have gotten out and scouted it, but we've both canoed a lot of miles, and despite its name the Strong is generally peaceful. So we just went with the flow. Pity.

We aimed for a slot in a river-wide clay-rock ledge where the water gushed as if from a big spigot. Looked pretty simple. The bow dropped into the torrent. But instead of shooting straight through, the canoe canted to the right and water slopped in over the side. As if in slow motion, it continued to fill until we both tumbled out. Although the Strong is mostly shallow, my feet went out from under me in a deep pool. We clung to the boat until we made it to a sandbar. As we emerged dripping wet, we both had the same question: how did that happen?

King and I walked back up to examine the rapid. A side current pushed the main flow onto a ledge just to the left of the drop. That's why the boat rode up on its side.

We pulled the canoe upstream for a do-over. This time as the bow entered the drop I muscled the boat hard to the right before it could ride up on the ledge. We slid through without mishap, regaining at least a measure of our soggy dignity.

More surprising to me than the rapid's trickiness was the fact that King would even attempt it. The former forester had a disabled left arm and can barely hold a paddle. In 1999 he was cutting a leaning pine with a chainsaw when the tree twisted and fell on him, shattering the bones in his upper left arm. A surgeon installed a metal rod, but it broke. Then a staph infection set in, hurting as badly as the original injury.

Nearly three years later the bone wasn't healed, and King had to wear a rigid, jointed brace on the arm. He had only minimal use of the hand, plus problems with his shoulder and back. Yet when I invited him on a float, he jumped at the chance.

King had been active all his life, canoeing, bicycling, hiking. He was full of adventure stories, like the time he'd been floating Arkansas's Buffalo River and heard a hideous scream as a doe deer tumbled down the bank, neck slashed by predator's fangs. Or the time he went backpacking in Homochitto National Forest after an ice storm, just to revel in the beauty. Or the workday he tripped on a vine and landed in a brush pile face to face with a cottonmouth moccasin. Or walked up on a six-foot coiled rattlesnake, its head "as big as the back of my hand." The year he and his son Jason drove and hiked through Glacier National Park. The time they canoed the Homochitto River under a full moon.

King had hoped someday—now that he was injured—Jason would be able to take the lead role in their outdoor excursions. "Such was not to be," he said.

In 1996, Jason sustained massive brain damage in a car wreck. "He learned to eat one Rice Krispie at a time," King recalled, telling how he and his wife Sylvia would put a grain on Jason's lips and coax him to eat. Jason progressed from bed to wheelchair to walker to cane, eventually able to hold down a job working a floor machine.

Both King and son defied the odds. Doctors said King's main arm nerves were dead. They thought Jason would never be able to function. They were wrong in both cases. "I have to attribute that to God, to trust and faith, because I was really powerless to do anything. The doctors and nurses were powerless to do anything," King said. "Jason's recovery, too. We put it all in God's hands."

Neither of us had floated the nine-mile stretch of Strong River from Highway 28 near Pinola to Bridgeport Road east of Georgetown. The rapids got our attention. Though the rest of the river was slow, there was plenty to hold our interest.

We found the largest congregation of buzzards either of us had ever seen. For a mile along the remote, deep-woods river, black vultures inhabited one tree after another, flying up with creaking wings as we drifted near, swirling in the air like wasps disturbed at a nest. We estimated one hundred or more.

Then there were the white clay cliffs. King estimated them at 150 feet tall.

A flock of white egrets with a single blue heron preceded us downstream, stitching the haze with their graceful arcs. The thick air was lush with scents of willow, cypress, pine, and occasionally honeysuckle. Wildflowers glimmered orange and purple in the jungle green. Killdeer scampered at the water's edge. Hawks and great blue herons made cameo appearances. Deer snorted from both sides of the river at once as if communicating in code.

Although King's left arm was weak, fragile, and painful, he kept the limp hand propped on the top of his paddle and stroked continually with the force of his right arm. That's what I call a strong man on the Strong River.

BOGUE CHITTO RIVER

> The first river you paddle runs through you the rest of your life.
> It bubbles up in pools and eddies to remind you who you are.
>
> —LYNN CULBREATH NOEL

For many Mississippi naturalists and outdoorsmen, that first river, the stream that cuts a channel through the rest of their lives, is the Bogue Chitto River of southwest Mississippi. The name Bogue Chitto is a common place-name that means "big creek" in Choctaw.

> "Bogue Chitto" is used as the name of several creeks, rivers, and communities in Mississippi, including a maze of Bogue Chitto creeks at the headwaters of the Pearl River, a Bogue Chitto community between Brookhaven and McComb, and the Bogue Chitto River of southwest Mississippi and southeast Louisiana—a major tributary of the lower Pearl River.

The Bogue Chitto River begins in Lincoln County near Brookhaven with tiny east and west forks that come together like a wishbone to form a single stem. At first a logjammed creek, it extends southeast into Pike County, where it widens into one of the prettiest and most popular paddling rivers in Mississippi. It angles across Walthall County, meanders into Louisiana, and merges with the vast swamps of Bogue Chitto National Wildlife Refuge along the lower Pearl River. All told, that's 130 miles of river—69 in Mississippi and 61 in Louisiana.

An 1890 column in the Summit, Mississippi, *Enterprise* suggests that at that time the river was navigable by laden steamboats all the way from the Pearl River in Louisiana to Alford's Bridge near Summit, a distance of roughly ninety miles. Nowadays, you might be able to paddle a canoe between Alford's Bridge and Highway 570 in northern Pike County, but even then it is liable to be shallow and logjammed.

Still, it's a sweet five-mile stretch. A few steps above Alford's Bridge, Beaver Creek slips into the Bogue Chitto from the west, having escaped its confinement at Lake Dixie Springs. This realm of green shade and chatterbox water seems like a preview of heaven with birch and sycamore trees reaching across the Bogue Chitto in places to form a canopy. The water is usually clear enough to spot fish darting from sandy shallows to opaque depths.

The Bogue Chitto is a popular river for canoeing and tubing.

There aren't too many logjams on the next four-mile segment between Highway 570 and Highway 44 east of McComb. This stretch is a fine one, except perhaps for the sound of machinery from Sanderson Farms, a poultry processing plant just visible from the river. Sanderson Farms built the plant in 1993 along with a $3 million four-stage treatment plant to handle the seven hundred to eight hundred thousand gallons of wastewater it discharges each day.

Mudworms and Rotten Cheese

The Bogue Chitto provides good fishing. Flathead catfish of fifty or more pounds have been caught, though most are much smaller. The river also harbors channel cats and a few blues. The Bogue Chitto also offers excellent fishing for largemouth and Kentucky red-eye bass, red-bellied and bluegill bream, even

The Bogue Chitto River

crappie. River bass typically go one or two pounds, but sometimes lunkers up to seven pounds get caught.

For bait, some local fishermen use a type of worm apparently found only in the Bogue Chitto and other streams in the lower Pearl River Basin. Referred to locally as mudworms, they make great bait but aren't widely known. The bluish-gray, square-bodied worms live in leafy muck alongside spring branches. Dig them with a potato fork in the early spring and you'll have bait aplenty. At up to two feet long, a single worm can bait ten to fifteen hooks. But if you're digging and you see one, grab it quickly or it will vanish underground.

A biologist said it appears to be in the genus *Haplotaxida*, which is just science-speak that means they're first cousins to earthworms and leeches. One old-timer said, "Way back yonder folks would say, 'There's a good crop of mudworms because the hogs are fat.' Hogs would root in the mud, look like they'd be standing on their head in the hole because they'd be eating those worms."

Another unusual catfish bait is rotten cheese, commonly used with a type of trap called a slat-basket.

"If the river is muddy today, there'll be a hundred pounds of fish," said the late cheese vendor Sam Thomas of Pike County. "One trap will feed two families a year."

Thomas learned about fish trapping as a child. In 1944, his family bought 360 acres, mostly on the east side of the river, from the Federal Land Bank and a Magnolia bank for ten dollars an acre with a third of the amount as down payment—a price considered high at the time. The land, since divided, includes the modern-day Bogue Chitto Water Park. Thomas grew up learning to fish in the river and recalled "watching people fishing on the river in boats, and a few people who had illegal wire fish traps."

The boats were wide, flat-bottomed, and homemade from cypress planks. The traps were three or four feet square, baited with foot-square chunks of cottonseed meal. When one was full of fish, it took two men to lift it. Unlike wooden slat traps, wire traps had a major disadvantage—snakes can't get out.

"You do not want to turn a trap over in your boat with a live snake in it—a mad snake," Thomas said.

Thomas used trotlines until a friend noticed wooden slat traps embedded in sandbars between Highways 98 and 48 after every flood. "Trotlines were not doing as well as he expected, so he tried one trap," Thomas said. "Instead of three or four fish a week, he was getting forty or fifty fish in one trap twice a week."

Thomas learned the most effective methods of trapping, like where to position it.

"You can set your trap six feet this way or six feet that way and not catch anything," he said. "Once you find your sweet spot, you stay with it."

He would set his baskets in the outside of a curve in the riverbed where the bottom is hard. A trap placed on an inside curve can fill with sand and gravel in high water.

"The fish coming upstream will swim right up that channel," he said, referring to the deep side. "If you set your trap there, you're going to catch fish, and you won't lose your trap."

A typical slat basket is five feet long with a wooden throat at one end. The fish enters, then passes through a funnel made of plastic strips into the main part of the box.

Thomas noticed that he caught exclusively blue cats, each about one and a half pounds, in his traps in the Bogue Chitto River. He said he caught more than 1,700 pounds one year in a single trap. Muddy water is best, clear water worst. Traps will work in large ponds and lakes but really need some current to the water.

Some fishermen use cans of dog food with holes cut in the metal for bait. Thomas was a rotten cheese man, so much so that he became a vendor. "I was buying it from somebody else, driving fifty miles to get it," he said, noting that the cheese comes from waste scraps in Wisconsin factories. "I said, 'I'll just buy a truckload of this and sell it to other people.'"

Thomas also sold slat baskets for sixty-five dollars each.

In Mississippi, slat baskets are tightly regulated, requiring a commercial fishing license, a separate license and tag for each trap, and specific parameters for trap size and placement.

Giant Sturgeon

A most unusual fish was found in the Bogue Chitto in 2005. On July 14 of that year, a group of Pike County canoers caught a Gulf sturgeon by hand, photographed it, and released it. They estimated the fish to be well over seven feet long and two thousand pounds. Paddler Kevin Tynes of Summit said the fish was in a deep pool of water with shallows on each end.

That August, wildlife officials from Mississippi and Louisiana converged on the river in hopes of locating the fish. The effort failed, but they said the presence of the sturgeon is a good sign both for the endangered species and for the river.

> Gulf sturgeon swim up rivers in late winter and early spring to spawn at the place where they hatched. They then go back downriver to a staging area before reentering the Gulf of Mexico in the fall. The fish don't eat while they're in the river. In the Gulf, they feed on invertebrates along the bottom.

The Louisiana researchers said they've tagged sturgeon as big as 7 feet, 11 inches, and 350 pounds in the lower Bogue Chitto River, while Mississippians have caught them up to 6 feet and 200 pounds in the Pascagoula River. The biggest obstacles to sturgeons trying to swim up the Pearl River into the Bogue Chitto are sills, or low-water dams, built on the lower rivers in 1956. The sills, along with a barge canal and a series of locks and dams, were meant to aid navigation back when companies around Bogalusa shipped gravel, paper, and timber down the Pearl. The locks and canal are no longer in use and have been abandoned. Sturgeon sometimes find their way past the sills, either swimming over them in high water, jumping them, or finding alternate routes.

Watch Out for Snakes

Snakes are far more common in the Bogue Chitto than are sturgeon. In and around Mississippi rivers it's not too hard to memorize all the venomous snakes because there are only six: three rattlers (pygmy, eastern, and canebrake), two moccasins (copperhead and cottonmouth), and one coral snake (eastern coral).

Most folks make do with learning a handful of rules of thumb about which snakes are venomous, such as: does it rattle, have a triangular head and slit eyes, or red bands touching yellow bands? Venomous. But that doesn't mean you should play with any round-eyed, round-headed snake you see. Even bites from nonvenomous snakes carry dangerous bacteria that can cause an infection.

It also doesn't mean you should kill any venomous snake you see. They play a role in their ecosystem, and some are even becoming endangered because people often grab a hoe and chop any rattler they hear. It is nice to know if a snake is dangerous or not, but it is best to leave any snake alone unless it poses an imminent threat to you or your children.

> A few years back, a McComb man took his new wife canoeing and camping on the Pere Marquette River in Michigan. Chatting with a nineteen-year-old river guide, he asked, "So, what sort of snakes do you have to watch out for around here?" The river guide responded, "I've never even seen a snake in my whole life." The McComb man replied that if the river guide ever felt a need to see a snake in a river, he should come check out our Bogue Chitto in southwest Mississippi during the summertime.

Holmesville History

The seven miles between Highway 44 and Holmesville contain a few easy pullovers but are otherwise mostly smooth going. Holmesville, now a rural community, was the first town in Pike County, established in 1816 as a county seat. Pioneers from Georgia, Tennessee, and the Carolinas built a log courthouse complete with a jail, stocks, hanging tree, and whipping post. In 1848, that courthouse burned and was followed by a brick building that still stands today in a large grass field a quarter mile west of the Bogue Chitto River on Pike 93 Central.

An annex was added in 1934, and renovations—including the removal of two chimneys—were made in 1974. "This is a rare example of an antebellum courthouse," said Malcolm Allen of the Pike County Historical Society. "This area right here played a vital role in the War of 1812." That war ran into 1815, with the greatest local participation in 1813 in response to the Creek Indian massacre of settlers at Fort Mims in Alabama.

> According to a historical marker at the red brick courthouse at Holmesville, "[d]uring the War of 1812, General William Carroll, en route to New Orleans, marched his Tennessee Militia through Pike County, crossed the Bogue Chitto River north of Holmesville and camped along Love Creek. While returning from New Orleans via this same route one of his men became ill, died and was buried near that same Love Creek campsite. By order of the United States War Department, this soldier's remains were disinterred and reburied in Chalmette National Cemetery in October 1908."

With the advent of the railroad in the 1850s, officials decided to shift the county seat west to the tracks, so the towns of Magnolia and Summit competed for the privilege. A court ruling favored Magnolia, and a courthouse was built there in 1875. That Magnolia courthouse, which burned in 1882 and was rebuilt in 1918, is on the National Register of Historic Places and is a Mississippi landmark. McComb, meanwhile, went on to become the largest town in Pike County, which was named for explorer Zebulon Pike of Pike's Peak fame.

Topisaw Creek

Below Holmesville, thirty-mile-long Topisaw Creek enters from the east. On the upper reaches of Topisaw Creek at Highway 570 sprawls Felder United

Methodist Church and Felder Campground—home of a historic Methodist camp meeting that's still ongoing.

> Translating names derived from Native American languages is seldom straightforward. It is agreed that the name Topisaw is derived from Choctaw, but proposed translations vary widely. It has been said that Topisaw may mean "peeled vines," "creek of many falling banks," or even "the place where they saw each other." More recent etymologies suggest that Topisaw probably refers to a "little chestnut tree."

The Felder Camp Meeting dates to 1843, but the religious gatherings go back to the early settlement of Pike County. "The year 1810 marks the beginning of a movement that brought many Methodists to Mississippi, among them [the] Felder and Sandell families. A church was formed, known as Felder's Church, and a camp meeting was held east of Magnolia in 1811," according to the April 12, 1956, edition of the *Magnolia Gazette*. "This church was finally dissolved, and the members went into other pioneer churches, at Holmesville, at Terrell's church near where McComb is located, at Gatlin's campground established on Bogue Chitto River in 1826, and at Felder's or Topisaw campground a few years later."

An article in the June 7, 1935, McComb *Enterprise* gives more specifics. "In 1843 John Felder with Christopher Hoover, Hardy Thompson, David Winborne, Matthew McEwen, Samuel Whitworth, Archie McEwen, and Silas Catchings established the Topisaw or Felder's Campground." The reporter goes on, "During the Civil War, the church and tabernacle were burned and not until 1881 were they rebuilt as they are today. John Felder and his wife are deeply devoted to their religion and to them the community owes much in the upbuilding of the Methodist denomination, and maintenance of the Church and Camp Meetings held there. Their sons and daughters were all Christian people of the same faith.

"In 1846, John Felder had a water mill constructed over Topisaw, upright saw, grist and cotton gin near the Camp Ground under the supervision of Luther Smith assisted by his sons Levi and Robert. John Felder died in 1876 and was buried near the campground in the family cemetery, which is situated on a hill overlooking the Camp Ground." By the 1920s the camp meetings saw attendance in the thousands, according to reports in the *Summit Sentinel*. The one hundredth anniversary was celebrated in 1943.

In 2018, the camp meeting celebrated its 175th year and dedicated two historical markers—one from the Mississippi Annual Conference of the United

Methodist Church, the other from the Mississippi Department of Archives and History. Both designated the campground an official historic site.

Topisaw Creek also once powered a grist mill, a cotton gin, and even an electric power plant. Dr. Charles Edward Felder of Brandon revealed the stream's illustrious past in a twenty-four-page booklet, *Pricedale, Mississippi: A Community Before Its Time*. Felder, who grew up in Pricedale, published the booklet in 2004; a doctor of psychology at Mississippi College, he interviewed numerous local residents and compiled photos and diagrams for his publication.

Pricedale is located on Highway 44 just east of Topisaw Creek, which runs into the Bogue Chitto River. Just north of Highway 44 is a now stagnant tributary of Topisaw known as Mill Creek. "Mill Creek first received its name because Indians in the area had a grist mill operated by a water wheel on that part of Topisaw Creek," Felder writes. "[W]hen the Indians were operating the grist mill on Topisaw, the creek at that time was probably flowing naturally down Mill Creek without a dam. At the time that the Pricedale community was developing other projects on Mill Creek, the main channel of Topisaw was simultaneously moving more toward the west and a dam became needed to keep a flow coming down the old channel."

A waterwheel also powered a cotton gin, one of many operations in once thriving Pricedale. Other enterprises included a sawmill, syrup mill, general store, post office, mule barn, rodeos, even a semipro baseball team with its own ballfield. Local athletes were paid to play baseball, and spectators were charged admission. "The Price Brothers baseball team was considered to be one of the best at the time, and many members of the community looked forward to attending the ball games," Felder writes.

Probably the most unusual operation was the power plant, which "provided electricity to residences, businesses, a church, and a school approximately ten years before electricity was available in other rural areas" in the mid-1930s, Felder reports. D. C. Price, the brainchild behind the plant, built a second dam below the old cotton gin dam about a half mile north of Highway 44, Felder writes. The only thing left now is a large piece of sandstone extending from the east bank.

Felder's booklet goes into considerable detail about how the plant worked, including diagrams. Water spun turbines that turned a shaft that powered a generator that charged twelve 6-volt batteries. "These batteries were then used to furnish the Pricedale electrical system with approximately 64-volt direct current electrical power," Felder writes. "Cedar poles with insulators and wires were used to transfer the electrical current in the air and serve electricity to the immediate Pricedale community plus D. P. Walker's store about a mile to the west and Carter's Creek School and Bogue Chitto Baptist Church approximately two miles to the east.... The electrical system at Pricedale drew attention from communities and towns far away, and many people who lived outside the area drove miles to view the homes and businesses at night."

Pricedale isn't quite as active nowadays, but being on a state highway it still gets plenty of traffic. There are a few small businesses, a couple of churches—and Topisaw Creek, shallower than it used to be, but still running clear and pretty through the rolling hills of southwest Mississippi.

Conflicts on the Water

Below the mouth of the Topisaw, the Bogue Chitto River slides toward US Highway 98 and two miles farther to Bogue Chitto Water Park. The now defunct Pearl River Basin Development District established the water park in the 1970s, and the river became wildly popular with tubers and paddlers, with all the attendant problems. On a given summer weekend, thousands of people would float the river—mainly from Highway 98 to the water park boat ramp—with the inevitable excesses of litter, profanity, and drunkenness. Landowners protested, saying that river access should be limited.

Prior to 1970, public waterways in Mississippi were governed by an 1896 statute that defined navigable waterways as at least twenty-five miles long and capable of floating a steamboat carrying two hundred bales of cotton for thirty consecutive days. In 1970, the state supreme court upheld a Pearl River County chancery court decision that declared Hobolochitto Creek private. The court ruled that the old statute "was intended to exclude small private creeks and streams, non-navigable in fact, and to declare navigable only streams actually capable of being navigated by substantial commercial traffic."

In an attempt to clarify the issue, the state legislature adopted an act in 1972 that stated the public had access to rivers that averaged three feet in depth along the thread of a channel for ninety consecutive days. The issue would not be resolved, however, for another twenty years.

In the meantime there were injury lawsuits, such as one for $14 million filed in 1984 by a man who dove from a cliff between Highway 98 and Bogue Chitto Water Park, breaking his neck. He sued Pike County, the Pearl River Basin Development District, and the owner of the land where the injury occurred, claiming they failed to warn river users of the danger. A judge dismissed the district and the landowner from the suit, leaving the county to settle out of court. The landowner, meanwhile, spent tens of thousands of dollars in legal fees.

Outraged landowners prevailed on the sheriff to bar access to the river on grounds that it was not a public waterway. The issue went back to court, and in 1988 a Pike County chancellor ruled the river to be private. The case went to the state supreme court, which in 1991 ruled the Bogue Chitto to be a navigable waterway open to the public. The ruling affected all rivers with a minimum one hundred cubic feet per second flow, which includes streams considerably smaller than the Bogue Chitto.

> The Commission on Environmental Quality publishes a map and a list showing all public waterways in the state. According to the law, on public waterways "the citizens of this state and other states shall have the right of free transport in the stream and its bed and the right to fish and engage in water sports."

Once the public got word they weren't likely to be arrested for trespassing, they returned to the river, and by the late 1990s problems had resumed. Law enforcement reacted, with plainclothes officers making numerous arrests on summer weekends.

In 2008, Pike County supervisors tried banning alcohol on the river, but canoe rental companies sued the county, and in 2010 the Mississippi supreme court said they could ban consumption but not possession. Nevertheless, the alcohol restrictions had a dual effect: they cut down on many of the problems but also hurt the recreation business, forcing some canoe rentals to close.

Don't Dive!

One of the dangers of the Bogue Chitto River is its high cliffs, such as one on private land south of Highway 98, where many people have sustained serious injuries when diving.

David Pickard of McComb was left a quadriplegic after a plunge into the river in 1973. He has words of warning for anyone who likes to jump into a good hole of water: "Don't dive!" He urges swimmers to "be careful. Use common sense. Don't do stupid stuff." Check out a hole of water before swimming. River bottoms can change overnight. A log can wash into a swimming hole. "Kids think they're invincible. They think it only happens to the other guy."

Pickard, then sixteen, was swimming with a couple of friends in the Bogue Chitto in the Holmesville area on August 5, 1973. A buddy swung out on a rope, partly back and dove. No problem. Pickard did the same thing. But the water was shallow and his head struck the bottom.

"It stunned me," Pickard recalled. "I didn't know what happened. It paralyzed me instantly. I couldn't get back to the surface."

Determined not to inhale water, he clamped his jaws shut and held his breath until he passed out. When he surfaced face-down, his friends thought he was playing—until one rolled him over and saw he had turned blue. Friends pulled him out and attempted CPR but couldn't get his mouth open. Pickard eventually came to and told them to call an ambulance.

He was taken to Southwest Mississippi Regional Medical Center in McComb, where it was determined he had a fracture to the C-5 and C-6 vertebrae in his neck. He then went to the University of Mississippi Medical Center in Jackson, where he spent five weeks. Doctors performed a temporary tracheotomy to help him breathe, but scar tissue formed in his trachea above the surgery and they were unable to repair it. Pickard did recover his ability to speak, using a microphone to amplify his whispery voice.

Pickard persevered. He passed his General Educational Development (GED) test in 1974, became a CB radio operator in 1976, and got his ham radio license in 1978. He became a life member of the Southwest Mississippi Amateur Radio Club and a member of the 599 DX Association. He got a computer in the early 1980s and ran a computer repair shop for five years, was appointed church elder at Faith Assembly of God around 1988 and elected deacon in 2006, received two certificates from H&R Block for passing its tax course, created eight websites, and sends out devotionals, prayer requests, and church announcements.

Pickard was not the first nor the last person to be injured diving into the Bogue Chitto. He offered words of hope. "Keep your hopes up. Keep your dreams up. You can't let it get you down," he said of paralysis. "It's not the end of your life."

Fun to Float

For paddlers, Bogue Chitto Water Park is a showcase with gorgeous woods, secluded campsites, rustic cabins, a pavilion, a hiking trail, picnic areas, and fine river views. The park is located south of Highway 98 between McComb and Tylertown, and there is a canoe and tube rental company just outside the gates.

On the river, high, forested banks provide a deep-woods feel, augmented by the presence of creatures like ospreys. The five miles between Bogue Chitto Water Park and Walker's Bridge Memorial Water Park just below Highway 48 in Walthall County constitute a picture of what a canoeing stream should be—narrow enough to provide shade, tricky enough not to be dull, with little sign of human presence until just above Highway 48, where camps appear. Many of the riverside houses are attractive, expansive brick or rustic wood, sheltering beneath water oak and beech trees. At some, white plastic pipes funnel artesian springs into the river, creating a cozy sound.

Half a mile below the Highway 48 bridge on the west bank, Walker's Bridge Water Park has a boat ramp, pavilion, and picnic area but no other facilities. The park is located half a mile south of Highway 48 between Magnolia and Tylertown. There are also privately operated campgrounds along the river—Hidden Springs Resort above Highway 48, Paradise Ranch RV Resort below it. Camps and riverside residences become more abundant in Walthall County as the river widens on the six miles from Walker's to Stallings Bridge west of Lexie and on three miles down to Dillon's Bridge west of Highway 27, the last bridge before Louisiana.

Magee's Creek

Magee's Creek, a nice paddleway in its own right, enters from the east a half mile above Dillon's Bridge after a thirty-mile passage through Walthall County. There are around 150 species of butterflies found in Mississippi, and a good number of them have been observed at Beechnut Nature Retreat along Magee's Creek north of Tylertown. Retreat owner Tammany Baumgarten of New Orleans leads occasional field trips at the property, sometimes with the help of Linda Auld of Harahan, Louisiana, also known as the Bug Lady.

Baumgarten is a landscape horticulturist who owns the cleverly named BaumGardens Landscape and Design in New Orleans. She bought a forty-acre tract north of Tylertown in 2011 and installed three cottages on it. Magee's Creek has flooded the property twice, but she has managed to nurture an array of raised beds and open-field plantings of flowers and vegetables.

On one of her field trips, a checklist for participants named thirty-two butterflies and thirteen skippers—six swallowtails, six whites and sulphurs, three hairstreaks, one blue, one milkweed, thirteen brushfoots, two satyrs, six spreadwings, and seven grass skippers. And that's not to mention the many bees and other insects Auld pointed out in and around Baumgarten's lush gardens.

"Some bees are general and some bees are specific," said Auld, author of *BugLady's Butterfly Summer*. "What really intrigued me is the okra bee, and they also call it the Jesus bee because it walks on water. They like okra, sunflowers, and gaillardia—Indian blanket. They also like mallow."

Farther south in Tylertown, Holmes Water Park borders Magee's Creek and features the "Trail of Seven Bridges" walking path, picnic areas, a playground, and an event center; it is known for its fabulous annual lighted Christmas display.

Magee's Creek flows south from Tylertown past Lexie and eventually into the Bogue Chitto a short distance above Dillon's Bridge. By this point, the Bogue Chitto is starting to look like a pretty wide river. Shade is a thing of the past, but so are river-wide logjams. Swift, log-studded bends look more dangerous than they did upstream, but the channel is broad enough to provide an easy route most of the time.

Heroes of the Bogue Chitto

Canoe and Trail Outpost is located at Dillon's Bridge with boat rentals and a campground. Wilmon Van Dan started the Outpost in 1977 when he teamed up with canoe outfitter Byron Almquist of New Orleans. In 1996, then-governor Kirk Fordice signed a proclamation recognizing Van Dan and the New Orleans Sierra Club for their long-standing efforts to pick up trash along the Bogue Chitto River and Magee's Creek. Fordice even designated September 7—the day of Van Dan's annual trash pickup—as Bogue Chitto River Day. Van Dan and Almquist also led groups on outdoor adventures around the nation, such as to Missouri's Current River, North Carolina's Nantahala National Forest, the Rio Grande, the Grand Canyon, and Arkansas's Buffalo River.

But in 2006, tragedy struck. Van Dan was changing a bulb in a thirty-foot-high security light at his home near the Bogue Chitto River around 8:00 p.m. when he fell to the ground and was severely injured. Fortunately his son Connor, then four, was there, and his dad had trained him well. "I remember he used to teach me a lot of stuff," said Connor years afterward. "At three years old I could pretty much crank a tractor, a bulldozer, anything."

The child ran more than a mile in the dark woods to get help, returning with a neighbor and two nurses. Wilmon had suffered brain damage but rallied more than anyone thought possible.

In 2007, Connor received the American Legion Auxiliary Youth Hero Award for his heroic rescue. After graduating from high school in 2021, he took over the family business and farm.

After his injury, Wilmon had a long road toward recovery. "When we took him home, for the first ten years he was great," his wife Kim said. "He wasn't the same, but his love for Jesus, his love for life was all the same."

Eventually he began forgetting things and having seizures, and he was bedridden the last eighteen months of his life before passing away in 2019 at home at age sixty-five. "He lived a long time. They told us I could never take him home," said Kim, who defied the predictions by doing just that. "He was a good guy and he loved Jesus and he was full of laughter. He loved life."

Connor recalls his dad teaching him to "work hard, very hard, and just be humble and trust in God." In addition to floating the river and helping at the business and farm, Connor played basketball and learned to fly an airplane.

"When he was an infant we would put him in a canoe," Kim remembered. By seven he could paddle on his own.

"I probably floated Magee's Creek thirty times this year," Connor said in 2020. "I get it naturally, I believe."

In 2012, Kim bought nearby Sweetwater Tubing and named the combined business Canoe and Trail Outpost/Sweetwater Tubing. When Wilmon started the business, canoes were the main boat used on the Bogue Chitto and Magee's Creek. Now it's sit-on-top kayaks. Inner tubes have always been popular.

Canoe and Trail Outpost has cabins and RV and tent sites, plus canoes, kayaks, and tubes. Connor's plans for the business are to "grow it, probably get more kayaks." Ditto inner tubes.

Over the years, Canoe and Trail has remained popular while other outfitters have come and gone. "The location, and I would say the primitiveness, keep the party crowd out; very family oriented," employee Caleb Barnes summarized.

Fifty Miles on the Bogue Chitto, by Patrick Parker

Early one Indian summer Friday afternoon a few years ago, the older Boy Scouts of Troop 124 of McComb and I put in at the Bogue Chitto River under the Holmesville bridge about a quarter mile east of the famous red courthouse. The goal of our expedition was to do a fifty-mile paddle over the course of three days while camping on sandbars and picking up any trash we came across.

Our logistics guy had to do something else with his trailer that day, so he dropped all of our canoes off that morning underneath the bridge with someone to watch them till we got there. When we gathered up our gear and crew and got to the river, we realized we had too many canoes, so the choice was to either operate a couple of canoes with one paddler or else tether the extra canoe to the back of one of our boats and ditch it when we got to the water park.

We decided to tow the extra boat, and that turned out to be a terrible drag because the tow rope snagged every stob in the water, wrapped our two boats like a hinge around tons of trees, and generally ran us into every obstacle there was.

It was slow going that morning, but eventually we passed the Topisaw Creek confluence a scant two miles below Holmesville. One Pike County outdoorsman had told me to be careful of eddies and strainers at that confluence. He'd made it sound to me like the ancient Greek story of Scylla and Charybdis—a narrow passage between a terrible sea monster and a fearsome whirlpool. Scylla and Charybdis (and the Topisaw confluence) were said to wreck boats and consume paddlers—but the monster must have been asleep that morning, and we glided past with hardly a side glance.

We finally made it to the water park and left the extra canoe high and dry for someone to come get. Unencumbered that afternoon but chased by thunderstorms, we continued past the water park and the Yacht Club campground, past Hidden Springs Resort, and past the confluence of the winsomely named Love and Sweetwater Creeks at Walker's Bridge.

As the sun was getting low in the west, we camped on a gravelly sandbar on the east bank with a deserted-looking camp overlooking us from atop the bluff across the river. While we were setting up, we discovered that the sandbar was littered with sandstone pipes. These geological oddities, which look just like iron pipes, are naturally occurring geological formations created when ferrous water percolates through sandstone, leaving concentric rings that over time form stony tubes.

The next morning the thunderstorms were gone, and in exchange we had sunburn weather. Each successive meander in the river plunged us into the cool, green shade of tall trees on steep banks, then exposed us to the glaring morning sunlight. We pulled our sun hats down as far as they could go and laid beach towels over our laps to cover our knees and feet—and paddled on.

As we passed the Magee's Creek confluence, some of the locals in our party declared that there was a story of a giant alligator that lived in that bend of the river, but just as the day before at Topisaw, the monster slept as we paddled by.

Sliding past Dillon's Bridge with the Canoe and Trail Outpost perched high up on the bluff, we slipped across the state line into Louisiana.

After making good progress throughout the morning, we stopped for a few minutes on a muddy sandbar just before a sharp westward bend in the river. It was pleasant to walk around and stretch and eat something, but we were under a feeling of time pressure. Every minute that we stayed on that sandbar was three hundred feet that we were not progressing toward our goal of fifty miles. So, we hopped back in our boats and pushed back out into the stream.

If you let a canoe drift along in the current, especially in a winding river, it will meander and spin out of control. They are much easier to steer when they are moving forward faster than the current, so as we floated out into the swiftly moving current and began to sweep around the bend in the river, we began paddling hard to get some momentum.

We were probably moving four or five miles per hour (that's pretty good speed in a seventeen-foot metal canoe) when we rounded a bend in the river and ran smack-dab into a maze of fallen trees and submerged tree stumps—and that's just the moment that the Scout in the front of my canoe looked down and discovered that at the muddy sandbar he had gotten dozens of leeches on his feet and legs.

To say he spazzed out would be putting it mildly. He dropped his paddle and started swiping at the leeches. It was apparent that we were not going to be able to stop in the middle of these rapids—and it was equally apparent that I would not be getting any assistance in maneuvering our boat through the logjam, so I set about trying to provide both power and steering.

It was at that fateful moment that our canoe ran head-on into a submerged log and stopped dead still instantly. People in a canoe behind us said it looked a lot like a car wreck: "One moment they were paddling right along and the next moment Pat was just gone."

The force of our collision ejected me from the canoe into the rapids, banging my left knee painfully on the gunwale of the canoe, plunging me into the chilly, autumnal, artesian waters, and leaving my Scout adrift in the canoe plucking leeches from his legs.

Fortunately, Scouts are always prepared, and in typical Scout fashion we were wearing our life jackets—you know, the orange horse-collar-style near-shore PFDs that make both Scouts and adults look like total geeks. Thanks to my geeky orange PFD, I didn't drown.

I finally got over the surprise of the sudden stop and the plunge into the cool water and clambered back into the canoe. The Scout in the front of the boat finally got all the leeches plucked out from between his toes. We never figured out where he waded that the rest of us hadn't, but he was the only one to get leeches on him.

The next day we took out at the state park just past Franklinton, Louisiana. We'd made our fifty miles, and the combination of logistical issues, sandstone pipes, and the attack of the leeches made that canoe trek unforgettable!

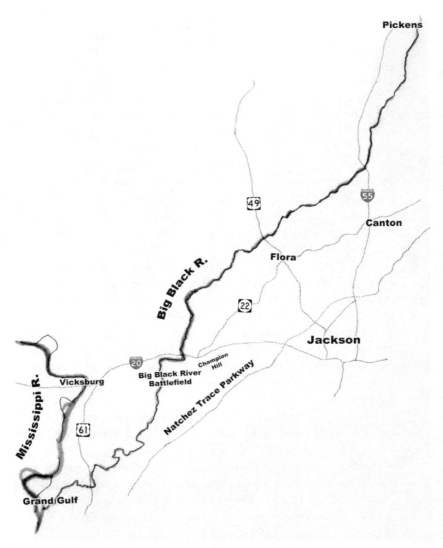

The Big Black River

BIG BLACK RIVER

> Wild vines... intertwine each other at the feet of these trees, escalade their trunks, and creep along to the extremity of their branches.... Often, in their wanderings from tree to tree, these creepers cross the arm of a river, over which they throw a bridge of flowers.
>
> —FRANÇOIS-AUGUSTE-RENÉ DE CHATEAUBRIAND

The Big Black is neither big nor black, but Medium Brown River just wouldn't sound as good. It was probably dark and clear when first discovered, but farming and logging have kept it muddied up ever since. Its main appeal to the modern paddler is its remoteness. Bridges are few and far between, with not much else but woods, fields, and swamp.

The 277-mile Big Black starts as a wiggly creek in Webster County. It flows generally southwest across the state before entering the Mississippi River near Grand Gulf between Port Gibson and Vicksburg. Despite its length and its name, it never does turn into a big river. It's hemmed in by the Yazoo River on the northwest and the Pearl on the east, both of which are major river systems.

> The Big Black River's headwaters amid small, tortuous creeks northeast of Eupora were the site of an Indian war in the mid-1700s that extirpated the Chakchiuma ("Red Crawfish") tribe, who may have been the ancestors of the Houma Indians of Louisiana. It would have taken a substantial threat or insult to make longstanding Choctaw and Chickasaw rivals team up against the Chakchiuma. This insult apparently came during the French-Natchez and French-Chickasaw wars when the Chakchiuma allied with the French. The survivors of the Chakchiuma were eventually subsumed into the Choctaw nation.

The Big Black serves as an informal dividing line between the low, flat floodplain of the Delta and the prairie and piney woods of central and southwest Mississippi. Being a product of both regions, the Big Black shows characteristics of both—the curvaceous bends and sandy soil of the Pearl interspersed with the channelized stretches and deep mud of the Delta.

Deprived of substantial tributaries, the Big Black is largely rainfall dependent, so its water levels fluctuate wildly. In springtime it may be out of its banks from heavy rains, by summer so low the sandbars are rimmed with reddish mud.

The Big Black is a fine waterway for catfishing enthusiasts—one of the best in the state. Flathead catfish nigh sixty pounds and blue cats up to thirty pounds come out of its muddy waters.

"It clears a little bit, clear enough you can catch minnows in the summertime," said the late Jack Albin of Goodman, who coon hunted and catfished the Big Black for most of his life. "It's some big fish in that river. The biggest one I ever saw was fifty-nine pounds. It's a fellow caught a forty-pound one out of there . . . and a twenty-pound one between Goodman and Pickens."

> For twenty or twenty-five miles between Eupora and Kilmichael, the river is channelized into long, straight segments. Kilmichael's claim to fame is that it is where blues icon B. B. King was raised by his grandmother. Is there something about long, straight, severely altered rivers that incubated the Mississippi blues?

Sunset along the Big Black River (photo courtesy of Sam King Photography)

> The Big Black runs past the towns of Vaiden and West—which, incidentally, lies west of the Attala County community of Possumneck. Possumneck is one of many colorfully named Mississippi communities; others include Alligator, Arm, Buzzard Roost, Chickenbone, Hot Coffee, It, Money, Panther Burn, Soso, Turkey Foot Fork, and Whynot.

Below West, two tributaries come in: Jordan Creek from the west and Apookta (Choctaw for "doubled" or "forked") Creek from the east. By the time the river reaches Durant (named for 1930s Choctaw chief Louis Durant) twenty miles away, it's big enough for a canoe or johnboat.

Surprisingly, the Big Black does have some sandbars. But these aren't the deep, toe-wiggling sands found in the Pearl River Basin, rather more of a light coating over mud, like white icing on caramel cake. Even when disembarking at a sandbar, a paddler may wallow inches deep in muck. Paddlers may prefer to camp at Holmes County State Park between Durant and Goodman and commute to the river for day floats. The beautifully wooded 444-acre park straddles a range of hills between Interstate 55 and US Highway 51 and includes two fishing lakes.

Dreamy River

During the summer, the Big Black is often so low that ample sandbars are exposed, and the current moves along pleasantly in places—but in a few places, even paddlers may have to drag their shallow-draft vessels through shoals and around fallen trees.

The smell of willows and the hum of cicadas thicken the air. A red-eyed vireo—the most common bird in the eastern deciduous forest but rarely seen—chatters, "Look at me; here I am." Black damselflies and blue dragonflies dance over the water. Buzzards, deer, Mississippi kites, great egrets, kingfishers, rolling fish, a squawking great blue heron, a screaming hawk—all come and go as if in a dream.

Deep pools are good for trotlines, while sandbars provide a nice place to stretch your legs and swim. In the summertime the water is warm but more pleasant than sitting on the sand in steambath heat swatting mosquitoes and deerflies.

As darkness gathers, mosquitoes swirl around, and the woods chime with crickets. At dawn, a trotline may yield a nice-size blue cat. For breakfast, it's hard to beat thick fillets fried in butter, accompanied by hot coffee lightened with evaporated milk as the sun winks through the woods and a green heron screeches from the shadows.

Two sizable tributaries enter the Big Black on the Durant-to-Goodman stretch: Seneasha Creek (Choctaw for "sycamores there") from the east and Tacketts Creek from the west. Plenty of smaller sloughs offer access into the swampy environs flanking the river. Paddle up a quiet, shady channel, and you may startle a beaver out of its bank hole—or rather, it may startle you when it hits the water like a cannonball. The tree-gnawing rodents can weigh fifty pounds and have a habit of whopping the water with their tails for dramatic effect.

Folktales and Legends

Towering, vine-draped trees along the river hint at the virgin forests that inspired French author François-Auguste-René de Chateaubriand to write the famous novel *Atala* in 1833. That in turn inspired the name for Attala County (people didn't pay much attention to spelling in those days) on the river's east bank. The novel is a Romeo-and-Juliet-type love story about two Native Americans, a Muscogee princess named Atala and a brave named Chactas from the enemy Natchez tribe. Chateaubriand waxed extremely eloquent in depicting a realm that sounds like a cross between the Amazon rainforest and the Garden of Eden.

The real history of the area's Indians is less romantic. As settlers encroached and craved more land, they gobbled up Choctaw territory—five million acres at the Treaty of Doak's Stand in 1820, and the rest at the Treaty of Dancing Rabbit Creek ten years later. By then, the village of Bluff Springs was established near modern-day Durant, complete with ferry, sawmill, general store, distillery, and grist mill.

Bluff Springs was named for fresh-flowing water near the Big Black, and the area has other such sites as well, which are said to have emerged following the great 1811 earthquake. Nearby Earthquake Springs six miles south of Kosciusko supports this tradition. Red Bud Springs to the east became the town of Kosciusko, incorporated in 1836. Resort hotels grew up around Castalian Springs in Holmes County and Artesian Springs north of Canton in the mid-1800s. In the latter half of the century the railroad arrived, paralleling the Big Black a mile or so to the west from Vaiden south to Way, where the river swings southwest under the tracks.

> If you had been camped on the Big Black River near Vaughan on April 30, 1900, you might have awakened to a crash that went down in history. J. L. "Casey" Jones was a hot-rodding engineer known for his willingness to take risks. That night, late on his southbound run from Memphis to Canton, he ran through a stop signal and suddenly saw a freight train crossing up ahead. He ordered his firemen to jump just before his "Cannonball" rammed into the freight, killing Jones. Later, a railroad employee, Wallace Saunders, wrote "The Ballad of Casey Jones," which became a nationwide hit and propelled Jones to legendary status. The Casey Jones State Museum at the community of West tells the story of Jones and the railroad's glory days with artifacts and an authentic steam engine.

The forests along the river are no longer as awesome as they were in Chateaubriand's day—there are depressing stretches of cutover and fields without a buffer of trees—but there are still some impressive water oaks and cypresses along the banks. Other common species are river birch, notable for its curly bark, and maple, the leaves of which flutter brightly in the wind as their silvery underbellies are exposed. In the spring you'll see native azaleas, pink as strawberry ice cream; cross vines, whose red-throated yellow flowers drape trees and logs; and dewberries, whose red thorny-velvety vines and white blossoms blanket the edges of sandbars before yielding fruit in April and May.

> Visitors who want a hint of the area's truly ancient forests can go to the Mississippi Petrified Forest in nearby Flora. This privately owned park has outdoor features exhibiting fossilized logs seven feet thick. There is also a museum, gift shop, picnic area, and campground.

Long, Lonely Miles

The river continues past Goodman and Pickens. At Highway 16 more than twenty miles below Pickens, it turns southwest under Interstate 55. Distances between bridges grow even greater below Highway 16. It's thirty miles to Highway 49 south of Bentonia. Plenty of sloughs and oxbow lakes provide detours, with views of wildlife, including abundant waterfowl.

Photographer and history buff Sam King of Madison owns property on the Big Black between Highways 16 and 49. "There was an old Indian crossing that became a road later between Yazoo City and Livingston on the Madison County [south] side of the river between Highway 16 and Highway 49," he said. "At that crossing on the Madison County side was the county seat for Yazoo County for some years before it was moved to Yazoo City. That site is now the location for the wastewater treatment facility for the Nissan plant. The town of Livingston was the county seat for Madison County at that time [later moved to Canton] and has now been rebuilt."

From Highway 49 to Highway 27 west of Utica unwind sixty-two long and lonely miles. The river is broken by rural Cox Ferry Road, I-20 at Edwards, and Old Highway 80 at Bovina. Farm fields continue past Highway 49, along with hardwood forests and bluffs. Woods along this stretch have been logged in recent decades and don't reach the size found in some areas along the river. The Bogue Phalia (Choctaw for "long creek") enters the Big Black from the south about five miles below Highway 49. Paddlers can go up it a bit during higher water levels, but it's generally blocked by logs. Cox Bridge crosses about halfway on the forty-nine-mile stretch from Highway 49 to 80.

The river crosses I-20 and swings west to parallel Old Highway 80. Campbell Swamp extends to the right several miles below Fisher Ferry Road, with impressive stands of cypress and tupelo gum. Rocky Springs on the Natchez Trace Parkway a few miles to the southeast provides a base camp for day trips on the Big Black and nearby Bayou Pierre. Some twenty-six miles below Fisher Ferry Road, the Big Black passes under Highway 61, where the river changes character.

Champion Hill

In the Civil War, the lower Big Black River was the location of a pair of battles that would unlock Vicksburg to a siege by the Union and lead to the fall of Vicksburg less than two months later. General Grant's Union forces crossed the Mississippi River at the port of Bruinsburg, or Petit Gulf, south of Vicksburg, but before attacking their ultimate objective they made a wide loop by way of Jackson, Raymond, and Champion Hill to secure their flank.

Champion Hill was a plantation house at a major crossroads about twenty miles east of Vicksburg, hard between the arms of Bakers Creek and Jackson Creek, two tributaries of the Big Black. It was here that Grant's army surprised General Pemberton's Confederate forces in the midst of a confused march to Raymond. Despite being a preliminary skirmish on some relatively unknown hill by a creek, the action was violent and the results disastrous for the Confederacy, which was forced to withdraw to the Big Black—the veritable doorstep of Vicksburg.

General Grant later commented on the Battle of Champion Hill: "While a battle is raging, one can see his enemy mowed down by the thousand, or the ten thousand, with great composure; but after the battle these scenes are distressing." Union general Alvin C. Hovey dubbed Champion Hill "the Hill of Death," describing a wild confusion of dead and dying men and horses and the scattered "cannon and debris of an army." It is said that there were so many dead Confederate horses on the battlefield that the Union forces could not get to all the cannons they had captured during the fight. General Hovey's evocative "Hill of Death" moniker stuck and is now used in commemorative signage at the battle site.

The next day at the Big Black River, General Pemberton ordered Brigadier General John S. Bowen to lead a rear guard in covering the retreat of the main army into Vicksburg. Major General John Alexander McClernand's Union troops swarmed and routed Bowen's rear guard resoundingly. Pemberton commented upon seeing the loss of the Big Black Creek bridge: "Just thirty years ago I began my military career . . . and today . . . that career is ended in disaster and disgrace."

A scant month and a half later, Pemberton would be forced to surrender to General Grant nearly 30,000 officers and men, 172 cannons, 60,000 firearms, and the Gibraltar of the Confederacy—Vicksburg. The Father of Waters once more ran "unvexed to the sea," as President Abraham Lincoln put it.

Lincoln would also issue a public written apology to General Grant for having doubted his tactics leading up to the Siege of Vicksburg: "When you got below [Vicksburg], and took Port-Gibson, Grand Gulf, and vicinity, I thought you should go down the [Mississippi] river and join Gen. [Nathaniel Prentiss] Banks [at New Orleans]; and when you turned Northward East of the Big Black, I feared it was a mistake. I now wish to make the personal acknowledgment that you were right, and I was wrong."

Lower Big Black

Below Highway 61, the Big Black winds on toward Allen and straightens out as it enters the Mississippi River floodplain. Forests give way to large farm fields, with camps along the river. A road runs along the north bank for a few miles, large enough for eighteen-wheelers carrying logs or soybeans. An abandoned boat ramp at Karnac Ferry on the southeast bank about nine miles below Highway 61 is the last take-out before the Mississippi. Five miles below Karnac, the river empties into the Mississippi about a mile above Upper Grand Gulf Landing.

Alligators are commonplace in the Big Black, usually noticeable by a head just above the water. The distance in inches between nose and eyes is supposedly the gator's length in feet. That is, if there are twelve inches between the nose and eyes, the reptile is twelve feet long. In 2012, David Ard of Summit caught a 12-foot, 2-inch, 560-pound gator in the Big Black near Port Gibson using a rod and reel with a snag hook. It took four and a half hours to reel the behemoth in.

Along the banks on this lower stretch, deer mosey in the woods, great blue herons croak, buzzards flap from the shadows, and white egrets perch on trees. Trucks rumble down a farm road on the north bank, churning up dust. Mostly, the banks are lined with woods, including pecan trees with trunks three feet thick. An unusually high bluff is probably the old Mississippi River bank before it moved a mile or so west.

Karnac Ferry

Although the Big Black is infamously muddy from start to finish—the only rocks being the occasional smattering of gravel amid the muck—just upstream from Karnac Ferry, big clay rocks form an island seventy-five feet long by fifteen across. The rocks break when struck, revealing light-colored clay inside. On the outside they're colored from countless deposits of silt. Mussel shells aplenty lie among the rocks. The catch is, they're only visible when the river is extremely low, like late summer.

When the water is low, long dirt banks stretch down from an old boat ramp to the brown river. Sometimes the water level is so low that dirt and weeds continue another seventy-five yards or so past the old concrete boat ramp to the water's edge.

One story is that Native Americans rolled the rocks off a bluff to make a crossing place. That seems as good an explanation as any for the phenomenon. There is no sign of a nearby bluff they could have been pushed off of, but riverbanks move substantially over the years, and it easily could have caved in. When the fall or winter rains come, the Big Black rises, and once again this mystery sleeps in the murky depths.

Grand Gulp

Approaching the Mississippi River, the quiet, cozy world of the Big Black opens out to a breezy view of distant sandbars and towboats pushing barges. Up ahead in the Mississippi is a churning mass of water historically known as Grand Gulf.

> Legend says that Grand Gulf was originally called Grand Gulp because of a boat-swamping whirlpool at the mouth of the Big Black. There's rarely a whirlpool these days, but the current still looks dangerous. When a boat leaves the sluggish Big Black and enters the swift Mississippi, it feels like mashing down on a gas pedal.

Less than a mile down the Mississippi River on the east bank is Grand Gulf Military State Park. This park provides a fascinating historical account of the namesake settlement, which started as a French village on the Mississippi River in the early 1700s. It grew into a major port city during the cotton heyday in the 1800s but returned to village status after a yellow fever outbreak in 1843, a tornado in 1853, and a shift in the Mississippi River channel that washed away much of the town. Then came the Civil War, and Union troops torched what was left.

The four-hundred-acre park opened in 1962. In addition to historical exhibits, it has a campground and a beautiful hiking trail with views of the Mississippi River. The huge cooling towers of the Grand Gulf Nuclear Power Plant about a mile to the south provide a stark contrast to the rustic setting.

Honoring the Fallen, by Ernest Herndon

An unusual ceremony took place at Grand Gulf Military State Park in 2002 when members of the Sons of Confederate Veterans (SCV) dug up and reburied two Black Union soldiers to prevent their graves from collapsing into a ravine.

"We want to see to the fallen. It doesn't matter to us which side they were on," said Ed Funchess, a member of the Stockdale Rangers SCV Camp of McComb.

SCV members exhumed the remains at the military monument, placed them in body bags, and stored them at a McComb funeral home. During Black History Month in February, they reburied the remains with military ceremonies in new wooden coffins under cleaned and repaired tombstones.

Funchess became interested in the situation after reading an article by Walt Grayson in *Today in Mississippi* magazine about the grave of Jackson Ross in Grand Gulf Cemetery. Over the years a gully had widened to within a couple feet of the grave, threatening to collapse it into a thirty-foot ravine. A little investigation revealed that a grave on the other side of the gully, belonging to Wesley Gilbert, was likewise threatened.

Three SCV groups, or camps, got involved: the Stockdale Rangers, the Colonel Moses Jackson Camp of Liberty, and the Brookhaven Light Artillery. Several members went to the park to look over the situation.

One option discussed was lining the sides of the gully with concrete riprap, but Funchess said that would be costly and unfeasible. It would be simpler just to dig up the graves and rebury the remains elsewhere in the cemetery. "We felt like the only thing that could be done to save these guys, outside of spending $100,000, is to exhume them," he said.

Funchess wrote a proposal and got approval from the Mississippi Department of Wildlife, Fisheries, and Parks, the Department of Archives and History, the State Department of Health, and the Claiborne County coroner. Meanwhile, he tried to pin down more information about the soldiers.

According to the tombstone, Jackson Ross served in Company I of the Forty-Seventh US Colored Infantry Regiment, Eighth Louisiana Infantry. A search of government Civil War records on the internet revealed a Jackson Ross in the Sixty-Fourth and one in the Forty-Eighth but none in the Forty-Seventh. Wesley Gilbert was in Company E, Fifty-Second US Colored Infantry Regiment, Second Mississippi Infantry. Funchess could find no Wesley Gilbert in the Fifty-Second records, but he did find a John

Gilbert and an Armistead Gilbert. He speculated that John and Wesley were the same person, since John Wesley is a common given name.

To exhume the soldiers' remains, a worker used a mini-backhoe to get as close as possible to each grave, and the rest was done with hand tools, much like an archaeological dig. Pike County coroner Percy Pittman donated military body bags to hold the remains, and the Catchings Funeral Home of McComb stored them until the reburial. Funchess and fellow SCV members Wayne and Ben Parker built a pair of white pine coffins based on a design from the 1800s. The SCV invited the Sons of Union Veterans and an African American SCV unit from Clinton to attend.

Funchess said that, though the Civil War left long-lasting divisions in American society, animosity between Union and Confederate soldiers ended quickly. "Everybody was happy and there was a reconciliation almost immediately between the opposing forces," he said.

He said the Sons of Confederate Veterans were glad to rescue the graves of Black Union soldiers. "We don't care who they were," he said. "They were soldiers who were combatants in the Civil War, and they need to be taken care of."

NORTHEAST MISSISSIPPI

Thine eyes are springs in whose serene and silent waters heaven is seen.
—WILLIAM CULLEN BRYANT

Northeast Mississippi is a geographic anomaly. Whereas most of the state is alluvial floodplain, loess bluffs, or piney woods, the southernmost foothills of the Appalachian Mountains erupt through the northeast corner of Mississippi, producing much different surface geology and paddleways, with different characteristics than the other regions of the state.

The Bear Creek Valley is, in some ways, the epicenter for the geological oddity of northeast Mississippi. Particularly in Tishomingo State Park, giant stone boulders protrude from hillsides and lie tumbled as if a giant unseen infant had left toy blocks half-stacked.

The Tennessee-Tombigbee Waterway joins the Tennessee River in the farthest northeast corner of Mississippi to the Tombigbee River, which eventually empties into the Gulf of Mexico near Mobile, Alabama. The Buttahatchee is one of its more beautiful tributaries.

A little farther west are the Wolf and Hatchie Rivers, both of which come into their own across the line in Tennessee.

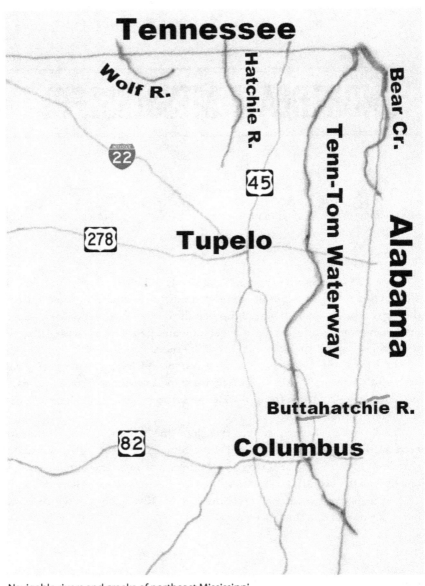

Navigable rivers and creeks of northeast Mississippi

BEAR CREEK

Prior to the mid-1880s, the town of Eastport was the northeasternmost settlement in Mississippi. Eastport was quite a trading hub during the early 1800s, lying as it did near the confluence of the Tennessee River and Bear Creek, and conveniently close to the Natchez Trace. Like many once prosperous river towns in Mississippi, Eastport declined after it was bypassed by the railroad in the late 1800s.

Bear Creek is not only beautiful in its own right; it runs through the heart of one of the state's loveliest parks—Tishomingo State Park. This eighty-mile-long creek starts in Alabama, where it and its tributaries are dammed to form several reservoirs. It enters Mississippi near Red Bay, Alabama, and swings north, which can be confusing since most Mississippi streams flow south, west, or east. It passes through Tishomingo State Park, which straddles the Natchez Trace Parkway, before crossing back into Alabama into an arm of Pickwick Lake on the Tennessee River.

> Tishomingo State Park is a natural place to camp near Bear Creek, with developed and primitive campsites, a forty-five-acre lake with paddleboat and fishing boat rentals, cabins, group camping, nature trails, an 1840s-era log cabin and pond, rock climbing, disc golf, canoe rental, and dulcimer festivals, among other attractions.

The landscape is rocky and hilly, and portions of Bear Creek scoot over rocks for some exciting swifts. Other stretches are long, straight, and currentless. Outside the park's borders, paddlers encounter fields and thin stands of forest, but inside the park they're enclosed in a canyon of towering trees, lush green in the summer and stunningly colorful in the fall.

In Mississippi, Bear Creek offers several floats, but by far the most popular is from Dennis to the park. The popular six-and-a-half-mile section is serviced by the park's canoe rental. The next leg, from the park to Highway 30, is around six miles. Paddlers could handle both stretches in a day, but for float fishing—Bear Creek is also a prime float-fishing stream—allow a day for either.

Below Dennis, Bear Creek makes a huge loop northwest and back southeast, then angles northeast and reenters the park. Remains of an old Confederate bridge stand just inside the park boundary. Rock and gravel shoals make for fun paddling when the water level is normal but may require some towing during low water such as in the fall. The take-out is at the swinging footbridge at the southeast end of the park.

Below the footbridge, the creek remains within the park for several miles. For a long piece below the swinging bridge there is almost no current, surprising in this rocky hill country. Shortly before the Natchez Trace Parkway bridge, the water quickens at a row of rocks that looks like a crude attempt to block the river. And that's exactly what it is—a Native American fish weir. It still works, in a way, as the area below the swifts is a great spot to cast for bass. When the creek leaves the park, the change is obvious as farm fields appear.

> During the Civil War, Eastport, Iuka, Burnsville, and the surrounding creeks, namely Bear Creek, Indian Creek, and Yellow Creek, would play peripheral parts in larger, more notable actions—namely Shiloh and the sieges at Corinth. Eastport was shelled from the Tennessee River and taken by General Sherman, and the Battle of Iuka was fought with the Confederates backed up into the swampy headwaters of Indian Creek, a Tennessee River tributary near Iuka.

When Pickwick Landing Dam was built in 1938 at Counce, Tennessee, it raised water levels and changed topography on Bear Creek for ten miles south past Eastport and as far east along the Tennessee River as Muscle Shoals, Alabama. The old town of Eastport was inundated, and now all that is left is a marina and some camphouses along the southern arm of Pickwick Lake.

The Tennessee-Tombigbee Waterway is a great canoeing destination.

TENNESSEE-TOMBIGBEE WATERWAY

Long straight canals. Broad expanses of open water. Locks and dams. Barges and cabin cruisers. The Tennessee-Tombigbee Waterway may not sound like much of a paddleway, but think again. This stretch of water offers superb vistas, top-notch campgrounds, and passes through excellent wildlife areas. The Tenn-Tom, as it's called, links the Tennessee and Tombigbee Rivers in northeast Mississippi and continues all the way to Alabama's Gulf Coast. Appearances to the contrary, it's definitely worth considering for paddlers willing to set aside their usual criteria and try something different.

> The Tennessee River was named after a Cherokee Indian village called Tanasi near the headwaters. The name Tombigbee is thought to come from a Choctaw phrase meaning "box maker," presumably because of a wright who lived or worked near the river.

The Tennessee is a major tributary of the Ohio River and thence the Mississippi River. As such, it has been a major paddleway for as long as people have lived around here. Only a tiny segment of the Tennessee River lies within the bounds of present-day Mississippi, defining about ten miles of the northeasternmost corner of the state from its confluence with Yellow Creek to its confluence with Bear Creek.

Ten miles north from Eastport along the Tennessee River lies the mouth of Yellow Creek. As with Bear Creek, when the Pickwick Landing Dam was built, the lower (northernmost) eight or ten miles of Yellow Creek became a tortuous lake that swells in places to nearly a mile wide. Yellow Creek is worth exploring in and of itself—its rocky bluffs are draped with forest that shows gorgeous colors in the fall—but this swollen, winding arm of Pickwick Lake is also the northern terminus of the Tennessee-Tombigbee Waterway.

The southernmost headwaters of Yellow Creek come temptingly close to the northernmost headwaters of the Tombigbee River, which heads up in northeast Mississippi and winds southeast to the Gulf of Mexico at Mobile, Alabama. So it seems inevitable that someone would eventually come up with the idea of bridging the thirty-some-odd-mile divide between the rivers, cutting off up to eight hundred miles for boat traffic that would otherwise have to follow the Tennessee, Ohio, and Mississippi Rivers to get to the Gulf. Indeed, this canal idea was first studied in the 1870s during the administration of President Ulysses S. Grant, but the project would not come to fruition until a century later when work began in 1972.

Completed in 1984, the waterway cost $1.8 billion in tax dollars to build. Neither the Suez nor the Panama Canal can match the Tenn-Tom when it comes to earthwork. Builders moved more than 307 million cubic yards of dirt, nearly a third more than the Panama Canal. The 150 million cubic yards of earth from the Divide Cut itself—the canal across the topographic divide between the two river valleys—exceeded Suez Canal excavations.

Mississippi can claim more than half of the Tenn-Tom, which extends from Pickwick Lake to Demopolis, Alabama. From Yellow Creek to Columbus is 115 miles, and another 25 miles to the Alabama line. J. P. Coleman State Park lies a few miles southeast of Yellow Creek on Indian Creek, while Pickwick Landing State Park is just over the line in Tennessee.

The 234-mile series of canals, lakes, and river is chock full of hunting, fishing, camping, and recreation areas. It can be paddled straight through, better yet in segments, or best of all explored piecemeal from base camps. A good many paddlers enjoy the waterway, including some long-distance through-paddlers, though technically camping is only allowed in designated camping areas. Most Tenn-Tom campgrounds are designed for drive-in visitors, not long-distance paddlers.

The Tennessee-Tombigbee Waterway is not just a canal.

> As mitigation for the massive Tenn-Tom project, the Corps of Engineers set aside eighty thousand acres along the waterway and another eighty-eight thousand acres elsewhere in Mississippi and Alabama. Examples include the Mahannah and Twin Oaks Wildlife Management Areas in the Delta and the Ward Bayou WMA near the coast. The Corps spent some $50 million on first-class recreational facilities and campgrounds. There are boat ramps galore. With the exception of the Divide Cut, access is never a problem on the Tenn-Tom, which makes options unlimited for exploring the waterway.

Wildlife abounds along the waterway. Deer splash across shallow inlets. Geese raise a ruckus like a dog kennel with a loose cat. Bald eagles soar in silent majesty. Rabbit hunting is popular in brushy areas along the levees, and squirrels are plentiful in the massive hardwood forests. The Tenn-Tom draws abundant waterfowl, and there are deer and turkeys galore. Bass, crappie, and bream fishing are excellent. Jug fishing and tightlining for catfish are common.

> The Tenn-Tom hosts several species of wildlife more commonly associated with northern climes. Loons visit in late winter. Bald eagles nest all along the waterway and can be seen wheeling overhead. Small numbers of smallmouth bass can be caught in Bay Springs Lake. And walleye inhabit spring-fed tributaries, though they are protected and must be released if caught.

At the south end of the Yellow Creek arm of Pickwick Lake, the waterway narrows into the Divide Cut, a 280-foot-wide, 12-foot-deep, 23-mile-long canal between the Tennessee and Tombigbee River valleys. With high levees lined with rock—the gray rocks known as riprap or revetment, used to prevent erosion—the cut offers few places to take a boat out of the water. And the long, straight channel funnels the wind, usually out of the south. All of this makes the Divide Cut the least enjoyable portion for paddlers. On the plus side, the Corps has built fishing areas along the cut in the form of concrete spillways where tributaries enter the canal. Fish tend to gather beneath the cascading water.

There are some interesting sites along the Divide Cut, but they're inaccessible from the steep-banked, rock-lined waterway. Rather, they can be checked out from the road. Developed hiking trails flank both sides of the waterway most of the distance from Yellow Creek to Holcut. Woodall Mountain, located east of the Divide Cut near Iuka, is the state's highest peak at 806 feet, and 794-foot Lebanon Mountain just to the west of the canal near Baldwyn is Mississippi's most prominent (steepest) peak.

> "Follow the Drinking Gourd" is a traditional African American code song that reputedly gives instruction to escaping slaves on how to navigate the three-hundred-some-odd miles along the Tombigbee River from south Alabama to the Ohio River. The song advises them to follow the Drinking Gourd (the Big Dipper) northward along the banks of the Tombigbee, watching for trail markers on dead trees until the river ends between two hills (Woodall and Lebanon Mountains). It further advises them to keep going north, because just on the other side of the divide they will find where the little river (Yellow Creek) joins the big river (Tennessee), which will take them to freedom.

Holcut Memorial Overlook on the east side of the waterway marks the site of a community that was displaced by waterway construction. A short distance away, the Divide Overlook Area stands at the crest between the two drainage systems. Both places, located off Highway 364, provide sweeping views of the countryside.

The trickling headwaters of Yellow Creek near Holcut are only a handful of miles north of the community of Paden on Mackeys Creek, which is the headwaters of the Tombigbee River. It is this proximity that made this location so attractive for the Divide Cut.

Series of Lakes

At mile marker 421, the Divide Cut opens out onto 6,700-acre Bay Springs Lake, one of the most beautiful spots on the waterway. The beach-rimmed, piney-woods lake sprawls nine miles long and less than a mile wide, with countless coves big and small. While heavily used on summer weekends, at off times such as an autumn weekday the lake may be virtually deserted. This is the kind of place to make a base camp and spend days boating, fishing, hunting, or swaying in a hammock with a good book. Piney Grove Campground on the west bank even offers primitive campsites on an island close to shore. There are also boat ramps on both sides of Bay Springs, six recreation areas, two picnic areas, a marina, a beach, and a visitors center.

The Jamie Whitten Lock and Dam at Bay Springs looks imposing but is simple even for paddlecraft. Below the exit gates, a new vista awaits: a three-hundred-foot-wide channel leading to G. V. "Sonny" Montgomery Lock Pool three miles away. On paper, the lock-and-pool section of the Tenn-Tom looks scarcely worth seeing. In reality, it's lonely and wild. The section consists of five narrow lakes, or pools, linked by canal, with the levee along the west side. The Sonny Montgomery Pool is just two and a half miles long, and its thirty-foot lock is small potatoes after Bay Springs' eighty-four-footer. A two-mile canal leads to six-and-a-half-mile-long John Rankin Lock Pool. To the west is the old Tombigbee River, a wiggly channel of mostly dead water. Beaver Lake Recreation Area is to the east. The Divide Cut and Canal Section Wildlife Management Areas provide long buffers of semiwilderness, while several marinas offer sanctuary for boaters.

Fulton Lock Pool, a mile below John Rankin Lock, stretches six miles, with the Jamie L. Whitten Historical Center—which showcases the history of the Tenn-Tom—and Fulton Campground on the east. The canal between Fulton and Glover Wilkins Lock Pool stretches six miles, with Bean's Ferry Recreation Area on the east bank. Glover Wilkins Lock Pool is nine miles long and skinny, in places no wider than the canal. The Smithville boat ramp and fishing pier are located at the dam. It's three miles to Amory Lock Pool, the smallest at two miles long, bordered on the southeast by the town of Amory and a boat ramp and arboretum.

> Amory was originally known as Cotton Gin Port and had been a jumping off point for the expeditions of French explorers Jean-Baptiste Le Moyne de Bienville and the Marquis de Vaudreuil in the early 1700s.

Rejoining the River

Five miles below Amory Lock, the canal joins the Tombigbee and quickly changes character, becoming muddy with big, vine-draped woods—alligator and cottonmouth country. As the river expands into eight-mile-long Aberdeen Lake, numerous swampy channels branch off, providing opportunities for exploring. Then the lake widens, and handsome residences outside the town of Aberdeen come into view on the west. Blue Bluff Recreation Area also extends along the west bank with campsites.

After the lock at Aberdeen, paddlers encounter alternating stretches of canal and river for sixteen miles en route to Columbus Lake. The river is wide and lonely, with forest looming on each side. Tree-shaded channels branch off as canals slice through bends on the Old Tombigbee. Paddlers can stay on the main channel or go around for a more scenic route.

The Buttahatchee River enters from the east and is worth exploring. By this point, however, the woodland quiet is shattered by frequent flights from Columbus Air Force Base. Town Creek Campground is located to the west a few miles past the Buttahatchee. There's also a campground at DeWayne Hayes Recreation Area on the east bank a couple of miles from Town Creek. Columbus Lake also features another recreation area and marina.

Because of its numerous islands, Columbus doesn't really feel like a lake until its final two and a half miles, when it opens up. With several creeks coming in from the west, it, too, offers exploring potential, though the presence of houses along the shore diminishes the sense of wildness. Luxapalila Creek enters from the east about two and a half miles below the John C. Stennis Lock and Dam at Columbus. The Lux provides a day float from Caledonia Steens Road just north of Steens to Highway 50 in Columbus, with a few logjams in the first mile or so.

The Tenn-Tom continues twenty-five miles downstream from Columbus before crossing the state line into Alabama. Aliceville Lake—where the Plymouth

Bluff Environmental Center is located—straddles the border. The waterway proper ends at Demopolis, and boat traffic follows the Tombigbee River on to Mobile, three hundred miles from the Mississippi line.

> Columbus, lying between the confluences of the Tombigbee River with Luxapalila Creek and the Buttahatchee River, has an extensive Civil War history. Columbus was used as a hospital city for wounded soldiers after the battles at Shiloh and Corinth and is now said to have one of the finest collections of antebellum homes in Mississippi, second only to perhaps Natchez.

A Host of Tributaries

South of Columbus, a host of tributaries flow east across the state line into the Tombigbee. The Noxubee River gathers creeks like Woodward, Jordan, Wet Water, Shotbag, Yellow, Hashuqua, Plum, Dry, Macedonia, Running Water, Shuqualak, Wahalak, Shy Hammock, Big Scooba, Little Scooba, Flat Scooba, Bodka, and Qudby en route to the Tombigbee. South of that, the 110-mile Sucarnoochee River absorbs Sucarnoochee Creek, Pawticfaw, Blackwater, Ponta, and Alamuchee, among others.

> Keith Baca's excellent book *Native American Place Names in Mississippi* (University Press of Mississippi, 2007) helps unravel some of these place names. Hashuqua means grass growing, Shuqualak means beads, Wahalak is to branch out, Scooba is reed brake, Bodka means wide, Sucarnoochee is hog river, Pawticfaw a place where wild animals shed their hair, Alamuchee a little hiding place, Noxubee a stinking river—and Tombigbee means box maker, which could also refer to a coffin or wooden chest.

Locking Through

Ten locks drop the water level 341 feet between Pickwick and Demopolis. This feat of engineering is based on centuries-old principles. Man-made canals date to ancient times and flourished during the 1700s and 1800s, though most have since closed as roads and railroads sprang up. Locks were in use at least as early as the 1400s, when artist and inventor Leonardo da Vinci built six in the canals of Milan, Italy. The Tenn-Tom locks are based on the same hydraulic principles that George Washington used in the C&O Canal. A standard 110-by-600-foot chamber is drained from the bottom, rather like pulling the plug out of a bathtub. It takes about ten minutes for millions of gallons of water to refill it from the upper end via gravity feed.

At eighty-four feet, Bay Springs Lake has the highest of the Tenn-Tom's locks and the third highest east of the Mississippi River. Others on the waterway range from twenty-five to thirty feet. The locking process is safe and easy for paddlers, though sometimes intimidating to the uninitiated.

Barges are among the most common lock users, typically carrying such products as steel (for the mill in Columbus), logs, wood chips, salt (for chemical companies), fuel, and coal. The anticipated amount of barge traffic never arrived on the Tenn-Tom, though barges are more plentiful when the Mississippi River is low and they need an alternate avenue to the Gulf Intracoastal Waterway.

Other vessels include personal watercraft, bass boats, small sailboats, houseboats, and yachts. Even cruise ships and Mississippi River passenger boats have traveled the waterway. Fall is snowbird season, when yachters bring their vessels down the waterway bound for Florida or beyond. Then flat-bottom boats come out as hunters take advantage of miles of wildlife management area, much of it accessible only by boat. In early spring come the fishermen; then the snowbirds return. Recreation season hits full swing from Memorial Day to Labor Day weekends, with hordes of motorboats.

Northeast and north-central Mississippi contain several creeks and small rivers that spend much or most of their time in neighboring states but are still worth a look, including the Wolf River, Hatchie River, and Buttahatchee River.

A kayak glides through a Wolf River cypress swamp.

WOLF RIVER

The Wolf River, obviously distinct from the Wolf near the Gulf Coast, heads up in Holly Springs National Forest northwest of Ripley. It runs west and then north into Tennessee near Michigan City, turning west toward Memphis, where it empties into the Mississippi River.

The twelve- to fifteen-mile Mississippi state stretch is a logjammed creek, but a segment in Tennessee passes through the four-thousand-acre Ghost River State Natural Area, an impressive cypress swamp where the river spreads out and markers on trees show the way through.

The Wolf continues to provide good paddling after it exits the swamp until it enters the environs outside Memphis. The stream flows surprisingly fast, its speed in part the result of a 1960s Corps of Engineers channelization project that shortened the river a good fifteen miles. Still, the Wolf is one of the few west Tennessee streams running more or less naturally for most of its ninety-mile length, and it provides a refreshing corridor of forest amid the ever-expanding subdivisions of Memphis and suburbs.

HATCHIE RIVER

The Hatchie River is born between New Albany and Booneville. Only 38 of the river's 238 miles are in Mississippi. It crosses into Tennessee at the Hardeman-McNairy County line. In Tennessee, the Hatchie meanders northwest toward Brownsville, then swings west to the Mississippi River near Covington. The Hatchie is even less tampered with than the Wolf, remarkable compared with the straight-line channelized routes of so many west Tennessee streams.

> *Hatchie* is Choctaw for river—the name is often attached to descriptors, such as Tallahatchie, Buttahatchee, or Pelahatchie.

One of the best floats on the Hatchie is the twelve miles from Highway 76 to Highway 70 near Brownsville, Tennessee, where it passes through the 11,556-acre Hatchie National Wildlife Refuge, which lines the river for twenty-four miles. In its final miles, the Hatchie also goes through the 7,394-acre Lower Hatchie River National Wildlife Refuge.

BUTTAHATCHEE RIVER

The Buttahatchee River (Choctaw for "sumac river"), a tributary of the Tombigbee, provides good paddling and fishing but has been heavily affected by gravel mining on the lower end between Highway 45 and the Tennessee-Tombigbee Waterway. The 125-mile-long river starts near Sulligent, Alabama, and crosses into Mississippi near Greenwood Springs, with about half its length in each state. At Greenwood Springs it joins Sipsey Creek, another Alabama stream that comes in from the north.

The stretch from Caledonia to US Highway 45 north of Columbus is locally considered the best float on the river, though gravel shoals require occasional portages. The Buttahatchee is characterized by its variety. It features long, wide, straight stretches with no current, almost like lake paddling. Then it swerves and shoots among cypress knees into a green tunnel between park-like woods. The river widens and slows as it passes a gravel bar. The streambed alternates between gravel and mud, so even when clear, the water is slightly dingy. Fishing is good in the Buttahatchee, which provides habitat for catfish, crappie, bream, and bass alike.

Gravel mining has scarred the lower river and left numerous shoals. Because of the mining, the river has shifted course dramatically over the years, moving as far as three-quarters of a mile. Columbus Air Force Base, built during World War II, lies just south of the lower Buttahatchee, and the air traffic can be distracting if not intrusive as planes touch down and take off frequently.

DeWayne Hayes Recreation Area is located on the east shore of Columbus Lake south of the mouth of the Buttahatchee. The area around Caledonia is a countrified suburb of Columbus, with attractive brick houses springing up among shade trees next to cotton and hay fields.

A Taste of the North Woods, by Ernest Herndon

One year in the spring I camped on an island in the North Woods, complete with clear water, the cry of a loon, and crisp morning air. That's the North Woods of Mississippi, by the way. Bay Springs Lake northeast of Tupelo is the closest I've found to the real North Country without leaving the Magnolia State.

I first experienced Bay Springs Lake when my buddy Scott Williams and I paddled Mississippi's portion of the Tennessee-Tombigbee Waterway on a 120-mile trip from Pickwick to Columbus. Bay Springs was so beautiful that I felt like canceling our trip plans and staying there for the rest of our time. Instead, I vowed to return someday when I had time to explore. You might say Bay Springs was on my bucket list.

So on a Monday before Memorial Day, Scott and I launched our boats at a ramp near Piney Grove Campground and paddled a couple miles around a point to an island where primitive camping is allowed. The entire area is regulated by the Corps of Engineers, and camping is only allowed in campgrounds. A friendly ranger told us the island had been a haunt for noisy, drunken partiers until officers cracked down. It's still popular on holiday weekends. We were glad to find it deserted.

The island is maybe half a mile long and a quarter wide and covered in woods. For some reason the Corps saw fit to cram all eleven campsites right together. Maybe that's because there's a beach there, but signs warn of the purported dangers of swimming and wading. Another sign tells campers to call in and report their campsite upon arrival on the island. To add to this regulatory mishmash, the island lies just offshore from the main campground, but you have to paddle the long way around to get here. Regulations.

The cool breeze off the lake blew our frustrations away as we pitched tents, ate black beans and rice, and settled back under a half moon while night fell. A soft wind from the South carried the clean scent of trees and water, as crickets chirped sleepily in the woods.

Since Bay Springs Lake is part of the Tenn-Tom Waterway, one or two towboats pushing barges rumbled past in the night, sweeping the water with their lights. The next morning we paddled across the lake and into a long cove with countless smaller coves branching off it. The air was cool as thunderstorms rumbled in the distance around us.

After lunch we returned to the main lake, where we were greeted by warning whistles from a pair of ospreys guarding their nest in a tree that leaned far out over the water. Scott paddled closer to take photos as the big birds swooped over him threateningly.

Our intrusion must have upset the natural harmony, because the storms that had kept their distance now rolled onto us with a blast of wind, thunder, and hammering rain. We hunkered down in our boats across the lake from our campsite, but we were so miserable we finally decided to paddle on over despite the weather. Bad plan. Thunder crashed overhead, and the wind was so strong it took everything I had to force the canoe into it—and that's not to mention the buckets of cold rain.

That's not the kind of bucket list I had in mind. We survived the crossing, though, and half an hour later were basking under blue skies and sunshine in our hammocks. A loud cry sounded just offshore, and we looked over to see a loon floating and diving.

More rain came through in the night, but mostly gentle enough to sleep to. We woke to a crisp morning that reminded me of Minnesota, or maybe Michigan, Canada, or the Adirondacks of upstate New York—in other words, North Country.

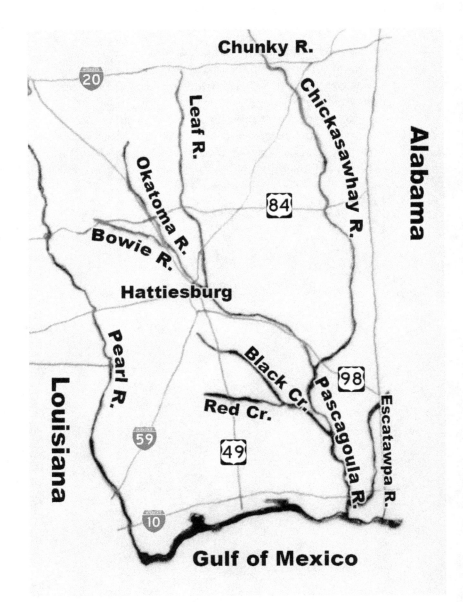
Navigable rivers and creeks of southeast Mississippi

SOUTHEAST MISSISSIPPI

Plans to protect air and water, wilderness and wildlife are in fact plans to protect man.
—STEWART UDALL

Surrounded by more than three-quarters of a million acres of wildlands—national forest, wildlife management areas, wilderness areas, national wildlife refuges, and nature preserve—the southeast corner of Mississippi is dominated by the Pascagoula River.

The Pascagoula is notable as the last undammed major river system in the lower forty-eight states. It also boasts a wealth of fine tributaries, including the Leaf, Chickasawhay, Chunky, and Escatawpa Rivers; and Okatoma, Bowie, Black, and Red Creeks, among others.

PASCAGOULA RIVER

> Swamps and bogs are places of transition and wild growth, breeding grounds, experimental labs where organisms and ideas have the luxury of being out of the spotlight, where the imagination can mutate and mate, send tendrils into and out of the water.
>
> —BARBARA HURD

If there is one river in Mississippi worth seeing from top to bottom, it's the Pascagoula. This southeast Mississippi waterway is the last major river system in the continental United States unaltered by dams, channelization, levees, or other human impact.

North of Mexico, only thirty-five such natural large river systems remain in the Western Hemisphere, all of them in Alaska and northern Canada except one—the Pascagoula. That puts it in a category with such far-north streams as the Stikine, Yukon, and Noatak Rivers. Although the Pascagoula does have some dams in its uppermost headwaters—such as Little Black Creek Water Park, Lake Bogue Homa, and Okatibbee Lake—the river and its main tributaries still run free, at least for now.

One prominent fisheries professor has likened the ecological significance of the Pascagoula River to that of East Africa's Serengeti grasslands, Vietnam's Mekong Delta, and South America's Amazon Basin. It's also comparable to the Florida Everglades, Georgia's Okefenokee Swamp, Alabama's Mobile-Tensaw Delta, Louisiana's Atchafalaya Basin, and Texas's Big Thicket.

> In order to understand why the Pascagoula has been compared to such places, one must understand its major tributaries. The Pascagoula's uniqueness includes geological and paleontological treasures like the Chickasawhay River, wildlife habitats like Big Cedar Creek, and national wilderness areas like those on the Leaf River and Black Creek.

The river's unique status was documented in the November 4, 1994, issue of *Science* magazine. Authors Mats Dynesius and Christer Nilsson surveyed all the large river systems in the Northern Hemisphere and found that only 39 percent of those were not affected by dams and channelization. A color map accompanying the article illustrated the situation vividly. The lower forty-eight states are almost completely blood-red, indicating river systems whose flow

The Pascagoula River is one of the last pristine rivers in the Northern Hemisphere.

has been strongly affected—except for a plume of green in the Deep South of the map, where the Pascagoula flows.

The Pascagoula is an ecological holdout partly because Mississippi is one of the poorest and least developed states. But it's also because of some astute and far-sighted political maneuvering in the 1970s that resulted in an environmental coup—the setting aside of much of the land bordering the Pascagoula into state wildlife management areas. Donald Schueler's 1980 book *Preserving the Pascagoula* tells the complex story behind the groundbreaking accomplishment involving the Nature Conservancy.

The Pascagoula is now bordered by the 37,124-acre Pascagoula River Wildlife Management Area and the 9,494-acre Ward Bayou WMA. It's also flanked by other impressive swaths of public land: the 501,000-acre De Soto National Forest, 940-acre Leaf Wilderness Area, 5,000-acre Charles M. Deaton and Herman Murrah Nature Conservancy Preserves, 5,000-acre Black Creek Wilderness, 19,273-acre Mississippi Sandhill Crane National Wildlife Refuge, 18,500-acre Grand Bay National Estuarine Research Reserve, and 7,000-acre Grand Bay National Wildlife Refuge—more than three-quarters of a million acres of wildlands.

As for paddling in the Pascagoula watershed, there are opportunities aplenty: the Chickasawhay and its tributaries the Chunky River and Buckatunna Creek; the Leaf and its tributaries the Okatoma, Bowie, Tallahala, and Bogue Homa; and the Pascagoula itself along with Black Creek, Red Creek, and the Escatawpa River. All these provide excellent, slow-water, deep-woods paddling, with occasional rapids to liven things up. While the Pascagoula is just 80 miles itself, its major tributaries, the Leaf and Chickasawhay, are each well over 150 miles long.

The Bread People of Singing River

The word "Pascagoula" appears to be a derivation of the Native American words *pasca* for bread and *okla* for people. When French explorers visited the Pascagoula tribe in late summer 1699, the Indians fed them bread made from corn and "a grain that grows on canes"—cattails, perhaps—along with buffalo, bear, and deer meat, and peaches, plums, watermelons, pumpkins, and a succotash of corn and beans. Pascagoula men and boys went naked while women wore loincloths made of Spanish moss. They lived in round huts with dirt walls and bark or leaf roofs.

The Pascagoula Indians were generally peaceful except for occasional wars with neighboring tribes such as the Biloxis. Mississippi's coastal tribes headed west after the 1763 Treaty of Paris. Groups of Pascagoulas moved to Lake Maurepas and the Amite River in southeast Louisiana, the Red River and Bayou Boeuf in central Louisiana, and on into East Texas and Oklahoma, with the last identifiable tribe members reported in 1914.

That ending—assimilation into other tribes in rural America—is less poetic than the "singing river" legends that still circulate around Pascagoula and adorn such edifices as Singing River Hospital and Singing River Bridge. The legends purport to explain a musical noise sometimes heard on the river.

According to the most common version, when the disease- and war-ridden tribe realized they faced extinction, they decided to commit mass suicide. They held hands and, singing, waded into the water, never to be seen again. A little research reveals similar legends concerning Biloxi and Yazoo Indians and escaped African slaves in Georgia. The story existed even among the Pascagoulas about an earlier, ancestral tribe. According to that one, the ancestors emerged from the sea to live a gentle, harmonious life, but shortly after Hernando de Soto's army came through in 1539, a missionary appeared and began to teach them their version of the gospel. One moonlit night, a mermaid goddess arose from the water and summoned her children, telling them she would never surrender them to a foreign way of life.

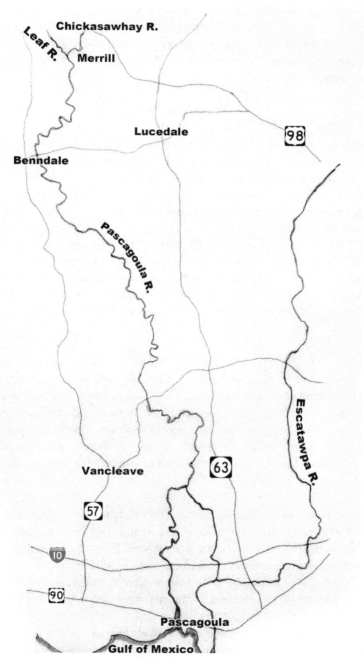

The Pascagoula and Escatawpa Rivers

About the only discernible seed of truth in all this is a 1726 account of several people drowning in the Fish River, as the east branch of the Pascagoula was then called. It's possible that incident fueled the legends. As for the mysterious noise, many people say they've heard it (including author Herndon), but the cause remains unknown.

Entering the Swamp

Paddlers can launch on the Pascagoula River just below the confluence of the Leaf and Chickasawhay Rivers at the community of Merrill on the east bank. After a few miles of private land, the Pascagoula River WMA begins, and public land dominates most of the rest of the way. As with the Mississippi River, there are just a few bridge crossings and several remote landings, both public and private.

On the stretch from Merrill to Highway 26, the Pascagoula retains elements of hill country, with high bluffs, pine trees, and only intermittent swamps and bayous among the big, beautiful sandbars. Big Black Creek enters from the west about three miles above Wade-Vancleave Road, carrying with it the waters of Black and Red Creeks from the piney hills of De Soto National Forest.

> About twelve miles downstream of Highway 26, the river slips past the community of Basin, where White Creek and Reed Flat Creek join the Pascagoula. Basin used to be known as Helveston, which is still a common surname in Mississippi. A few miles south of Basin, the river passes by the first county seat of Jackson County, Old Americus. Nothing remains of this settlement except a crossroads. Big Cedar Creek pours into the Pascagoula here, draining waters from around Lucedale and Agricola.

From Highway 26, the Pascagoula grows increasingly swampy as it enters the Ward Bayou WMA. The river curves east and does some serious meandering before turning back south at Cumbest Bluff. It continues south for several miles, then seems to come to a dead halt—but closer inspection shows a branch leading off to either side. This is the beginning of the West and East Pascagoula Rivers, which pass Gautier and Escatawpa, respectively, before pouring onto the Gulf of Mexico at Pascagoula Bay.

Below the east-west split, the river scarcely flows at all as it twists through dense woods, cypress swamp, and marsh. On the west river are Ward Bayou

The Pascagoula River is enjoyed by paddlers and fishermen.

and Poticaw Landing with a concentration of camps, houseboats, and bait shops. From the split to the mouth of the river, shores are likely to be muddy. The river is subject to tidal fluctuations, meaning unsecured boats can float away overnight. A couple of miles above Interstate 10, boaters can take Swift Bayou to the left (south) and follow it to Creole Bayou, which leads to the right under the interstate and back to the main river, thus cutting off one huge bend. From here, it's a hard pull on windswept water big enough for shrimp boats. Less than a mile above Highway 90, a broad channel to the left connects back to the east river. There are boat ramps at Highway 90 crossings, plus Shepard State Park on a bayou off the river on the west.

The East Pascagoula River (aka Fish River), meanwhile, joins a broader channel coming out of several bayous, then runs south alongside the towns of Escatawpa, Moss Point, and Pascagoula, with development and industry including Ingalls Shipyard. Two miles farther, the East Pascagoula River splits, one channel joining the west river, the other going east and south to a ramp at River Park just north of Highway 90. Amid this labyrinth, the lower rivers are joined by numerous bayous, creeks, sloughs, and dead lakes.

Seasons in the Swamp

On a swampy river like the Pascagoula, it makes a big difference whether you paddle during low water or high. Both seasons have their charms. In the floods of late winter and early spring, the river can easily get out of its banks, which is ideal for exploring by boat.

As you paddle down the river, watch for openings into the woods. Machete and compass come in handy for getting the boat through walls of canebrake, though beware of snakes that like to coil up on bushes above the water. And be aware that a cottonmouth making its lazy way across the surface is not likely to be intimidated by a mere canoe or kayak. Poke a paddle at it and you may get to see the white interior of its mouth and its slivered fangs.

Such thrills aside, it's enchanting to drift through a flooded forest, especially in late winter and early spring when dogwoods, red maples, and redbuds are in bloom. The narrowest passage may open onto a lake shaded by giant cypress and tupelo gum trees, which are often hollow. Camping during high water may mean settling for a spot just an inch or two above the level of the river in big woods.

In low-water time, such as October, sandbars abound. Even on a sandbar, though, you can tell you're in swamp country by the hordes of mosquitoes waiting in ambush in the willow thickets. While low water makes it harder to venture into the backcountry by boat, it allows for exploring on foot, revealing such wonders as a four-foot waterfall tumbling from a jungle clay bank.

Among other factors for which the Pascagoula is memorable is the likelihood of seeing a swallow-tailed kite. These graceful, distinctive birds range from extreme southeast Mississippi along the Gulf Coast down to Florida and on to southern South America. With slender wings spreading up to fifty inches edged at the rear in black, and a long, sharply forked black tail contrasting with white body and forewings, the kites are instantly identifiable. They inhabit wetlands, feed on insects and reptiles, and skim the water to drink. They like to ride the air currents, and their presence gives evidence of a fine, wild place.

Groundbreaking Documentary

Not surprisingly, the Pascagoula has drawn the attention of numerous documentary filmmakers. In 2003, Mississippi Public Broadcasting and the Nature Conservancy joined to showcase this wonder in *The Singing River: Rhythms of Nature* on Mississippi Educational Television (ETV). The film begins with awesome images of the river, including aerial shots that show just how vast the basin is. It's a view travelers can glimpse when driving across the high-rise bridge on Interstate 10 near Moss Point.

The documentary tells the intriguing story of how the river came to be protected, unlike so many others nationwide that have fallen prey to clear-cutting, channelization, damming, and other projects.

Also helping protect the river is the rare Gulf sturgeon, a giant fish that uses the Pascagoula system to spawn. Conservationists used the sturgeons' presence to block a proposal to dam the Bowie River, a Pascagoula tributary, in the 1990s. The film shows University of Southern Mississippi researchers netting and studying the weird, prehistoric-looking fish, then releasing them. Other species get attention, too, from massive alligators to some of the three hundred species of birds that frequent the swamp.

The film outlines the prehistory of the river basin, from ancient times when it all lay beneath the Gulf of Mexico to more recent days when Native Americans carved arrowheads from riverbed rocks. Although many people contributed to the documentary project, ETV's Kirk Loy was the driving force, serving as producer, director, editor, and photographer. Loy filmed everything from underwater fish scenes to swimming alligators and from soaring eagles to billowing thunderheads. Conservationists said they hope the documentary will spur people to appreciate the Pascagoula and make sure it continues to be preserved.

Film and Print

In 2010, filmmakers Alison Fast and her husband Chandler Griffin visited the Pascagoula River WMA while filming the Gulf oil spill. Griffin is the founding director of Barefoot Workshops, which provides courses in documentary filmmaking. Fast is a Peabody Award–winning television producer who has worked for NBC/Universal, BBC Worldwide, and MTV. She is the program director of Barefoot Workshops. Their projects have taken them all around the world.

One of their main points of interest regarding the Pascagoula River was a US Department of Energy proposal at the time (since abandoned) to withdraw fifty million gallons of water from the river a day for five years to hollow out the underground Richton salt dome as a storage site for the Strategic Petroleum Reserve. After much opposition, the plan faded, but there was considerable irony to it when the 2010 Gulf oil spill was washing up at the mouth of the Pascagoula. You might say the river was threatened by oil from above and below.

The couple drove to an oxbow lake, a perfect example of the Pascagoula's majestic cypress swamps. With author Herndon serving as their guide, they launched a pair of canoes in the lake as the sun set over the cypress trees.

The beauty was beyond description. They weren't talking anymore, just looking. Fast had set one camera on a dock for time-lapse photography and held another in a canoe, recording the sights and sounds of the swamp. The silence was blissful—though silence is the wrong word for the symphony of crickets, cicadas, bullfrogs, and other creatures.

The hours of filming resulted in a short documentary called *Pascagoula: River at Risk.*

The river has also been featured in books. In addition to Schueler's *Preserving the Pascagoula*, the river was profiled in Herndon's *Canoeing Mississippi* and described in depth in the travel narrative *Paddling the Pascagoula* coauthored by Herndon and Scott B. Williams. Both books were published by the University Press of Mississippi. As described in *Paddling the Pascagoula*, Herndon and Travis Easley canoed the Leaf while Williams kayaked the Chickasawhay, and they met up at Merrill to continue to the Gulf coast.

Mississippi paddler David L. Pugh also paddled the river in 2017 and wrote *Voyage of Freedom: Kayaking to the Coast.*

Scouting a Movie Location, by Ernest Herndon

I've often wondered what it would be like to be a professional canoe guide. I got a taste when I served as Swamp Guide to the Stars. I assisted Scott B. Williams in leading some Hollywood movie producers into a Pascagoula swamp to scout possible filming locations for *Free State of Jones*, which came out in 2016 starring Matthew McConaughey.

Our clients were Gary Ross, Robin Bissell, Diana Alvarez, and Phil Messina, all of California. Ross, the writer and director, also wrote the screenplay for *Seabiscuit* and authored such movies as *Pleasantville* and *Big*. Bissell was likewise involved in *Seabiscuit* and *Pleasantville*. Alvarez worked on a long list of TV shows including *The Highlander* and *The Practice*. Messina's credits include *Ocean's Eleven* and *Ocean's Twelve*.

They initially contacted Mississippi River canoe guide John Ruskey of Clarksdale. Ruskey referred them to me but I was busy the weekend they needed to visit, so I referred them to Scott. Scott and Travis Easley took Gary and associates on a preliminary scouting trip. Later, Scott enlisted my aid—in particular, my canoes and pickup truck—for a swamp trip.

Scott had located some good backwaters off the Pascagoula River south of Lucedale, so one evening I loaded three canoes onto my truck—two on a roof rack, one in the bed—and at 6:00 a.m. the next day headed east to meet Scott at a convenience store near Hattiesburg.

"They're running late," he told me when I arrived.

We had planned to meet our clients at 8:15 a.m. at Rose's Barbecue on Highway 49 just south of Highway 98. That got pushed back to 9:00, so we drove to Rose's and drank coffee. At 10:00 they showed up in a rented SUV. Diana apologized for being late.

We drove to the swamp an hour away. As we surveyed a picture-perfect cypress lake, Phil and Gary expressed doubts. This was too open. Did we have something thicker?

Scott, who had already checked out the area, told them it was thicker on the back side. So we launched the canoes, Scott and I fielding questions as we paddled.

"Do alligators live here?"

"Yep."

"Do they attack people in boats?"

"Not usually."

At the end of the lake, I spotted a six-foot gator swimming, which prompted much excitement. It didn't attack, though.

We landed and got out. Scott and I led the way, hacking through underbrush with machetes, our rubber boots sinking in the mud. We found a fine stretch of dry swamp with cypress and tupelo gum trees. Cypress knees rose everywhere. Phil and Gary framed scenes with their fingers, snapped pictures with their digitals. Diana took photos of insects.

The irony of the scene struck me. In the past I have hired local guides—Miskito Indians, New Guinea tribesmen—to lead me into the jungle. I recall Miskito Indians, carrying machetes and wearing rubber boots, waiting patiently as I snapped pictures and marveled at the scenery in the Mosquitia region of Honduras and Nicaragua. Now I was the local guide.

Meanwhile, Gary and Phil discussed scenes they would film. As we returned to the boats, I pulled out my banjo-mandolin, which I had brought along for ambience. Sitting in the back of a canoe, I picked "Bonaparte's Retreat," "Old Joe Clark," and "Lost Indian." I looked up to see the group listening appreciatively. Or maybe they were thinking about *Deliverance*.

Back at the truck, our clients whipped out their cell phones while Scott assembled the lunch they had specifically requested—wheat bread, pita bread, hummus, turkey, roast beef, baby Swiss cheese, cheddar, Dijon mustard, lettuce, tomatoes, regular and salt-and-vinegar chips, carrots, celery, cucumber slices, Planter's Deluxe Assorted Nuts, beef jerky, Diet Coke, and bottled water—while I opened my sardines and crackers and swigged from my canteen. They did offer to share with me, of course. But the difference in our respective backcountry meals was entertaining.

We scouted more lakes. At 4:00 p.m., Gary declared the trip a success. We shook hands all around and said we hoped to meet again soon. These folks had been fun to be with.

Then I began my long trip home, arriving after 8:00 p.m.—fourteen hours and 365 miles after I'd started. As I unloaded my canoes and gear in the dusk, being a professional guide didn't feel quite so glamorous.

Oh, and as for the location? They chose somewhere else for the movie.

ESCATAWPA RIVER

> Beauty [is like] the reflection in dark water of that silver shell we call the moon.
>
> —OSCAR WILDE

Like Black Creek and Red Creek, the Escatawpa River is a blackwater stream, its waters stained by natural tannic acids leached from vegetation. But Black and Red enter the Pascagoula from the west, while the Escatawpa comes in from the east.

Black and Red Creeks are shades of iced tea, but the upper Escatawpa is more like strong black coffee. Bordered by porcelain-white sandbars and gnarled cypress roots, the dark river gleams like an antique mirror in an old mansion. One man described it as spooky. Another called it miraculous. Either way, it's a wonder to behold.

The 125-mile-long stream, which is floatable for half its length, heads up along the Mississippi-Alabama state line. Topographic maps indicate it starts in Alabama, but the Corps of Engineers puts its headwaters near the community of Copeland, Mississippi, southeast of Waynesboro. Regardless of who can claim the exact birthplace, the upper half of the river lies in Alabama, flowing generally south parallel to the state line. It angles into Mississippi at Highway 98 and eventually hooks west into the Pascagoula River at Moss Point.

> Modern locals call this the Dog River, but the etymology of that name is unclear. The name Escatawpa derives from a Choctaw phrase meaning creek where cane was cut—*uski* for cane and *tapa* for cut.

There's a popular swimming hole at the put-in at Lott Road, a county road north of Highway 98. On the stretch from Lott Road to Georgetown Bridge Road, the stream is small enough to require some drags over sandy shallows and tight squeezes among logs. This can be a problem in late summer and early fall when water levels are low. Puppy Creek enters from the east just above Georgetown Bridge, boosting channel width as it continues to Highway 98.

Brushy Creek flows in from the west ten or so miles below Georgetown, another sizable stream that enlarges the Escatawpa considerably. Brushy Creek is floatable if there's sufficient water and you don't mind some pullovers. Escatawpa Hollow Campground sprawls along the east bank just past Highway 98.

As the Escatawpa widens, the intensity of its blackness diminishes. Still, it continues lovely and wooded from Highway 98 to Tanner Williams Road. Sandbars remain pleasantly small.

The Escatawpa grows noticeably swampy from Tanner Williams Road to a boat ramp at Highway 614. Bayous and oxbow lakes provide good side trips. Showy white spider lilies and titi (pronounced tie-tie) bushes bloom in late spring and early summer. Titi, also known as leatherwood, has drooping, finger-shaped clusters of white blossoms; it grows thick along riverbanks. Spider lilies stand upright, their three to seven white petals sparkling with leggy fringe. They flourish in lower, swampy areas such as the shores of oxbow lakes.

On the stretch to Pollock Ferry Road, sandbars diminish, banks sag, and the river is wide enough for motorboats. As a result, fewer people paddle here. This stretch is low-lying enough for flanking areas to merit names such as Red Oak Swamp, Reed Brake Swamp, and Island Swamp. Big Creek flows in below Highway 614, then Jackson Creek, both from the east. An oxbow lake at the mouth of Jackson Creek, known as Goode's Mill Lake, is a popular water-skiing spot. Interstate 10 crosses the river a couple of miles farther.

This lower river is the least appealing section to paddlers due to industry and motorboats, but ironically to the south and east lie the 18,500-acre Grand Bay Reserve and the contiguous 32,000-acre Grand Bay National Wildlife Refuge. This impressive swath contains coastal bays, saltwater marshes, maritime pine forests, pine savannas, and pitcher plant bogs. It harbors creatures like the Alabama red-bellied turtle, Bachman's sparrow, speckled burrowing crayfish, crawfish snakes, glass lizards, and diamondback terrapins, plus plants like sundew, wild orchids, Chapman's butterwort, pineland bogbutton, night-flowering wild petunia, giant spiral ladies'-tresses, and Harper's yellow-eyed grass. The reserve and the refuge—which are open to fishing and hunting—serve to protect a habitat that has shrunk drastically in recent years. After Pollock Ferry, the river turns west toward Moss Point, expanding into two-mile-long Robertson Lake on its final run to the Pascagoula River.

A Fishing Disaster, by Ernest Herndon

In an old episode of *The Andy Griffith Show*, Andy tells Aunt Bee he plans to go camping and fishing and asks her to pack a few things in his knapsack. She cheerfully obliges, even baking him an apple pie to take along.

I decided to try that approach.

"Honey?" I said to my wife, Angelyn. "I'm going camping for several days. How about throwing some stuff together for me, and maybe bake an apple pie while you're at it?" Suffice it to say her response did not resemble Aunt Bee's. So I decided to invite her along with me, apple pie or no. After all, we're always being advised to take a kid fishing. Why not spouses?

For our camping trip I chose the Escatawpa River, which crosses the Mississippi-Alabama line about fifty miles east of Hattiesburg. The stream was reputed to be scenic and secluded with pretty good fishing. I figured to put our canoe in the water at Lotts Road, a gravel lane near Citronelle, Alabama, and our destination was to be a take-out near Hurley, Mississippi, forty miles downstream.

My main concern was bugs. Insects like Angelyn. At home, as soon as she goes into the yard you can hear the blades of grass rustling as ticks, redbugs, and fleas begin crawling toward her. Plus, she's allergic to the heavy-duty repellents needed against hungry insects. I was also worried about heat, thunderstorms, and other discomforts that might make her want to swear off of camping.

After a couple hours paddling down the coffee-colored stream, I decided it was time to get out the tackle box. I picked up the new rod I had purchased in hopes of maximizing Angelyn's fishing enjoyment.

"Look up there and hand me that tackle box, would you?" I said.

"Tackle box?" she asked. "There's no tackle box up here."

"There's got to be," I said, but as my words trailed off I realized I had not, in fact, put it in the canoe. I must have left it in the driver's truck, which would be in Mobile, Alabama, by now.

Even Aunt Bee wouldn't have forgotten the tackle box.

My spirits wilted, but Angelyn wasn't fazed. As a non-fisherman she didn't know what she was missing.

We pitched camp on a pristine sandbar with no rain and few bugs. The night turned off chilly, just right for sleeping. We did get a thundershower the next day, but we quickly strung a tarpaulin lean-to and stretched out underneath for a nap.

As we approached Highway 98, the river grew murky from the runoff of rain-swollen tributaries. That meant the bass fishing wouldn't be good anyhow, so I didn't feel so bad about the missing tackle box.

We camped on another sandbar, strung the hammocks, and cooked a big supper. The trip was turning out to be pleasant after all. Then on the third day, I suggested that Angelyn take the stern.

The stern of a canoe is the steering position. While the Escatawpa is hardly treacherous, it's tricky in the bends where swift currents rush among fallen logs—and Angelyn had no experience steering.

Not to worry. She had me to teach her. As a self-taught paddler, I'd spent years figuring out such things as the J-stroke, guide stroke, sweep, reverse sweep, draw, and ruddering, not to mention how to spot shoals, crosscurrents, eddies, and submerged logs. With me teaching, I saw no reason why Angelyn couldn't learn all that by, say, lunchtime.

I explained everything, then left the steering to her. As she wrestled to guide the seventeen-foot-long boat, the woodland quiet was punctuated with splashes, thuds, mutters, and an occasional screech. But we didn't turn over, and by late afternoon she was dodging logjams handily.

We pitched the tent on another squeaky-white sandbar and slung the hammocks in a shady red-maple arbor at the edge of the river. My hammock extended over the water while Angelyn's stretched alongside it. The spot was water-cooled and bug-free. We took a swim, ate a big supper, and built a campfire. The mosquitoes didn't bother her any worse than they did me.

By the last day, Angelyn seemed at home on the water. She sat in the bow, shaded by a big straw hat, pausing to point out birds and plants. As we eased onto a cypress lake she thumbed through a wildflower field guide, identifying the plant life as we passed.

She was so relaxed she wasn't even bothered when an alligator slammed the stern of our canoe with its tail—at least, I assume that's what it was. The best I could tell, we'd backed over a gator lying on the shallow bottom. Judging by the sound of the whack and the cloud of mud in the water, it couldn't have been longer than, say, five or six feet.

Nope, Angelyn wasn't bothered. Not by the gator, the bugs, the rain, not even the forgotten tackle box. I'll take her over Aunt Bee and an apple pie any day.

CHICKASAWHAY RIVER

> The more tortured [the land] is by water... the more it attracts fossil hunters, who depend on the planet to open itself to us. We can only scratch away at what natural forces have brought to the surface.
>
> —JACK HORNER

The Chickasawhay River begins near the east Mississippi town of Enterprise where the Chunky River and Okatibbee Creek come together. From there it flows 158 miles to its confluence with the Leaf River, where the Pascagoula is born.

At this southernmost fringe of the Appalachian Mountains, the upper Chickasawhay slices through stone and mud, an intriguing region of waterfalls and alligators, cliffs and swamp. Boat ramps have been placed along the river, since it's generally inaccessible otherwise because of its steep banks. The prevalence of rocky shoals along the waterway makes motorboating difficult, and that's good news for paddlers. Except for the lower reaches where it becomes wide and deep, the Chickasawhay makes for pleasant floating, with good fishing and relatively little human contact.

> There are a couple of plausible etymologies for the word "Chickasawhay" (pronounced Chick-a-sa-HAY). The more evocative story is that it derives from a Choctaw phrase meaning "place where martins dance." That probably refers to a stretch of river known as King's Bluff, where martins build nests in the bank. More recent scholarship suggests that the river is actually named for the "Chickasaw" wild potatoes (*ahi*) that grow in that region (cf. the Leaf River tributary Oakohay, or "wild potato").

Thirty-Five Million Years on the Chickasawhay

One of the reasons that the Chickasawhay River is unique is that starting around the present-day community of Shubuta it vividly showcases the geological progression of time in its steep banks. The sediment at Shubuta is said to be about thirty-five million years old, and the farther downstream you go, the younger the deposits get until you get to around Woodwards about twenty river miles downstream, where the strata are around thirty-two million years old.

This means these steeply eroded banks of the Chickasawhay display the boundary between the Eocene and Oligocene epochs (about thirty-three to thirty-four million years ago) of prehistory perfectly, as if it were a diorama in a museum. This, in turn, makes the Chickasawhay one of the best places in the world for geologists and paleontologists to study the mass extinction event that marks the boundary between these epochs.

This geological uniqueness of the Chickasawhay was spotlighted in the outstanding 2018 Mississippi Public Broadcasting documentary *35 Million Years Down the Chickasawhay*, which features Mark Puckett, professor of geology at the University of Southern Mississippi; George Phillips, curator of paleontology at the Mississippi Museum of Natural Science; and James Starnes, geologist at the Mississippi Office of Geology.

Spanish Gold Seekers

On this river, things don't seem much different than during the days when Hernando de Soto and his army of gold-seeking Spaniards came through the region around 1540. The town of De Soto on the upper Chickasawhay was named for the conquistador, as was the national forest to the south, though whether he actually crossed the Chickasawhay is questionable.

De Soto and 650 of his troops landed near what is now Tampa, Florida, but from there their route is vague. Apparently they hacked their way north to Tallahassee, Florida, veered northeast into the Appalachians as far north as Knoxville, Tennessee, then back south into Alabama near Montgomery. They crossed into Mississippi over a swift, wide river, which most scholars believe was the Tombigbee but local residents prefer to think was the Chickasawhay. From there, they went on across northeast Mississippi to the Mississippi River. De Soto crossed it somewhere around Walls, just south of Memphis, looped into Arkansas and back to the Mississippi, apparently near Arkansas City, where he died of fever.

> The Spanish had several advantages over the Indians. First they had guns, clumsy things known as arquebuses, but they were so unreliable and inaccurate that they were mainly useful for making a loud noise. Horses, too, gave the Spanish an advantage, but not a tremendous one in the forest environment. Their steel and padded armor, however, made them virtually impervious to arrows. In one battle, De Soto was hit by twenty-one arrows, but since he was wearing padded armor, they merely stuck out like a pincushion while he continued to fight.

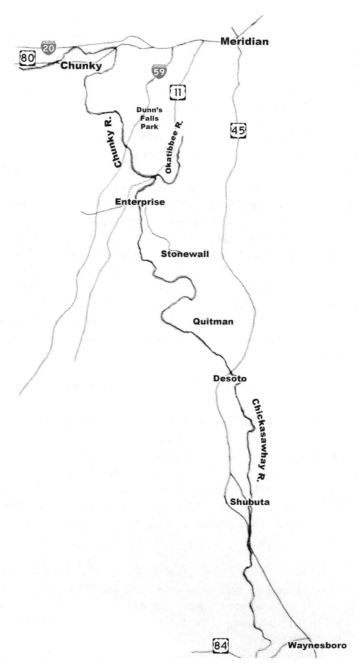

The Chunky River and the Chickasawhay River from Enterprise to Waynesboro

The Spanish wanted one thing: gold. And they didn't hesitate to kill, enslave, and torture Native American inhabitants, even hunting them with war dogs for sport. De Soto's general strategy when meeting Indians was to seize the chief and enslave the people. If they resisted, which they naturally did, he was swift to attack. Despite the depressing nature of De Soto's tactics, it's fascinating to contemplate the wilderness he encountered—and still possible to get a glimpse of it in the big woods along the Chickasawhay.

The highest launch point for paddlecraft is at Highway 513 in the town of Enterprise, less than a mile below the confluence of the Chunky and Okatibbee. Just below Quitman, Souenlovie Creek (derived from local Choctaw dialect meaning "leech killer") comes in from the west, a sizeable tributary. Next, Archusa (Choctaw, "little river") Creek flows in from the north through Archusa Creek Water Park, which has a campground.

The town of De Soto was named for the conquistador, of course, but it has a colorful history apart from the explorer. The area was settled in the 1830s and incorporated as a village in 1896. It remained thus until the legislature did away with village status in the state, since most such hamlets lacked a sufficient tax base to provide services. De Soto retains its village feel, with a historic old barber shop that operated from 1924 to 1964 and was restored in 1999. Also restored was an old artesian well where trains used to stop for passengers to drink.

The Smoky Water Yowani Choctaws

A large chunk of the Chickasawhay Valley was settled in the eighteenth century by a subset of Choctaws known as the Yowani. The Yowani were apparently a robust tribe because by the time French settlers encountered them in the early 1700s and set up the nearby settlement of Shubuta, the Yowani Choctaws had spread out in a broad five-hundred-square-mile swath from around Shubuta to near Pachuta, westward to the Bogue Homa area, and southeast to the juncture of the Chickasawhay and Buckatunna.

> Shubuta is a Choctaw phrase that means "smoky water." The Yowani Indians apparently got their name from the "caterpillars" that infested the area. Pachuta means "pigeons roost there," Buckatunna means "creek where there is weaving" (or reeds for weaving), and Bogue Homa refers to a "red creek."

The Chickasawhay River from Waynesboro to Merrill

A Frontier Travel Mystery

In the fall of 1787, a Frenchman by the name of Jean Delavillebeuvre left New Orleans headed on a mission of trade diplomacy among the Choctaw Indians in east-central Mississippi. He sailed to Bay St. Louis, then headed north for the villages of Yellow Canes and Grand Yazoo—in the vicinity of today's towns of Enterprise and Meridian, respectively.

Here's the catch—he made the trip from Bay St. Louis to Yellow Canes in eight and a half days.

The journey was described in the article "The Politics of Trade: Delavillebeuvre's 1787 Mission to the Choctaws and Journal" by Jackson historian Charles A. Weeks in the Spring 2003 issue of the *Journal of Mississippi History*. On an accompanying map, a dotted line traces the route from New Orleans across Lake Pontchartrain, through the Rigolets and along the Mississippi Gulf Coast. It continues up the Pascagoula and Chickasawhay Rivers to Yellow Canes, located near the confluence of Okatibbee and Chunky Creeks, and Grand (West) Yazoo to the north. The caption reads, "Jean (Juan) Delavillebeuvre's 1787 Mission to the Choctaws: Probable Route."

Note the word "probable." Jean's journal gives no details from the time he left the coast until he arrived at Yellow Canes.

According to his journal, Jean left New Orleans on September 27 "and dropped anchor at the entrance to the Rigolets at midnight, whence we set out two and a half hours after midnight, and after sailing all night arrived at Madame Asmar's at five in the evening, where we remained for two and a half days to arrange for rafts and to prepare for the voyage; and we left there on the 28th two hours after noon. We arrived at Yellow Canes the seventh of October at ten in the morning and stayed there two days."

A footnote to Weeks's article says that Madame Asmar's was located in the Bay St. Louis and Pass Christian area. It also says, "The use of bacs, translated here as 'rafts,' indicates that Delavillebeuvre and his party were traveling on rivers, no doubt the Pascagoula and the Chickasawhay."

The problem with that scenario is that it involves going 40 miles east along the coast to the mouth of the Pascagoula, then 250 miles upstream to Yellow Canes—nearly 300 miles. If Jean made the trip in the approximately eight and a half days he mentions, that's more than 35 miles per day, which is about the max a modern paddler would make—downstream.

Granted, the sort of recreational canoeing we do these days is different from frontier travel. Jean might have used rowboats powered by sailors, or long dugout canoes manned by Indians, and stayed in motion from dark to dark. But modern-day Miskito Indians travel the Coco River in Central America—

a river remarkably similar to the Pascagoula—and when they go upstream, they pole their dugout canoes at a painstakingly slow pace against the current. In comparison, twenty miles a day was about the most the Lewis and Clark Expedition made going up the Missouri River.

The key to Jean's mystery may lie in his description of what came next: "We left Yellow Canes the 10th at nine in the morning and arrived at Grand Yazoo the 13th with the utmost difficulty, our horses being extremely tired, injured, and lame."

Why would the horses be tired, injured, and lame from a three-and-a-half-day trip? Could it be because they had just ridden overland from the coast?

Those "rafts" Jean referred to were probably used for crossing St. Louis Bay—which is generally too shallow for a ship—to high ground, from whence they would ride. On land, that trip would have spanned less than two hundred miles, probably on a trail through open longleaf pine forest. That makes the eight-and-a-half-day travel time more reasonable. Author Weeks agrees that that's plausible: "After the mention of Madame Asmar it's a guess," he writes.

Of course, there's another possible explanation for the quickness of Jean's journey: "He lied," suggested a Mississippi outdoorsman. "Hunters and fishermen always do a little of that."

Sandbars and Bluffs

Sandbars increase on the 13.5-mile stretch from De Soto to Shubuta. There are about ten small sets of easy rapids on this segment, including a two- to three-foot drop-off and a roaring two-hundred-yard-long stretch at the mouth of Shubuta Creek called the Old Shubuta Races, three miles north of the town of Shubuta. These upper stretches of the Chickasawhay are particularly scenic, with high clay-rock walls and deep woods ranging from pine plantations to tropical-seeming jungle. The sheer bluffs are natural sources of springwater. In the springtime rainy season, water pours from the mossy clay walls, making it easy to keep canteens filled. Such springs often disappear during dry season, however.

Tributaries lead to Appalachian-style wonderlands with small, gushing waterfalls, caves, and dripping ferns. Even the sandbars are steep on the upper river.

The river grows gradually wider and slower below Shubuta, with many large sandbars. Buckatunna Creek, a floatable tributary, enters from the east a few miles below Chicora. Farther down, there are fewer shoals, but long, lonely stretches of woods are blissful to paddlers. Near Leakesville the banks grow muddy, and trotlining for catfish is popular. Halfway between Leakesville and the Pascagoula thirty miles downriver, Big Creek comes in from the northwest.

The ghost town of Winchester used to be the county seat of Wayne County. It was situated on Meadows Mill Creek near where it joins the Chickasawhay. One of the earliest settlements in the piney woods of eastern Mississippi, the Winchester of the late 1700s is described as having been a hub of political influence second only to Natchez. After Creek Indians massacred over five hundred settlers at nearby Fort Mims in 1813, alarmed residents of the Winchester area erected a fortification that would come to be known as Patton's Fort.

Despite serving as county seat for nearly fifty years, Winchester's political influence and trading and shipping situation waned as navigation up and down the Chickasawhay became less practical. But settlements rarely dry up and become ghost towns overnight, and even as late as the 1960s, one of Winchester's claims to fame was that it was the birthplace of country music star James O'Gwynn, whose songs include "My Name Is Mud" and "Bottle Talk."

Today, Old Winchester is buried in forest, and the only remaining sign of this once industrious site is a historical marker at nearby Highway 45 reading, "About one mile to the West. Site of Patton's Fort, 1813. Chartered 1818. Near old road from Natchez to Georgia. Became a thriving trade center, serving as county seat until 1867."

Buckatunna

Buckatunna Creek (sometimes spelled Bucatunna) flows 108 miles, but only 15 of them are floatable. Those 15 miles are interesting, though, as the creek is something of a Chickasawhay in miniature. Like the big river into which it flows, Buckatunna occupies a curious verge between rock and mud, with fern-draped stone walls next to Spanish moss–cloaked cypress trees. The water is stained by natural tannin common to southeast Mississippi streams, as well as chocolate-colored mud. Often slow and slightly murky with some deep pockets, Buckatunna is good habitat for catfish and bream.

The stream heads up just east of Meridian and runs south parallel to the Alabama line. It doesn't become navigable until a boat ramp at Denham Progress Road near the community of Denham east of Waynesboro. It's a little over fifteen miles from there to the Chickasawhay. Occasional logjams and shoals are always possible on a creek of this size, but it usually holds enough water to float a boat even in dry season.

Even though Denham is the highest put-in, you can paddle upriver from there since there is little to no current for a good ways. This stretch is lovely and intimate, lying shaded beneath rocky cliffs. Just below Denham, the stream is wider and shallower as it wraps around large sandbars. Big Red Creek flows in from Alabama before Buckatunna passes under Highway 45.

Local campgrounds include Maynor Creek Water Park west of Waynesboro and Turkey Fork Recreation Area in De Soto National Forest.

River Champion

David L. Pugh of Waynesboro had been working at a funeral home for nearly thirty years and serving as Wayne County coroner for twelve, and he was feeling buried by work. Those are demanding jobs, to say the least, and he needed an adventure to resuscitate him. He found one at his doorstep—the Chickasawhay River, which leads to the Pascagoula en route to the coast. So Pugh, an ardent kayaker, packed his boat and took off.

He penned an account of his 170-mile journey in a short but excellent book, *Voyage of Freedom: Kayaking to the Coast*. In the introduction, Pugh writes that he grew up camping and playing along a creek in rural Alabama. "At the age of seventeen, I started working at the local funeral home in Citronelle, Alabama, while still in high school. That marked the end of my backwoods outdoor living for a LONG time," he writes. "Along the way, I allowed the confining 'on-call' nature of the business to restrict my life."

Anyone familiar with the funeral business and a coroner's job can sympathize. Those folks are subject to being called any time, day or night.

"For a number of years I pretty much gave up hope (eventually even a desire) for any kind of personal life," Pugh writes. In his forties, he found himself twice divorced, overweight, with high blood pressure and no hobbies. "I was becoming increasingly miserable. I had a feeling of being trapped, incarcerated by life itself, or the lack of one," he writes.

In December 2013, Pugh ran across a diet program, signed on, changed his eating habits, and discovered new energy. He started working out at a gym, then bought a kayak and began taking short trips whenever he could. "I could go on and on from there about how kayaking changed my life," Pugh writes. "The easiest way to sum it up is to say kayaking was my tunnel out of the prison I'd been in for a solid ten years."

His short trips turned into overnighters and then weekends. He wanted more, so he began to plan the big one, to the coast. After much preparation, Pugh launched his fourteen-foot kayak on October 12, 2016, at Highway 63 in Waynesboro. The ensuing trip spanned eight days of freedom and adventure— lots of wildlife, sunshine, rain, mosquitoes, and occasionally people.

Here's his description of dawn on a sandbar: "I awoke feeling pretty good and crawled out of bed early. I packed my gear and loaded my kayak to one of the prettiest sunrises one could ask for. There's no way to describe the peacefulness and beauty in such an environment. Watching and being part of the transformation that takes place on the river, from the stillness of the night to the normal day chatter—well, it is magnificent to behold. In a very real sense, the rising sun and its glow seem to bring the river to life. The birds started their morning serenade, the furry animals of the forest begin scurrying and even the trees seem to sing as the breeze picks up."

The book is valuable not only for its vivid descriptions but for its inspiration to get out and have some adventures of our own. Pugh is a humble sort and presents himself as an everyman, not a tough-guy explorer, so he's easy to relate to.

He opposes efforts that might harm the Pascagoula Basin, like plans to dam two Pascagoula tributaries, Big Cedar Creek and Little Cedar Creek, to create a pair of lakes in southeast Mississippi. "I am very much, vehemently and emphatically opposed to it," Pugh writes. "I'm very proud of the 'uninterrupted free-flowing' status of the Pascagoula River! In my opinion, the Pascagoula has survived well enough by herself a few years longer than we have been alive. Who are we, as humans, to think she needs our help now? And across the board, most things we've put our hands to, concerning Mother Nature anyway have turned out to be not so good for her. But that's just me talking. What do I know?"

Floating the Chick, by Ernest Herndon

The Chickasawhay starts just south of Meridian along a seamline of Alabama stone and Mississippi muck. After more than 150 miles, it joins the equally handsome Leaf River, its twin to the west, and they form the Pascagoula.

My paddling partner Scott B. Williams and I had a springtime week to invest in the Chickasawhay, so we chose a 130-mile stretch from Stonewall to Leakesville. We were eager to see the "90-foot bluffs with rock boulders as large as automobiles . . . the nearest thing to mountainous terrain in south Mississippi," according to a Mississippi Department of Wildlife, Fisheries, and Parks brochure.

At our first camp, on a high bluff several miles downriver from Stonewall, we made the error of building a campfire on a deer trail. That night as I drifted off to sleep in the tent, I heard deer splash into the river on the far side, clamber up the bank, and snort indignantly at the embers in their path. One deer approached the tent, snorting fiercely, until I shouted, "Go on! Get out of here!"

Smart-alecky deer.

Hot coffee started a crisp day ushered in by a whipping cold front. We buttoned our jackets up, bent our chins down, and pushed our paddles into the brown river.

It's hard to break the rhythms of ordinary life to go on a canoe trip, or any trip. At first you feel disjointed, out of sync. But gradually you get into the flow, and the miles glide by. No matter what your moods are, you paddle through them all. Depression, exhilaration, contentment—stroke, stroke, stroke. A canoe, particularly a well-made one, is a dream boat. Fast and responsive, it slices the water gracefully even with a heavy load. Canoeing at its best can resemble lying in a hammock and getting exercise at the same time.

In one day we saw three alligators, each six to eight feet long, soaking up some sun in the brisk weather. They slid reluctantly into the cold river when our canoe approached.

We camped in Tarzan country, where huge, vine-draped hardwoods shaded palmettos. These woods were machete-thick. "And to think I go to other countries to see the jungle," I said. Scott laughed. He's guilty of the same.

I strung a hammock and read Psalm 121, thinking about the peace to be found in lonely places. We explored deep gorges where water cascaded over slippery clay, feasted on early dewberries like cruising bears, ate sandbar lunches, and dozed in the sun. We filled our canteens from cold springs pouring like open faucets out of rock-clay walls. Around us, beavers plopped from dens into water as we glided by. Imperturbable muskrats watched us like furry couch potatoes. Deer paused with ears up, then scampered into the woods.

The river became swampier but kept returning to its rocky theme like Richard Strauss's symphony *Also Sprach Zarathustra*. At last, small bayous began to feed the river. Like minks on a night-prowl, we turned up them.

A canoe is virtually soundless. In a deep, dark, narrow, currentless bayou, the tension mounts as you round a bend, knowing you could surprise anything—like musical wild pigs. Four of them, young and black, rooted nearsightedly under the trees, little pigs all in a row making a sound like this: "Uh! Oooh! Uh! Oooh! Uh! Oooh!" I don't know why, but I had the impression the first and third little pigs were going "Uh!" while the second and fourth were going "Oooh!" When they saw us, they scampered off, but not like we were the big bad wolf or anything. Later, as we headed back down the bayou, the four musketeers burst through the bushes, in a major hurry to take care of business. Back on the river, a sow and piglet hightailed it for the woods, panicking up a whole herd of wild hogs.

On sandbars we saw footprints of bobcats, otters, raccoons, possums. One gator track measured nine inches. At night we heard coyotes and unidentified roars. And once again, we violated woodland etiquette by putting our tent on a deer trail. I was awakened from my dreams by a deer as indignant as Miss Manners at a tobacco-spitting contest. Standing so close to the tent I could hear it breathing, it began to snort. Loudly. Continuously. Rudely. In different directions. Make no mistake, it was giving us a cussing.

"People must not hunt out here much," Williams said the next morning. "I've never seen deer so hostile."

If the deer were brash, the people were not. Though we only saw a handful in a week's time, local fishermen demonstrated flawless southern courtesy. One man even offered us a just-caught catfish.

When we finally saw the bridge at Leakesville, it was with regret at leaving the Chickasawhay and its creatures. But it felt good to have seen such fine country.

CHUNKY RIVER

> By the time it came to the edge of the Forest, the stream had grown up, so that it was almost a river, and being grown-up, it did not run and jump and sparkle along as it used to do when it was younger, but moved more slowly.
>
> —A. A. MILNE

The Chunky River is the northernmost canoeable tributary in the vast Pascagoula River system. It feeds the Chickasawhay River, which joins the Leaf River to form the Pascagoula. It is characterized by long, still stretches alternating with gentle, rocky rapids. The area lies at the fringe of the Appalachians, and it looks it. The rocks, cliffs, ferns, and hardwoods appear more Tennessee than Mississippi.

The Chunky—named not for a portly pioneer but for a Choctaw ball game called *chenco*—rises in the hills northwest of Meridian, crosses Interstate 20 west of the town of Chunky, then swings east toward town, crisscrossing Highway 80. East of Chunky the river turns southeast to weave a crooked course past Interstate 59 south of Meridian and past Highway 11 to join its smaller sister, Okatibbee Creek, to become the Chickasawhay near Enterprise.

In all, the Chunky River and its main tributary, Chunky Creek, flow fifty-five miles, of which some twenty-one provide good paddling—at least when water levels aren't too low. While rocky ledges provide exciting chutes to pilot a boat through, in low water, which includes much of summer and fall, they can scratch up a boat hull and mandate frequent towing.

Few people float east of the town of Chunky because the river there is so shallow, but some wade-fish or fish from the bank. Some of the biggest bass often come from such narrow stretches.

> The upper stream was the site of the Chunky River railroad disaster of 1863 when a bridge collapsed, dropping a troop train into the river and killing nearly a hundred Confederate soldiers. Doolittle Cemetery on Highway 80 west near Newton commemorates the dead with stone markers.

Fine Fishing

The first place to launch a boat into the Chunky is at Highway 80 just east of the town of Chunky. The river swings north and back south to the highway to make a loop known locally as the Seven-Mile Bend, though in fact it covers three river miles and just half a mile on the highway. For many years, this stretch was the site of the Chunky River Raft Race and Festival, in which people competed with all sorts of homemade vessels.

From a paddling perspective, this segment is the most trouble-free on the river, slower and deeper than farther downstream. Even so, there are a few pullovers due to rock ledges. Because of this, spring is the easiest time to float the Chunky, not during floods but afterward when the water is leveling out.

Some holes on this stretch are ten or twelve feet deep. Such spots harbor big catfish. One hand-grabber hauled in a fifty-seven pounder. Bank fishermen use live bait like pond perch to catch spotted cats up to twenty-eight pounds. Cane-pole fishermen hook bluegill and red-bellied bream with worms. Bass fishermen drag small lures like black and yellow H&H spinnerbaits and dark green or black-with-white-stripes Tiny Torpedo topwater plugs across rapids or over logs to catch Kentucky redeye and largemouth.

Farther down, the Point-to-Stucky after a nineteenth-century member of the Dalton Gang, who ambushed travelers at the crossing and left their bodies in the river. The old bridge, first built in 1847, is a Mississippi landmark.

Dunn's Falls

Below Stucky, the Chunky passes Dunn's Falls Water Park, one of the state's outdoor gems. The park is notable for a sixty-five-foot waterfall that pours from a millpond dam down a rocky cliff into the Chunky. In 1854, Irish immigrant John Dunn diverted a stream down the bluff to create a waterfall to power a mill. He built a three-story cotton factory, and the operation grew to include a gristmill, distillery, blacksmith shop, and hat and clothing plant. The Confederate government commandeered the business during the Civil War to make goods for the war effort.

> There is a long-running legend that John B. Stetson learned his hat-making skills at Dunn's Mill and perfected his now famous Stetson cowboy hat there. The Stetson company responded to this tale with a statement that John B. Stetson never visited Dunn's Mill.

After the war, the miller's business eventually faded, and now the spot is a sixty-nine-acre park. A reconstructed mill wheel and millhouse stand by the pond and the waterfall. The pond is full of catfish. Nearby is a picnic area and primitive campground in a beautiful grove of hardwood trees. The water park also has a few short nature trails for meandering up and down the riverside.

On these rugged slopes you may see low-growing heart plants, the valentine-shaped leaves of which when broken smell like a blend of sassafras and licorice. Large winter huckleberry bushes grow along the banks in abundance, loaded with small, black berries in December. Unfortunately there's nowhere to launch a boat at the park because it's a steep drop to the river.

Big Sam

Frontiersman Sam Dale once roamed these woods and canoed these waters. A renowned trailblazer, the six-foot, two-inch Dale was a formidable adversary known as Big Sam to his Native American enemies. His career in the Old Southwest, as Alabama and Mississippi were then known, was full of adventures, none more thrilling than a famous canoe fight in 1813 on the Alabama River. Legend says that Dale fought six Creek Indians to the death with knife and rifle while standing with one foot in his boat and one foot in theirs.

Big Sam Dale eventually settled in Lauderdale County, fifteen miles north of Meridian. The community that grew up around him was known as Daleville. He served as a delegate in the 1816 convention that divided the Mississippi Territory into Mississippi and Alabama, and later served in the Mississippi legislature. He died in 1841 in his late sixties. The residents of Daleville moved their community two miles north to locate nearer to a school. A statue of Dale now stands at Daleville.

The Father of Country Music

Another local resident was a musical pioneer. Jimmie Rodgers, born in 1897 in rural Pine Springs just north of Meridian, is considered to be the Father of Country Music. Also called the Singing Brakeman and America's Blue Yodeler, Rodgers went to work for the railroad in his teens until tuberculosis forced him to retire in his twenties. By then he'd been informally schooled in banjo, guitar, and vocals, and he pursued a musical career. After a few false starts, his career took off when he recorded "T for Texas." For the next six years he was a national phenomenon. It's said that Depression-era Americans bought a Jimmie Rodgers record along with their flour, sugar, and coffee, his music considered as essential as groceries. He died of tuberculosis in 1933, and his legacy affected generations of musicians, evidenced by the top country acts who still perform his songs. There is a Jimmie Rodgers Museum located in Meridian.

Plenty of Surprises on a Chunky Float, by Ernest Herndon

The plan called for a canoe, a clear river, lots of bass, and sandbars for camping.

One out of four isn't bad.

When Steve Cox and I floated the Chunky River of east-central Mississippi one September weekend, we found muddy water, few fish, and one sandbar in twenty-five miles of river. We also came across one of the more interesting pieces of water I've encountered in the state.

The Chunky is a swift, rocky stream. You can launch at Highway 80 between Meridian and the town of Chunky, reportedly the site of a field where Indians played a ball game by that name. You can take out at bridges along the way or float all the way down to the Chickasawhay River, which is what we did.

While the Chunky is normally clear and shallow, recent heavy rains prior to our float made it high, muddy, and fast. My canoe zoomed down a three-mile bend in an hour with us barely paddling. We coasted over rocky ledges that are normally so shallow they require portaging or careful maneuvering.

Steve actually dozed off as we approached a bridge at the community of Point. But he woke when we neared a roaring rapid, bounced down a drop of one or two feet, and took some water from standing waves. Reverend Jerry Gressett of McComb, who hails from Chunky, had warned us about this spot. Fortunately the water was high enough to minimize the impact.

Midafternoon we found a big sandbar, an island actually, and made camp. Steve cooked up some dirty rice, and we watched a half moon slant downward through thick mist silhouetted by mimosa fronds.

Next morning the river had dropped a foot but was still too muddy for good fishing. Plus, a cool front was moving in with gusty winds and clearing skies. Muddy water, cool front: that's a double whammy against catching bass.

We passed Dunn's Falls, a high waterfall on the left bank beside a restored gristmill. The area is now used as a water park. But as the miles went by we found nary a sandbar, just a strip of mud to stop on for lunch. By late afternoon we reached Okatibbee Creek. We paddled up the tributary in hopes of finding a campsite, but the current was so stiff it felt like getting a sudden weightlifting workout.

In less than a mile we spotted a tiny clay-rock shelf just big enough to land on, and climbed a high bank into the woods to camp. I kindled a fire, baked sweet potatoes in the coals, and cooked yellow rice, corn on the cob, onions, and field peas on my camp stove. After supper we paddled upriver until logs blocked the way, then returned for some campfire sitting.

A gang of crows woke me to a golden dawn. I whipped up sausage and cheese grits, then Steve accidentally caught a bass on a white beetle spin while testing his fishing rig. Conditions must be improving.

We drifted down the Okatibbee to the Chickasawhay. The two streams ran together for awhile, then surprised us by splitting again.

We took the right channel and things got mighty interesting. The water raced under a canopy of cypress and water oak, hissed over shoals, sliced around logs, parted at islands.

Steve caught another bass on a popping plug, and I hooked one on a white spinner. The fishing was just starting back. The water was clearing, the weather moderating. Another day or two and it would be prime, classic October river bass fishing. Unfortunately, our trip was about over.

The channels finally rejoined to form the wide, slow, muddy Chickasawhay, which led us to our take-out at the town of Stonewall. Sometimes what you get is better than what you expected.

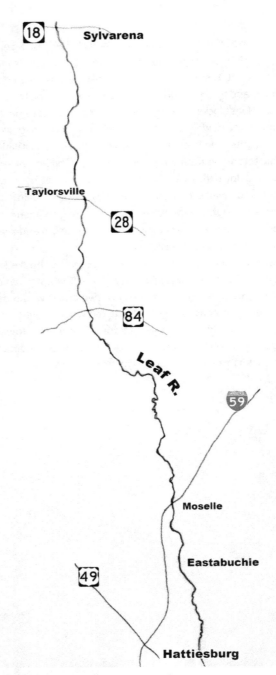

The Leaf River from Sylvarena to Hattiesburg

LEAF RIVER

> Wilderness areas are first of all a series of sanctuaries for the primitive arts of wilderness travel, especially canoeing and packing.
>
> —ALDO LEOPOLD

Appropriately enough for a river named Leaf, this major Pascagoula River tributary starts near the town of Forest in Bienville National Forest. It meets West Tallahala Creek a few miles south of Highway 18 and grows to a sizable river as it continues south and east past Hattiesburg en route to its juncture with its western twin, the Chickasawhay. The two rivers each flow more than 150 miles through southeast Mississippi before merging at the community of Merrill to form the Pascagoula River.

> This region of Mississippi is rife with Native American place names, mostly Choctaw. The Leaf River was known by the Choctaws as Eastabuchie, meaning "river of fallen leaves." Bogue Homa, sometimes spelled Bogue Homo or Bok Homa, means "red creek." Tallahala probably refers to "standing stones," while Tallahoma means "red rock." Oakohay means "wild potatoes," and Chickasawhay refers to "Chickasaw potatoes." All of these paddleways eventually swell the Pascagoula River, the name of which refers to a small tribe whom the Choctaws called "Bread People."

On the upper river north of Taylorsville, the Leaf is a shallow, rocky creek. Rapids alternate with long, slow stretches where the water barely moves as it slides across a sandy bed. Mossy clay banks rise on either side, topped with sycamore, river birch, water oak, hickory, cypress, and beech trees. Spicing up the greenery in the springtime are the white blossoms of dogwoods and fringe trees and the pinks of native azaleas. Buffalo fish flit through the water, snakes curl across the surface, moths dance in the sunshine. As night falls, woodpeckers call and barred owls whoop.

About two miles below Highway 28, Oakohay Creek enters from the west, making the route pretty much wide open for paddlers. The nearby town of Hot Coffee was named for the bracing beverage dispensed by an innkeeper's wife in the 1800s.

A paddler negotiates the rapids on the upper Leaf River.

Cradle of a Free State

Just after gathering the waters of Oakohay Creek, the Leaf River passes under Highway 84 right on the county line between Jones and Covington Counties. In the nineteenth century, this location was known as Reddoch's Ferry, and during the Civil War it became known as Devil's Den or Deserter's Den, the swamp hideout of famous Union supporter Newt Knight.

In 1862 in the aftermath of the disastrous defeats at Shiloh and Corinth, Confederate soldier Newton Knight deserted and headed back to his home in Jones County. Accompanied by other Confederate deserters and claiming that the Confederate government didn't have the right to conscript them against their will in the first place, Knight set up a mixed-race community in northern Jones County. Based in the Leaf River swamps, he and the other deserters of his company violently defended their homes and families from Confederate authorities, largely successfully.

Knight's activities were popularized by Professor Emeritus Victoria E. Bynum's 2003 book *The Free State of Jones*, and the 2016 feature movie of the same name that starred Matthew McConaughey as Knight.

> One can roughly triangulate Knight's guerrilla activities between the Devil's Den at Reddoch's Ferry, Knight's homeplace ten miles northeast near Taylorsville on the edge of Jasper County, and the Jones County seat of Ellisville about fifteen miles southeast of there. The upper Leaf River and its tributaries run all through this triangle, including Etehomo (or Etahoma) Creek less than a mile from the family cemetery where Knight is buried. Etehomo comes from a Choctaw phrase meaning "red wood" or "red pole," apparently referring to a marker (either boundary or funerary) similar to the red-painted boundary marker that gave Baton Rouge (French for "red stick") its name.

Wildlife Ups and Downs

The Pascagoula watershed, including the Leaf River Valley, is part of the native distribution of the majestic longleaf pine (*Pinus palustris*) that used to grace the pine savannah from easternmost Texas to southernmost Virginia. It is estimated that this range included nearly ninety million acres of longleaf pine with its profusions of 18-inch tassels decorating the tops of straight, 150-foot-tall trunks.

> In his *Thousand-Mile Walk to the Gulf*, John Muir writes about hiking in the pine barrens of southern Georgia: "In 'pine barrens' most of the day. Low, level, sandy tracts; the pines wide apart; the sunny spaces between full of beautiful abounding grasses, *liatris*, long, wand-like *solidago*, saw palmettos, etc., covering the ground in garden style. Here I sauntered in delightful freedom, meeting none of the cat-clawed vines, or shrubs, of the alluvial bottoms. Dwarf live-oaks common." Reading Muir gives a glimpse at what the realm of the longleaf pine (including the Leaf River Valley) must have been like prior to the arrival of Europeans.

This vast tract was traditionally managed by Native Americans who used controlled burns to get rid of underbrush, keeping the land perpetually in pine barrens. However, when European Americans arrived, their de facto policies of

The Leaf River from Hattiesburg to Merrill

fire suppression and logging without removing debris created large buildups of flammable debris, leading to catastrophic wildfires large enough to destroy the longleaf pines, allowing the subsequent progression to a climax forest of mixed pine (typically loblolly) and hardwoods.

More recently, there have been efforts to repopulate the region with longleaf pines. As early as 1936, a McComb *Enterprise-Journal* article describes an initiative of the Civilian Conservation Corps and the US Forest Service to reforest the area with thirty million trees from a nursery at nearby Brooklyn, Mississippi. In the 2010s, the US Department of Agriculture Natural Resources Conservation Service made financial assistance available to landowners to repopulate their lands with longleaf pine. By the end of the decade, the initiative had resulted in the restoration of more than 350,000 acres of longleaf forests.

Longleaf pine is not the only local species that had to be run nearly to extinction before it could be managed to thrive. In the 1920s and 1930s, white-tailed deer were extraordinarily rare in this area. They had been overhunted nearly to extinction by 1900. According to another *Enterprise-Journal* article from 1949, the Leaf River Wildlife Refuge was used to breed and relocate white-tailed deer to bring the species back from eradication.

Double-Decker Rapids

Big woods and occasional high, powdery sandbars line the Leaf as it continues from Highway 84 to Highway 588. The woods along the river range from swampy cypresses to dense canebrakes to tall pines. Towering, seventy-foot bluffs and dense forest create a secure, closed-in feeling. The riverbottom swamps resemble tropical jungles, while high, piney bluffs suggest the Rocky Mountains, as if this part of Mississippi contained the continent's geography in miniature. This section of the Leaf features numerous swifts, not exactly whitewater but enough to give paddlers a good tossing. The largest is Gordon's Rock, a three- to four-foot runnable waterfall.

Below Gordon's Rock, a cypress slough on the east leads to an eight-foot waterfall in a narrow ravine with a cold pool of water underneath. Despite the flow, the slough appears as still as a pond. The springwater forms a fast, cold current along the bottom, leaving the upper, warmer level undisturbed.

As the river widens below Highway 84, paddlers may observe hawks carrying snakes in their talons, ospreys toting fish, deer sipping at the riverside, swallows circling above rapids, black vultures hulking on rock bars, kingfishers diving for minnows, turtles sliding along the bottom, herons and egrets taking graceful flight, turkeys fleeing in panic, and snakes pausing in mid-swim to stare at passing vessels that to them must look like the *Titanic*. Adorning the banks are red buckeyes, dewberries, honeysuckle, wisteria, yellow-top flowers, privet, black haws, trumpet vines, native azaleas, and mountain laurel. Springs trickle over rainbows of clay: pink, orange, yellow, rust, purple, brown, and gray. Rapids include a double-decker that drops two or three feet and a foaming chute a hundred yards long.

Tallahala Creek

Below New Augusta, two pleasant creeks flow in from the north: Tallahala and Bogue Homa. It's not often you find two such good-looking streams running side by side just a few miles apart.

Tallahala Creek is the longer one, starting twenty-some-odd miles north of Laurel and running due south. Bogue Homa Creek, to the east, gets going at Heidelberg. Bogue Homa is a blackwater stream, its clear waters darkened by tannic acid. Tallahala is clearer, with a tendency to muddiness, which gives it a blond complexion. The twin streams run parallel roughly five miles apart on their journey to the Leaf River.

Even though Tallahala Creek stretches 96 miles, little over 25 miles of it is easily floatable, and even those miles can be difficult in low water. Compare that to nearby Black Creek, which is about 130 miles long but offers 100 miles of canoeing. Tallahala runs down a narrow corridor of land, bounded on the west by the Okatoma Creek Valley and on the east by Bogue Homa Creek. As a result, Tallahala has few notable tributaries and never gets a chance to grow. It's not often used by either paddlers or motorboaters, despite the fact that it's an attractive stream with good fishing. Though not far east of the metropolitan areas of Hattiesburg and Laurel, neither creek is heavily used—nothing like the whitewater Okatoma to the west. The navigability of both creeks is heavily dependent on rainfall.

After its beginning fifteen miles west of Enterprise, Tallahala Creek doesn't pick up tributaries for quite a ways: Nuakfuppa Creek (possibly a Choctaw cognate of the Chickasaw word for "mudcat fish") east of Bay Springs, then Tallahoma Creek above Ellisville and Rocky Creek below it. Tallahala is not even remotely floatable until Highway 29 east of Ellisville, and even then logjams and shallows dominate on the stretches between Highway 29 and the Moselle to Ovett road. There, Tallahala becomes a bit wider, but shallows may require some wading. Motorboaters can't usually get far in any direction without grounding in gravel shoals, which pose little problem to a canoe—though a few fishermen keep small motorboats near their camps for running nearby lines or minnow traps.

The creek features stretches of cutover alternating with walls of big trees and high banks. In the spring, flowering bushes glow like cotton candy in the deep shade—mountain laurel, the waxy-leafed bushes blanketed with white pentagonal blossoms half an inch across speckled with pink, red, and purple. There are also native azaleas. Sometimes called wild honeysuckle, these have a pink honeysuckle-shaped flower, though there is an orange variety in southeast Mississippi. Also plentiful are hornbeam trees, sometimes miscalled ironwood, which look like stunted, twisted beech. Sandbars glow golden in the sunshine, and mossy banks drip with cold springs in the shade. A beaver-dammed spring branch alternates between clear, sandy stretches and muddy beaver pools from a series of dams. In a shallow cove, ice-cold water boils up from a saucer-sized circle of sand.

Bogue Homa Creek

Bogue Homa is Choctaw for "red creek." The red may have referred to the tannin-stained waters that, seen in daylight, give the stream the color of cola. Dipping a paddle in that dark river is like burying it in ink. Paddlers won't get far before they have to tow through sand and gravel shoals and slide over barely submerged logs. The black water doesn't help, either. It's so dark, it's hard to see submerged obstructions, like a hidden stump that can high-center a boat, leading to some Laurel-and-Hardy antics to get free.

This is a pool-and-drop stream: long, still pools alternating with fast chutes. That means paddlers have to work continually in the pools, then get out and drag through the swifts. Such difficulties are offset in part by the exquisite water, darting fish, absence of humans, and abundant birdsong.

When the seventy-seven-mile-long creek widens at last, paddlers float under mossy banks spouting springwater like marble fountains. Bream flutter on their round gravel beds, largemouth bass race over the sand, gasper goo (freshwater drum) lumber in front of a boat. Red-and-black pileated woodpeckers whirl up from a log. Overhead, swallow-tailed kites soar. These beautiful black-and-white birds have a sharply forked tail and narrow wings that spread more than four feet, but they rarely flap as they soar like kites on the air currents. As many as three at a time may put on aerial displays, swooping fifteen or twenty feet overhead, sometimes cleaning their talons with their beaks in midflight. A grunt from the forest sounds like a wild hog, and a loud splash is either a big turtle or a small alligator. Vine-draped water oaks rise as tall as skyscrapers; thick-trunked elm trees lean like bridge buttresses.

Near its mouth, the creek makes a fishhook curve to the right under a mountainous red bluff, and through a tree-arching tunnel the Leaf River appears, along with a broad sandbar and houses on stilts.

Bogue Homa's biggest calling card for the general public is a man-made lake on its upper extremities. The 1,200-acre Lake Bogue Homa seven miles east of Laurel just north of Highway 84 offers skiing, fishing, camping, and picnicking.

Haunts of Herons

The Leaf River widens considerably and sandbars become vast on the stretch from the community of Eastabuchie to Highway 42 at Hattiesburg. These sandbars are favorite haunts of great blue herons, one of the most common yet interesting birds encountered by paddlers. These four-foot-tall water masters inhabit wetlands from Mexico to southeastern Alaska.

Smoky-blue, black-capped, white-faced, orange-beaked, they were once hunted for plumage but are now federally protected. They're incredibly wary—just try to sneak up on one—and they are excellent fishers, studying the water without motion, then stabbing their prey with sharp beaks. When they catch a fish they flip it so it goes down head-first, its sharp fins safely flattened.

With their S-shaped neck and jerky stride, herons seem awkward, but when they spread their huge wings they rise off the ground like helium balloons, and in flight they're Boeings with six-foot spans. Adult herons have few natural predators because of their size, though alligators take a few. They like to build gigantic platform nests high in swamp trees such as cypress. In the summer you may see half-grown birds peering over the edge onto their green domain. At dusk, you'll hear them returning home with beating wings. Throughout the night they grunt, snort, bicker, and sometimes squawk raucously—a cantankerous, alarmist village. Follow their big, three-toed footprints on sandbars and you'll discover that for all its height, the heron takes baby steps. On the river you'll frequently see great blue herons flying ahead of you in slow, swooping rhythm. They seem content to live their lives deep in the forest, disturbing no one, disturbed by none.

At Highway 42, the Bowie River enters from the west, carrying water from two significant canoeing streams: Bowie Creek and Okatoma Creek.

At river's end, the pale, silty Chickasawhay River meets the dark, clear Leaf to form the Pascagoula River. Half a mile downstream, the old iron bridge at Merrill looms like a vision from the past. Beyond it, the Pascagoula stretches into a seemingly endless forest.

Here Comes the Judge

Below Highway 84, one riverside landowner is former federal judge Charles Pickering. In addition to his work on the bench, the former Mississippi senator is an outdoorsman who grew up along the Leaf River in southeast Mississippi. Pickering helped leave a legacy that nature lovers can appreciate: tens of thousands of acres along the Pascagoula River set aside in wildlife management areas.

"One of my earliest and fondest memories is when we would finish laying the crop by in the summer, I would go with my dad and neighbor and they would set trotlines," Pickering said.

When Pickering was around ten years old, the men found a catfish in a hollow log and decided to grab it. However, the fish was too far back to reach, so a teenage boy volunteered to help. "He tried to go up in there head-first to try to get that fish," Pickering said. "They eventually pushed sticks in that hollow log and tore a hole in the side of the fish, and then they got their hands in on the skin and they pulled him back to where they could get their hands in the gills and brought him out."

That fish weighed forty-eight pounds.

Pickering also grew up hunting along the river, as did his son Chip, who also went on to serve in Congress.

"I've carried Chip squirrel hunting along Mason Creek and the Leaf River," Pickering said. "We used to hunt squirrels with a dog, a little feist dog. We've eaten Vienna sausage and crackers on the Leaf River banks while we were resting during the middle of the day."

One of Pickering's biggest quarries was wild hogs, which invaded his land in the early 1990s. "We caught, trapped, or killed forty-eight hogs," he said. "We got them all except one, and then a neighbor killed that hog a few years later.

"They make it very difficult for deer and turkey because they consume the food supply for the deer and turkey," he said. "They root up food plots, tear roads up."

Pickering put his love for the river into action by participating in the effort to preserve the Pascagoula River, into which Leaf River flows. That effort, which was both complicated and groundbreaking, is detailed in the 1980 book *Preserving the Pascagoula* by Donald Schueler.

In a nutshell, the Nature Conservancy purchased some forty-two thousand acres of riverside land from the Pascagoula Hardwood Company and sold it to the state, which set it aside in wildlife management areas. Many people were involved, and Pickering was one of the sponsors of the legislation.

"You've got a tremendously large tract of land that's preserved for this generation and for future generations so that they can have a wilderness experience and maintain the beauty of it," he said. "I think it's very important that we have those kinds of areas that are available for the public, particularly as more and more private land is not accessible to the public."

Old Augusta Outlaws

Old Augusta was the site where a notorious nineteenth-century outlaw met his demise at the end of a hangman's noose. As J. R. S. Pitts reports in *Life and Confession of the Noted Outlaw James Copeland* (1909; University Press of Mississippi, 1992), Copeland was a member of a much-feared gang of outlaws that terrorized the South in the mid-1800s. He, Reverend Charles McGrath, and Gale H. Wages were three of the main players.

Reverend McGrath must have been quite a preacher. At his first revival at Natchitoches, Louisiana, in 1841, he "raved, and exhorted all to repent and turn to God; and after raving about half an hour called all his hearers that wished to be prayed for to come forward. The whole congregation kneeled down," according to Copeland. After the service, McGrath fleeced his hosts out of a new suit of clothes, saddle, saddlebags, and fifty dollars.

McGrath's con job as a preacher in Natchitoches was the first of many as he made his way to rendezvous with fellow outlaws in San Antonio, Texas. By that point, "he had made a raise out of the religious brethren of about $1,000, by begging, and they had paid for four fine horses for him, which was equivalent to about $500 more," Copeland related. "He would sell his horse, saddle and bridle, and go to his congregation and tell them he had been robbed of his horse and all his money and clothes. The people would throw into the 'hat,' and buy another horse, and fit him out with new clothes and money."

It almost sounds comical, like from the movie *The Gang That Couldn't Shoot Straight*, but there was nothing funny about these guys. Copeland, McGrath, Wages, and their cronies robbed, burned, beat, killed, and kidnapped people all over the southern United States.

McGrath was a master of disguises. When it was time to play the preacher, "McGrath took off his traveling hunting shirt and straw hat; put on his long, straight-breasted bombazine coat and his broad-brimmed black beaver, and gave us a sound of his colloquial benediction of (the hymn), 'Hark from the tombs, gentlemen,'" Copeland recounted.

The trio chose McGrath to con an Irish flatboatman into taking them on as deckhands for his trading voyage down the Mississippi River. Copeland then murdered the Irishman with a hatchet, and the three weighted the body with iron and threw it in the river.

When a feud later erupted among gang members, Copeland's faction solved it by ambushing seven members of the opposition.

"McGrath and I waylaid him and fed him with contents of two double-barrel shotguns, about 48 buckshot, and put him in a swamp near Eslaya's old mill," Copeland wrote of one enemy. Of another: "We took him into an old house near the old Stage Stand. We then put a rope around his neck, and we very soon squeezed the breath out of him."

McGrath and Wages got their comeuppance in 1848 when they were gunned down by fellow outlaw James A. Harvey. Copeland was arrested, imprisoned, and later hanged. While in jail, he dictated his story to Perry County sheriff J. R. S. Pitts, who wrote it down in book form. When word spread that Copeland had named many of his accomplices—some of whom were supposedly respectable citizens—they tried to assassinate Pitts, and when that failed they charged him with libel. They succeeded in convicting him, and Pitts spent three months in an Alabama prison. The book outlived the outlaws, however, and was reprinted in 1980 with an introduction by John D. W. Guice.

The Right Boat

Despite its size and length, the Leaf River is subject to shoals and logjams during low-water periods as far south as New Augusta. Floaters need a lightweight boat to get onto the upper Leaf and its tributaries, which include Okatoma Creek and the Bowie River. As with the Chickasawhay, sheer bluffs on the Leaf mean steep landing sites, and occasional shoals and swifts make the river rough on flat-bottom boats with motors.

A Mississippi boat builder, Bertis Goff of Moss Point, created a unique vessel tailor-made for the Leaf. A typical Goff boat has red cypress sides, a bottom made of half-inch marine plywood, and wooden chines or strips around the edges. "I use Weldwood glue putting that thing together," Goff said.

Three wooden strips running lengthwise under the bottom keep the boat from sliding sideways in turns. Goff used sinker cypress from the Pascagoula River when he could get it.

"I usually try to get the log myself out of the bottom of the river, and I had them sawed up," said Goff, a retired police captain for the town of Pascagoula who made around thirty boats over a fifty-year period. "I saw boats similar to it and I just decided I'd start. I always kept me a pattern of when to cut those sides."

He used stainless steel hardware and painted the boats with porch and deck enamel. "I ain't never had no trouble with them leaking," said Goff, who stored the boats out of the water.

Most of the boats are twelve to fifteen feet long and around four feet wide. "I ain't bragging on them, but there ain't no aluminum boat or nothing that will handle like that in the water," Goff said. "An aluminum boat, [if] you stand

Mississippi author and boat builder Scott B. Williams works on a wooden johnboat.

up, it's going to throw you out, just about it—no buoyancy. That boat, two of us can stand up on the side and it won't tilt."

While many people would call the vessel a johnboat, Goff called it a "batty." "That's all I ever heard a wooden boat called with a bow like that," said Goff. He didn't know if the word came from the French *bateau*, another term for johnboat.

Goff's son, Cecil Goff, carried on the tradition, building both wooden boats and paddles. The paddles are made from strips of oak, cedar, and cypress.

Gathel Hinton owns one of Bertis Goff's creations, which at first glance looks like a typical old aluminum johnboat. A closer look reveals it's made of wood and has sleek lines and sturdy construction. Hinton worked as the southern regional state lake supervisor for the Mississippi Department of Wildlife, Fisheries, and Parks, and also spent time patrolling the Leaf.

"It's built like a 1950s or '60s building method when plywood was used before the advent of epoxy," said Mississippi author and boat builder Scott B. Williams, whom Hinton hired to replace the wooden transom in his vessel. "It's a cross of traditional and modern construction because it has a plywood bottom, but it's assembled like a traditional plank-on-frame boat. It's put together with screws and stringers or chine logs where the bottom joins the sides, so there's no epoxy or fiberglass. It's pure wood.... It looks like a good, capable design."

"I love the stability in the water," Hinton said. "When you're traveling up the river and you get in those curves and you go back and forth, when you're in that boat you don't feel all that."

He also liked the coolness of wood compared to aluminum, which gets hot in the summer.

"I love to trotline, and that boat is low in the water in the front end, and that front deck is excellent for running trotlines," Hinton said. "It's unbelievable. You don't have to pull that trotline two or three feet out of the water."

Hinton would occasionally run across someone on the water who paused to admire the wooden boat. "There is a many a people come up to me talking, and we'll be sitting in the middle of the river and they'll say, 'Is that a wooden boat?' . . . It's just a good old working boat, that's all you can say about it."

Impressive Wilderness

The lower Leaf River floodplain lays claim to one of the state's two designated wilderness areas: the 940-acre Leaf Wilderness Area in De Soto National Forest. The wilderness designation precludes any mechanical activity, such as chainsaws and four-wheelers. The Leaf Wilderness is considerably smaller than the nearby 5,050-acre Black Creek Wilderness. Its only trail is just one and a half miles long and subject to seasonal flooding, since the area consists mainly of hardwood bottomland near the river.

However, the area's swampiness is its virtue, for it contains such wonders as a water oak five feet across at chest height. Unfortunately, the designated wilderness area does not border the river itself, coming only within about a quarter of a mile, a few miles above the juncture with the Chickasawhay. The best way to see it is on foot in the dry season, such as late summer or early fall. It lies east of Highway 57 south of McLain.

In 2016, the Mississippi Forestry Commission, in conjunction with the Nature Conservancy, announced the formation of the Leaf River Forest Legacy Tract, a 2,100-acre tract along the Leaf and Pascagoula Rivers. The property connects over 450,000 acres between De Soto National Forest and the Pascagoula River Wildlife Management Area—"the largest tract of contiguous protected lands for conservation in Mississippi." That puts it on a par with Great Smoky Mountains National Park's 522,000 acres.

A couple of campgrounds are located close to Leaf River. Big Creek Water Park off Highway 84 between Collins and Laurel has a 150-acre lake with developed camping and rental cabins. Lake Perry south of Highway 98 near Beaumont has primitive camping and a 124-acre state fishing lake.

Cold-Weather Camping, by Ernest Herndon

B. R. "Billy" Gibson of Baton Rouge and I had every reason to cancel our campout one February weekend. There was a 100 percent chance of rain Saturday and a 70 percent chance that night, with temperatures to fall below freezing. I've camped in those kinds of conditions enough that, when I have a choice, I usually opt out. But this time I suppose I was just too lazy to stay home. After all, I already had the truck loaded.

I drove toward our destination in a steady rain. Only when I reached the Leaf Wilderness south of McLain did the downpour pause. When Billy showed up, it started again.

Our plan was to hike the mile-and-a-half wilderness trail, then find a place to camp in De Soto National Forest. Every so often Billy and I get together to camp out, smoke cigars, and philosophize beside a crackling campfire. It's good for the spirit. But when we checked out some potential campsites in the national forest, all we found were pine plantations and boggy ground—nowhere decent to pitch a tent, no good wood for a fire. Temporarily giving up, we returned to the trail and went walking in the rain.

At just a mile and a half long, the Leaf Wilderness trail doesn't make for much hiking. But I wanted to see it anyway. The wilderness consists mainly of hardwood bottomland near the Leaf River. The trail follows a rim of high ground before veering off on boardwalks into the swamp. We had gone about half a mile when it disappeared underwater. With all the rain, water was ripsnorting out of the hills, submerging most of the area. When it came to hiking, this was a fair-weather wilderness.

Soggy, we returned to our vehicles and resumed our search for a campsite, alighting at Lake Perry, a state-managed fishing lake south of Beaumont. There were primitive campsites with a lake view and a mixed-hardwood forest nearby for firewood. Even though the temperature was dropping fast and the wind was whipping out of the north, we were out of options.

Our plan was to sling a tarpaulin to block rain and wind, and rustle up enough firewood for a "two-cigar fire," as Billy put it. Then we would start supper and pitch the tent.

Billy was skeptical we'd ever have a fire in these sodden conditions, but I had brought dry kindling—paraffin-soaked sticks sold in grocery stores for starting charcoal. We also found a stump with plenty of fat pine, which serves the same purpose. We soon had a fire, a hot meal, a tent pitched, and chairs under a tarp. Night fell. The temperature plummeted and rain continued to fall off and on, but we kept the elements at bay. By 10:00 p.m. the moon was flickering among the clouds.

The tent, a tight dome I bought in Alaska, kept the wind out, and we burrowed down in mummy sleeping bags. I confess, though, the bags were so old they'd lost a good bit of their insulating power, and I kept putting on more clothing throughout the night.

Winter camping is not especially popular in south Mississippi, and with good reason. When northern states are getting dry snow, we're soaking in a frigid rain. I've heard people say they prefer a Rocky Mountain winter to ours. Either way, the trick is being prepared.

That means bringing more clothes than you think you'll need, preferably wool or fleece, with a dry set for camp and long johns for the sleeping bag. It means a good-quality sleeping bag, sleeping pad, and tent. It means a tarpaulin lean-to for sitting, cooking, and fire watching. It means bringing dry kindling and taking time to build a fire right.

When you have a lean-to at your back, a fire at your front, hot food, a drink, maybe some cigars, and a friend, winter-weather camping becomes more invigorating than menacing.

Next morning, Billy and I found ice outside the tent. The clouds were gone, and a biting wind ushered the yellow sun up over the lake. Having survived, there was no reason not to celebrate. We headed straight for McLain, where a restaurant offered eggs, grits, biscuits, sausage, and hot coffee.

It's wise to quit while you're ahead.

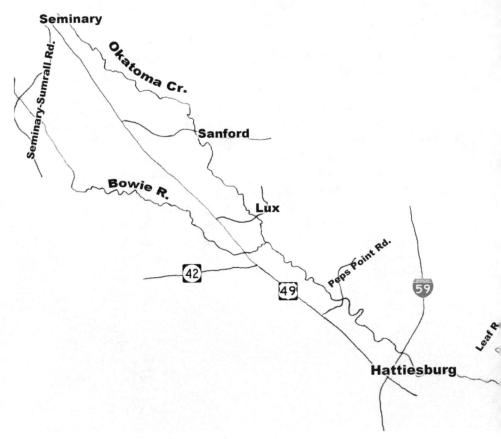

The Bowie River and Bowie and Okatoma Creeks

BOWIE CREEK

> All conservation of wildness is self-defeating, for to cherish we must see and fondle, and when enough have seen and fondled, there is no wilderness left to cherish.
>
> —ALDO LEOPOLD

Bowie and Okatoma Creeks start around Magee about halfway between Jackson and Hattiesburg. These two creeks swoop southeast like the *V* in a flock of geese. They converge northwest of Hattiesburg to form the Bowie River, which enters the Leaf just above Highway 42 at Petal. Bowie and Okatoma are both excellent for floating, though markedly different—Okatoma a heavily used quasi-whitewater stream, Bowie less traveled but strikingly beautiful.

Bowie Creek is smooth, clear, tree-shaded, and gorgeous. The seventy-mile-long Bowie—also spelled Bouie—heads up southwest of Magee and runs south. It doesn't become navigable until Seminary-Sumrall Road, and even then there are some logjams and shoals. Jungly woods, high banks, and murmuring springs combine to create a sense of eerie isolation. The stream is placid until a low, runnable waterfall about half a mile above Highway 589, where the current quickens. By Highway 589 the creek is easily floatable, small enough to savor the deep-woods experience, big enough to avoid logjams, far removed from downstream development. Yet not many people float it, mainly local fishermen in johnboats.

Big woods line the river, with oaks, cypress, beech, and magnolias. There is evidence of logging—sun-bleached stretches where locust and sweetgum riot like boisterous youngsters. But fortunately those rude tangles give way to the quiet, thoughtful shelter of older forest. In such an environment, paddlers are likely to encounter wildlife: a wild turkey exploding off a branch overhead; a swimming snake submerging at the sight of humans; a big owl rising off a leaning birch to the safe heights of the treetops, where it watches with wise, wary eyes.

A half mile above Highway 49, the creek takes a one- to two-foot plunge over a clay shelf. From 49 it's a scant mile to the junction with Okatoma Creek; another fifteen or so—passing under Interstate 59—to the Bowie's juncture with the Leaf. The pretty, woodland scenery and good fishing continue for most of this section, but below I-59 development picks up considerably.

A low-head dam of concrete rubble is used to reroute water for industrial use just north of Highway 42. The spot is swift, deep, and dangerous, and a number of deaths have reportedly occurred there. Better to portage around. Huge gravel mining operations have scarred these lower reaches, muddying the water and leaving many borrow pits alongside the channel.

In the late 1990s, a dam was proposed just above the confluence with Okatoma Creek. In 1999, the Pat Harrison Waterway District, the cities of Petal and Hattiesburg, and the Forrest County Board of Supervisors teamed up to study a $12–$30 million, 1,200–2,000-acre reservoir. Supporters said southeast Mississippi needed the new water source to handle the growth of development. Opponents, including Dr. Stephen Ross, then professor of biological sciences and curator of fisheries at the University of Southern Mississippi, said the dam would harm rare fish species such as the huge Gulf sturgeon and the tiny pearl darter and Alabama shad, which use Bowie Creek for spawning.

The Gulf sturgeon, listed as a threatened species, is a long-snouted, bony-plated fish that can reach eight feet in length and twenty-eight years in age and weigh more than two hundred pounds, though forty pounds is considered average. It's mind-boggling to picture such a behemoth in the small Bowie. However, there are other big fish in the stream, such as a 37.82-pound striped bass that held the state record until a 39.6-pounder was caught in the Pascagoula River. Gulf sturgeon numbers have dropped largely due to such habitat degradation as dredging, pollution, decreasing water tables—and dams. Radio tracking indicated a spawning site right about where the Bowie reservoir was proposed. A dam there would likely have destroyed one of the few places left where they reproduce.

Another argument against a Bowie River dam was the fact that the Pascagoula is the only major river system in the lower forty-eight states as yet undammed in its main branches. A dam across the Bowie would have ruined that distinction.

Such dilemmas exemplify how lack of recreational use can actually threaten a river. Although serious paddlers naturally fear what can happen to a stream when crowds discover it, also to be feared is what can occur when a stream goes unnoticed and unappreciated. In such a situation there may not be enough voices raised against plans to dam, mine, channelize, or otherwise damage it.

OKATOMA CREEK

Study how water flows in a valley stream, smoothly and freely between the rocks.
—MORIHEI UESHIBA

Most of Mississippi's neighboring states have whitewater. Alabama, Tennessee, and Arkansas all boast rivers with respectable rapids. Louisiana has just one (Bayou Toro), but it makes up for it with abundant wetlands. Several Mississippi streams have occasional chutes and drop-offs, but only one is renowned for its whitewater—Okatoma Creek.

> Like many Native American place names, Okatoma is not straightforward to translate. Some older stories have the name coming from *oka* for water and *katoma* for stench, thus "stinking water." It's hard to imagine a creek with a rapid, clear flow becoming stagnant and stinking. Other scholarship suggests the name could have other, vastly different translations, including "shining water" or "foggy water."

Though Okatoma Creek can claim whitewater status, it doesn't take itself too seriously. The fact is, Okatoma is a regular Mississippi creek that happens to have some rapids—just four notable ones on the popular thirteen-mile stretch between Seminary and Sanford. This modest series of adrenaline thrill-providers draws huge crowds, making Okatoma one of the most popular floats in the state. On a summer Saturday, canoe rental companies may easily put in hundreds of customers. And 95 percent of them will capsize before the trip is done. That's not because the rapids are particularly daunting—they're all Class II or, at most, borderline III. Rather, it's because most Deep South floaters lack experience in running whitewater, which is hardly surprising considering how little there is in the region to practice on. Besides, for most people, capsizing just means getting pleasantly wet on a hot day.

Most of the sixty-mile-long Okatoma is not whitewater at all. It heads up east of Mendenhall and runs southeast toward its rendezvous with Bowie Creek northwest of Hattiesburg. It's not floatable until Kola Road just south of Collins, and that stretch is subject to logjams, though there are periodic efforts to clear it out. There are no rapids here, just a pretty, forested creek disturbed only by the hum of traffic from busy, four-lane Highway 49 a short distance to the west.

Running Rapids

The town of Seminary is where crowds converge for the thirteen-mile run to Highway 598 at Sanford. The first rapid is about a mile downstream. Rock shoals block most of the river just beneath the surface, but a quick glance reveals a fairly easy passage to the left.

This run is a fun warm-up for the Chute, a mile and a half farther on. As with the first rapid, the Chute's outlet is a narrow channel to the left. But then the boat must make a hard right to negotiate a second drop, all at roller-coaster speed.

The third challenge, two miles below the Chute, is Okatoma Falls at Fairchild Landing, a straightforward plunge of two or three feet. As long as paddlers keep their bow forward and head down the tongue of the wave, it's usually no problem, though standing waves may toss a few cups of water into the boat.

The fourth rapid comes up quickly as the creek narrows into a tree-lined gorge. Keep the bow pointed downstream and expect water to splash in over the sides.

The stretches between these thrills are surprisingly slow but interspersed with smaller rapids. The six-mile stretch from Sanford to Lux offers fewer thrills but still some challenges. Below Lux there is a one- to two-foot waterfall and a couple sets of rapids within the first half hour before the creek slows as it curls toward Bowie Creek.

Okatoma whitewater has more benefits than providing a thrilling ride. The deep pools below the first rapid and below Okatoma Falls are popular swimming holes. Fishing is typically good around any fast water, especially below the Chute, though hordes of paddle-clanging boaters can give the fish lockjaw. Go on a weekday and drag a lure through the rapids to tempt one of the one- to three-pound bass common in the creek. Or use a fly rod or cane pole for bluegill. As for catfish, monsters up to fifty-two pounds have been hauled from the creek's deep holes.

Dealing with Crowds

Though Okatoma Creek is popular among floaters, one aspect is not so popular with many: it's located in a dry county. Some paddlers have long complained of harassment and illegal searches by overzealous law enforcement officers on Okatoma, but that's OK with the law enforcement officers and the outfitters that supply the paddlers.

"That's the reason church groups are able to go there, because they pretty much know officers are going to be on this creek all the time. It's a good family-oriented place," said Pat Butler, formerly of the Mississippi Department of Wildlife, Fisheries, and Parks. "There's a tremendous amount of church groups, Boy Scout groups, different clubs and organizations going down there, and that's what we're doing down there is trying to keep it safe for everybody to enjoy."

Even with dry status, officers find the usual array of problems, including drugs, littering, public drunkenness, underage drinking, and alcohol-related injuries. But while possession of alcohol is illegal, officers use discretion, Butler said. "We don't go and search everybody coming down this creek. It's basically people out in the plain view with alcohol, wide open, right in everyone's face; then we enforce alcohol. There's so many canoes coming down the creek, you're not going to search every one."

Ronnie Robinson operated a nearby canoe rental business for decades and agreed that conservation officers use good judgment in enforcing alcohol laws. "Our local game wardens know how to handle it, and they've done a great job with it," Robinson said. "And that's why we have so many church groups."

However, Robinson doesn't believe that outlawing alcohol alone is the answer to river problems. "I don't think wet or dry makes a difference. I think it's the way the businesses promote, whether they put up with it or not," he said. "You've got good people that come and they're going to bring one or two cold beers, and for them to come down a creek and not be able to drink one or two beers and enjoy themselves, you're cutting down on their fun. When you make it dry, you stop those people."

Law officers write plenty of tickets for public drunkenness, littering, and profanity regardless of whether alcohol is illegal. Robinson said that outfitters should stress the importance of obeying the law to their customers. He has refused to serve intoxicated customers when necessary. Also, his family floats the creek regularly to pick up trash and clear out logs.

Robinson said that law enforcement is the best solution to creek problems. "Get with your law enforcement and let them hit them hard. You don't want drunks on it if you want it to where church groups come on your place," he said.

Robinson said his business did fine without alcohol.

"One drunk will run ten church groups off, and a canoe rental doesn't want that. If they [rental companies] can think far enough ahead, good country folks that want to bring their families and bring their church groups and all and go on a day on the creek don't want to be around a bunch of folks out there drinking. If they did that, they'd go to a bar."

Going Slow in Fast Water, by Ernest Herndon

The best advice I ever got on canoeing whitewater was from a guy who had never floated a whitewater river. His advice: "Backpaddle."

The adviser was the late Walter Neil Ferguson, who lived on the Bogue Chitto River and fully comprehended hydraulic principles even though he'd never been near the Nantahala, Ocoee, or Colorado. His point was: when approaching a rapid, slow down—don't speed up like most people tend to do. When you think about it, that makes perfect sense.

The problem with rapids is they take you full-speed over rocks. The remedy is to slow down enough to maintain control of your boat and minimize impact. Virtually nobody does this, however, as I observed one May weekend on Okatoma Creek.

Robert Spillman of Gloster and his children Trey and Krystal and I camped at Lake Mike Conner near Collins and the next day went to Okatoma. The most-run stretch is the thirteen miles from Seminary to Sanford, two towns just east of Highway 49 north of Hattiesburg. There's good public access at Seminary, but at Sanford you have to pay a canoe rental to park and take your boat out.

The canoe rental business maintains a fleet of school buses and hundreds of rental boats. When we arrived before 8:00 a.m. on Saturday, a crowd was already assembling at the store. We paid our fee and hustled, eager to beat the mob. But by the time we launched our two canoes at Seminary, the first busloads were already arriving. Everyone was dressed almost identically, in white T-shirts, dark shorts, and either tennis shoes, neoprene booties, or river sandals.

Robert and I resembled relics from another time. I wore khaki pants stuffed into rubber boots and a loose brown T-shirt, and he wore his usual work uniform of navy pants and a pale blue striped shirt with the name of his air-conditioning company on the pocket. While some of the customers looked forward eagerly to getting wet, our plan was just the opposite.

We took off down the placid, green-shaded river. The first rapid comes up within a mile, a roaring three-foot drop over a rock shelf. It looks daunting, but just slip down the left side—resisting that impulse to paddle hard—and let the bow drop down into thundering whitewater. No problem.

The most challenging rapid on the river is the Chute. We backpaddled to a standstill, surveying it, then eased down the far left side. The current makes a hard right, then a hard left, with little room for error. A slight deviation and you can roll over.

But with my young partner, Krystal, remaining perfectly calm, we managed it. Trey and his dad then came through so easily you'd think they'd had years of whitewater experience. Like Ferguson, Robert has that country-boy comprehension of water that enables him to deal with tricky currents without ever losing his cool. We pulled up on the ledge to watch the crowd.

The first boat to come through obviously contained an experienced group leader, for we heard him shouting instructions to his bow paddler. Despite his experience, he had never learned Ferguson's advice, however, and they barreled through like the devil was chasing them. Their speed almost cost them. Though they made the first turn, they were going so fast they rode up onto submerged rocks and just did bounce off. The leader then landed and rushed back so he could bark instructions at everybody else.

The next boat missed the first turn entirely and careened up onto the ledge—a convenient escape valve for many paddlers. They hauled their boat out of the way and toted it around the rapids. A third canoe made the turn but hit the side of the chute and flipped. The life-jacketed paddlers bobbed up and wrestled their swamped vessel through deep, churning water. Of the next half-dozen canoes, only one got through the rapids. All the rest ran onto the ledge and had to be portaged. Our curiosity satisfied, the Spillmans and I continued downriver.

Far more interesting to me than Okatoma's rapids were its masses of mountain laurel in bloom, the intoxicating scent of honeysuckle and privet, the conversations with my pals, the cool breeze and blue sky, the gleaming hulls of turtles lined up on logs—none of which required speed to appreciate.

Many consider Black Creek the finest paddling in the southeastern United States.

BLACK CREEK

The clearest way into the Universe is through a forest wilderness.

–JOHN MUIR

Black Creek is without a doubt the finest paddling stream in the State of Mississippi. For most of its length, Black Creek is ideal paddling size. The current is just right, neither foaming whitewater nor stagnant bayou, lively enough to keep you alert without distracting you from the scenery.

On Black Creek you can paddle for days and remain within a Deep South wilderness of towering pine trees, gushing springs, glistening sandbars, and occasional cypress swamps. Nor does this glory end with a whimper. Running in a southeasterly direction south of Hattiesburg, Black Creek joins the lovely Red Creek to form Big Black Creek, which empties into the mighty Pascagoula River with its awe-inspiring swamps.

The 132-mile Black Creek flows through the 501,000-acre De Soto National Forest, including the 5,050-acre Black Creek Wilderness, the larger of Mississippi's two federally designated wilderness areas.

A twenty-one-mile stretch of the creek is a National Wild and Scenic River. Black Creek is known for its bream fishing; the woods are full of game. The state's longest hiking trail, the forty-one-mile Black Creek Trail, roughly parallels the creek to the south. Primitive campgrounds accessible by road are located along the river. State Highway 29 passes to the west of the wilderness area, with various rural roads branching off into the national forest. In short, you can float, fish, camp, hike, hunt, or just take a scenic drive through this beautiful part of southeast Mississippi.

Loads of Color

This stream is called Black Creek because of its tannin-stained waters. The tannic acid comes from a blend of acidic vegetative matter—particularly acorns and oak leaves. Blackwater streams abound in varying shades throughout the Deep South from southeast Mississippi to southeast Georgia and beyond. The latter's upper Suwannee River, for instance, resembles cola, while Mississippi's Red Creek is more like honey.

Black Creek's tannic luster is highlighted by small white sandbars beneath green forest walls speckled in the springtime with creamy white blooms such as titi bushes, southern catalpa trees, and Virginia willow, and pink with mountain laurel, native azalea, and occasional invasive mimosas. Curly-barked river birches bow before tall spruce pine, water oak, hickory, ash, and their royal kin. Sweet-smelling coastal rosemary and edible sawbriar shoots garnish the forest's edge, and gravel bars reveal geologic history with fossilized tiny crinoid plants, relics from the epoch when this region lay undersea. There's no sea salt now in the ice-cold springs that tumble from clefts in the pine-strawed bluffs.

On the river, there are plenty of signs of wildlife. You might spot a river otter, a covey of quail, a drove of turkeys, or a fat cottonmouth snake wriggling into a hole in the bank. Tracks of alligators, coyotes, deer, beaver, and raccoons mottle the sandbars.

As you drift along the creek agape at these wonders, you may miss the well-camouflaged nonvenomous water snakes curled in the lower limbs of overhanging bushes—six-footers aren't uncommon—but you're less likely to overlook a pair of nervous wood ducks swimming up ahead, especially when they panic and fly back upriver in such haste you almost feel their feathery wingbeats near your cheek.

Wilderness Banquet

The clear stream abounds with bream and bass, both of which can be caught on ultralight rigs, fly rods, or cane poles. Farther downriver toward the Pascagoula, fishermen use limb hooks to catch catfish.

There are other wild foods if you know where and when to look. Late August and early September is time for muscadines. The luscious wild grapes grow along virtually all Mississippi streams, but they're most accessible along waterways like Black Creek, which has plenty of sandbars. Muscadine vines, which have characteristic grape leaves, climb trees along the riverside to absorb sunshine. When they dangle directly over the water, it's nearly impossible to get the fruit. But when they hang over bare ground like a sandbar, you can load up. The prime method is to shake the vines, which causes the fruit—along with dirt, bark, and ants—to rain down around you. Throw sticks at the uppermost reaches to knock down the rest. Some people spread a bedsheet on the ground for easier collecting.

Pawpaws ripen the same time muscadines do. The small trees, with large leaves similar to those of hickory, thrive in the shade of tall hardwoods along riversides. Their oblong, greenish-skinned, creamy-fleshed fruit tastes like a cross between pear and banana. Harvest by shaking the trees and picking the fruit up off the ground, taking care not to get bonked on the head.

Quince are ready to pick in the fall. Being sour, they fare better as jelly, though some people relish the tart taste, especially with salt. Persimmons lose their bitterness after the first frosts of late November. The trees are easily identifi-

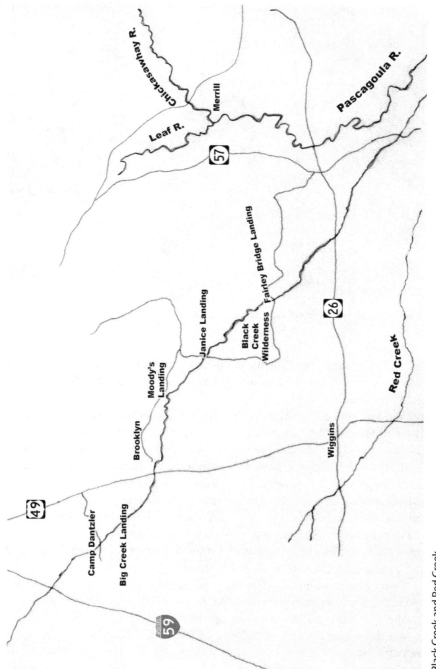

Black Creek and Red Creek

Black Creek above Dantzler Camp is often logjammed.

able because leaves fall off while the orange fruit still clings to the limbs. Few fruits are more bitter than an unripe persimmon, few more delicious than a fully ripe one.

Wild winter huckleberry, which is actually a blueberry, produces in February and March and grows right on the riverbank. Other huckleberries mature from April to June. Mayhaw, a tree that produces a tart red berry used for jelly, is ready in early April. It prefers swampy areas. Wild strawberries spring up from the ground in sunlit areas in April and May, though they have little flavor. Much tastier are dewberries, first cousins to blackberries, which are especially prolific along sandbars beside rivers at the same time of year. Wild cherries drop in late April. They tend to be tiny, but trees that get plenty of moisture may produce fruit big enough to snack on. Blackberries abound in May and June in tangled, chiggery, snaky thickets.

From May through July, American plums can be found in sunny margins such as the edges of clearings; sloe plums, dusty blue-gray in color, come ripe in the fall. Crabapples are sweet enough to nibble by June or July. Mulberries, which grow on trees and are beloved by birds, are edible in July. Maypop, a lemony fruit with lots of seeds, ripens on ground-running vines throughout the summer and stays ripe into the fall. Elderberry bushes, which favor moist

Black Creek provides camping in designated improved campsites or on the many sandbars.

soil, produce bold, white flower clusters starting in May, and tiny, black berries from late July into early September. The berries are edible but leave an inky stain and cause an allergic reaction in some people. They can be boiled with sugar to make juice, which can then be turned into wine.

Fruits just scratch the surface of edible wild foods. Others include cattails, pecans, walnuts, acorns (palatable when the tannic acid is leached out), arrowhead root, daylilies, sawbriar shoots, dried goldenrod seed, and many more.

Town and Country

The uppermost practical put-in for paddlecraft is ten miles south of Hattiesburg at Churchwell Road. The bridge lies outside the borders of the national forest, and the first five miles or so of creek pass through private land, mostly forested. This upper segment can get really low in dry weather, with swift, clear water flowing over a bed of gravel a few inches deep. The beauty of canoes, kayaks, and other paddlecraft is that they draw so little water. Because of its remoteness, the predominance of private land, and the more technical paddling required, local canoe outfitters have largely stopped servicing that bridge as a put-in.

As the creek widens and deepens, one camp after another appears, perched on the riverbank. After a few miles, the national forest begins. Sandbars make for good camping. Coyotes may wake you in the night, and perhaps a siren or a motorcycle. This stretch of Black Creek flows toward busy, four-lane Highway 49 and is bounded by other roads as well, so traffic noise isn't uncommon on this upper part, especially late at night when everything is still.

Eight miles below the bridge lies Big Creek Landing, which marks the beginning of the forty-one-mile Black Creek hiking trail, which rambles in and out along the stream's south side en route to its eastern end at Fairley Bridge. In 2005, Hurricane Katrina devastated De Soto National Forest, reportedly destroying 75 percent of the timber. Remaining trees were widely spaced, with a jungle of undergrowth underneath. A number of pine trunks snapped off halfway up. Still, there are plenty of trees to identify if you decide to take a walk, such as laurel oak, pignut hickory, tung oil, sourwood, dogwood, beech, holly, Eastern hop hornbeam; and loblolly, longleaf, shortleaf, spruce, and slash pines.

Five miles below Big Creek Landing is the town of Brooklyn, where a canoe/kayak/tube rental company does a steady business. The stream runs between broadening sandbars and high bluffs on the five-mile leg from Brooklyn to Moody's Landing, which is located on the north bank. The creek is narrow and shallow enough in places to require tricky maneuvering, even the occasional portage, but not enough hardship to make you question the worth of the trip. Here and there a massive tree may block the river, forcing paddlers to swim their boat under or tote it around. The US Army's Camp Shelby sprawls just a short distance to the north, sometimes providing a background thunder of artillery.

A Real Wilderness

Black Creek becomes a designated National Wild and Scenic River at Janice Landing, and the 5,050-acre Black Creek Wilderness Area spans the stretch from Janice to Cypress Creek Landing. Less than a mile below Janice, Beaverdam Creek enters from the south, an impressive little brook worth exploring on foot, either by wading or following the segment of the Black Creek Trail that loops around it.

A few miles farther down, Cypress Creek runs in from the north just above Cypress Creek Landing. Hickory Creek enters from the north about a third of the way along the reach from Cypress Creek Landing to Fairley Bridge, which marks the eastern end of the Black Creek Trail. All of these landings—Big Creek, Moody, Janice, Cypress Creek, and Fairley—have Forest Service primitive campgrounds, not that paddlers need them because sandbars are available along the creek.

> Just south of the Black Creek Wilderness, there used to be a community known as Red Hills. It must have grown up during the boom of immigration to the Mississippi Territory that occurred in the first couple of decades of the 1800s. Red Hills was situated somewhere near the Old Federal Road that carried soldiers and immigrants from Georgia and the Carolinas to Mobile and Natchez. The only thing that remains of the Red Hills community is a small cemetery nestled in the tall pines of De Soto National Forest. Nowadays, you could drive right up to the old Red Hills Cemetery on Forest Road 318, but the best way to get a feel for some of what life must have been like is to hike it. Starting at Fairley Bridge Recreation Area east of Wiggins, pick up the hiking trail going northwest alongside Black Creek toward Brooklyn. Follow the trail for about three miles to the three-way intersection of Forest Service Road 318-B, the Black Creek Trail, and the Florida Gas pipeline. Turn right onto 318-B and follow it for about a fifth of a mile (350 yards or so), watching on the left for the cemetery. The cemetery is often overgrown, but someone has blazed the trunks of the surrounding trees with white paint. The cemetery contains grave markers for eight people who lived between 1798 and 1898—the Fairleys and Brelands, Pearces and Byrds who settled the area in the early 1800s.

The river widens a bit on the run from Fairley to Highway 26 with the addition of Deep Creek from the east, Barney Branch from the west, then Mill Creek and Flat Branch from the east. A few miles below Highway 26, on the nineteen-mile stretch to Highway 57, Black Creek exits the national forest, but the change is not dramatic. More noticeable is the creek's gradual evolution toward swampiness.

Below Highway 57 it slows, and soon cypress trees outnumber pines, with Spanish moss dangling over the browning current. Springs continue to freshen the river, but they leak from low slippery-clay shelves rather than high red-clay bluffs, and sizzle with mosquitoes. Below Highway 57, Black Creek merges with Red Creek, and the two form Big Black Creek, a short outlet to the Pascagoula River.

Hurricane on Upper Black Creek, by Patrick Parker

One June a few years ago, Boy Scout Troop 124 of McComb embarked upon what we thought would be a five-day, fifty-mile canoe-packing trek along Black Creek from the bridge at Dantzler Camp (Churchwell Road) through the Black Creek Wilderness to the Highway 26 bridge outside Wiggins.

It seems to me that whenever we go on any prolonged trek like five days on Black Creek, there is this frantic feeling at the last moment. We run in circles wondering what we've forgotten and what we need to be really prepared. Even if we've been planning and preparing for months, there's still that feeling of doubt just before the start. After you leave the house, there is a stab of fear when you remember that one thing you forgot. It's too late to turn around, but you can still stop by the store to pick up that last thing. But then there is the actual moment when you step off the edge. When you push off into the river, there's no going back, only forward. Amazingly, the feeling of dread falls off when you can only go forward.

I watched a BBC documentary series titled *Ray Mears' Bushcraft* in which the bushcraft expert was talking about long canoe voyages such as Canadian fur traders used to make. He hints that old-timey canoeists experienced this same preparatory dread, and that they developed ways to counteract it.

Mears said, "On a good day's paddling I expect to cover many miles, but the fur traders would always start their journeys with a short day. They would make camp only a few miles into their journey. That way, they'd have the opportunity to use most of the kit that they'd be taking with them. If anything was missing, it wouldn't be too far to go back and get it. It was known as 'The Hudson's Bay Start.'"

Our route on Black Creek had its own built-in Hudson's Bay Start. From Dantzler Camp, it is only about eight miles (four hours) to Big Creek Landing, so we planned to stop there the first night. We didn't figure to hike back for anything we'd forgotten, but there would be good road access at Big Creek, so our ground crew could bring us any missing items (like insect repellent).

The guidebooks and the pros tell me that the current is faster moving and requires more canoe skills between Dantzler Camp and Big Creek. That seems correct. About five minutes below Dantzler, just after we rounded the corner out of view of our departing ground crew, we ran into a huge pine tree that had fallen completely across the river. It was a formidable obstacle for the more novice canoeists in the group, but we took our time and worked together, and soon we had finished pulling the canoes over the tree and were on our way.

We passed the Little Black Creek confluence soon after that. It was dumping a lot of water into Black Creek, and the boost in current was thrilling for a few moments. There were only one or two more obstructions between Dantzler Camp and Big Creek Landing, but one of them clotheslined me clean out of the boat, and my wife, Elise, jumped in to keep us from capsizing. We still shipped a lot of water and had to swim the canoe a couple hundred yards till we were able to beach it on a gravel bar and bail out.

Along the way, lots of little springs squeeze themselves out of tall clay banks, adding to the flow of Black Creek. There is even a spring of cold, clear water erupting from between the concrete slabs of the boat ramp at Big Creek Landing.

There were mosquitoes by the millions. It had rained a lot lately and the Forest Service had apparently not been able to mow the campground regularly, so the mosquitoes had some additional habitat in the tall grass. Ray Mears also mentions mosquitoes in his BBC documentary. "Blackflies and mosquitoes plague every warm-blooded creature around here. In the 1950s, the Canadian government carried out tests and discovered that an exposed forearm could be bitten 280 times in just one minute. So my bug jacket may make things hot and sweaty, but it is an essential item of clothing." That day, the horseflies made me wish I'd brought my baseball bat—I think I may have just been able to knock a few out of the air.

Anywhere there are mosquitoes, you will find that dragonflies and damselflies like to hitch a ride on your gear or your hat as you glide down the stream.

We saw hummingbirds flitting about in the top of a large mimosa tree, and we saw red velvet ants (actually a kind of wasp), both winged males and wingless females.

Around nightfall, our phones started blowing up with emergency alerts and messages from our ever vigilant ground crew, warning us that Tropical Storm Cindy was going to be an issue. The clear, starry night gave lie to the weather reports. It was simply unbelievable that after such a perfect day there would be a tropical storm to wreck our outing. But we made sure everything was secure, prepared ourselves for a deluge, and spent a sticky-hot, mosquito-miserable night waiting for the rain.

The rain never came because apparently Cindy was hanging out in the Gulf of Mexico gathering her strength before making a run inland. I think we probably could have made the float from Big Creek to Moody's Landing before the storm arrived, but my sense of adventure gave way to caution. Canoeing Black Creek while a tropical storm is spinning up might have been a grand adventure for skilled adults with knowledge of the river, but I figured the Scout moms would have deposed me from my job as scoutmaster if I'd dragged their children another eleven miles down that river into the Black Creek Wilderness.

As it was, we loaded our canoes up and skedaddled, and barely made it home before a single drop of rain fell on us. Everyone was safe and sound and able to canoe another day, but sadly we were only one-fifth as dirty and stinky as we should have been by the end of this adventure.

RED CREEK

Any meal is a good meal when you're on a good river.

—EDWARD ABBEY

Red Creek heads up in De Soto National Forest around Lumberton and flows southeast near Wiggins, roughly paralleling Black Creek to its north until the two creeks merge to form Big Black Creek and then enter the Pascagoula.

At eighty-six miles, Red Creek is shorter and shallower than its sister stream, and passes through less national forest, but it's still a gem. As their names suggest, Red Creek is a bit lighter in color than Black. But that may be less the color of the water than the fact that Red Creek is shallower and sandier. Thus, when its tannin-stained water flows a few inches deep over white sand, it's paler than Black Creek.

Red Creek exits the national forest and is first floatable at Highway 26 west of Wiggins, though paddlers may still encounter some shoals and logjams. By Highway 49, it's still small but rarely requires portaging. Studded with exquisite sandbars, Red Creek flows several miles to the rather remote City Bridge, then on to Highway 15 at Ramsey Springs. A couple of miles before Highway 15 near Ramsey Springs, it reenters national forest, where it flows for about ten miles. The creek also runs through a substantial chunk of Red Creek Wildlife Management Area on its lower portion. Below Ramsey Springs, the stream widens almost imperceptibly, deepening and darkening until, past Vestry, bayous appear with mammoth cypress trees.

Below Highway 57, Red Creek lies within the realm of the Pascagoula swamp. Floating this stretch during high water is a ticket to some great backwater exploration. The final mile or so before the juncture with Black Creek flows within the Pascagoula River Wildlife Management Area. When the creek is out of its banks, paddlers can venture into the forest and explore at will, a delight provided you have a machete and compass or GPS.

Red Creek is the perfect foil to the image many non-Mississippians have about the state. Visitors to Mississippi tend to expect mud, mosquitoes, moccasins, and moonshiners. What they find on Red Creek is white sand, fewer mosquitoes than in many other states, an abundance of nonvenomous critters, and not a single *Deliverance*-type character.

"I've never seen so many trees in one place—ever," Michigan paddler Seth Lambert said after an exploratory hike. Red Creek is satisfying from a paddler's perspective. Seth's father Dave had canoed many a whitewater river in Montana but still seemed challenged by Red Creek's obstacle course of submerged logs and branches, hairpin bends, and sandy shoals. These are intermixed with long, still stretches just right for lazing. In the aquarium-clear water you can see creatures on the creek bottom several feet down, such as snakes wriggling along the sand and big turtles gliding like raptors.

As for fishing, a Mississippi Department of Wildlife, Fisheries, and Parks brochure ranks the creek as generally poor due to the shallowness of the stream. It's a nice place for wading with a fly rod for bream or small bass. Below Highway 15, the creek is deeper and provides better habitat for spotted bass, bluegill, and catfish.

Unlike Black Creek, Red Creek doesn't have its own parallel hiking trail, but the Tuxachanie Trail comes within five miles. The twelve-mile path, located a mere thirty-odd miles north of Gulfport, provides a wonderful sampling of coastal pine savannah, characterized by sandy soil, longleaf pine trees, and broad views. The route has been declared a National Recreation Trail. The mostly flat path has a loop on the east end and crisscrosses the Bigfoot Horse Trail, allowing for day-hike possibilities. Outdoorsmen who want to mix floats down Red Creek with hikes on the Tuxachanie Trail can find a convenient base at POW Camp, a small lake and national forest primitive campground located along the trail not far south of Red Creek. A trail visitor, Brian Moore of Los Angeles, marveled at the intricate details within the "cathedral of pines," as he called it: the miniature canyon carved by the Bigfoot River (a small, sandy creek), a woodpecker's relentless hammering, white fungus growing on dead wood, clusters of insect-devouring pitcher plants.

From Snowfall to Sunbathing, by Ernest Herndon

When we walked to the Highway 26 boat ramp at Red Creek one Friday in early March, I didn't like what I saw. The narrow stream ran fast and high, several feet above normal. Add the winter storm warnings we'd been hearing, and a three-day canoe trip seemed ill advised. Yet here we were, victims of our schedules.

"Are we mice or men?" demanded Kemal Sanli, standing beside Wyatt Emmerich and Jeff Steevens. We talked over our options and agreed to try it. That's men for you. We unloaded canoes and gear, then Kemal and I drove toward the Highway 15 bridge thirty miles downstream to leave my truck.

It was nearly 3:00 p.m. when we slid our two canoes into the jet stream that was Red Creek. Usually the creek is narrow and clear, with countless sandbars. Now, at least four feet higher than normal, it was muddy and stretched between sheer banks.

We rounded the first bend and, a quarter mile later, encountered the very type of obstacle I had feared. A fallen tree lay halfway across the river on the right, and just downstream a barely submerged log lay halfway across on the left. We'd have to zig left and zag right to avoid being swept into the log.

In the stern, I ruddered us to the left, then Wyatt and I dug in with our paddles. But the current pushed us hard sideways, and we struck the log bow-first. Fortunately our momentum carried us over. We swung the boat around to wait on Jeff and Kemal. They tried the same maneuver and ran up sideways on the log, perfectly positioned for a capsize. But they kept their cool and, after a wobble or two, slid safely over.

Woodland scenery unfolded as we zipped past. A wild turkey flew across the river; a deer bounded up the bank; hawks and buzzards soared overhead against the gray sky.

We camped on a south-facing sandbar. Kemal built a fire, and I grilled jalapeño deer sausage. As dark fell we huddled around the fire in the ripping northwest wind. Something cold and damp peppered my face, and I pointed my flashlight up to see tiny snowflakes.

My camping buddies represented a wide range of personalities. Wyatt—owner of numerous newspapers—is the Philosopher. He sits cross-legged in front of the campfire like an Indian chief and expostulates knowledgeably on a mind-boggling variety of topics. Jeff—at the time, environmental toxicologist for the Corps of Engineers—is the Scientist, able to discourse on subjects ranging from nanoparticles to neurotoxins. Kemal—credit manager for the Lion Oil Company—is the Master Camper, chopping wood, building and tending fires, cooking superb meals, even carving a sitting area into a sloping sandbar. They call me Bayou Man and expect me to know the answers to any river-related questions, which often leaves me scrambling to come up with a reply. We're an unlikely gang, I reckon, but we all turn into Tom Sawyers and Huck Finns when we get out in places like this.

By dawn the sky had cleared and the wind slackened. Geese honked as Kemal fried bacon and eggs over the fire, served up with sweet rolls and coffee.

On the sun-washed river, blooming red maple trees contrasted with shiny green magnolias and freshly budding oaks. Yet many trees were broken and fallen, a legacy of Hurricane Katrina, which slaughtered forests all across this part of the state in 2005.

We zipped under Highway 49 at Perkinston, and by the time we passed City Bridge and stopped at a sandbar for lunch, the air was so warm that I took off my shirt to catch some rays. We lunched on jerky, sardines, sandwiches, and chips and napped on the sun-heated sandbar. But whenever a breeze blew or a cloud passed over the sun, the air felt instantly chilly.

That evening, we made camp on a narrow sandbar below an island. This was a lonely place, the sand riddled with fat bobcat tracks—two-inch-wide round pads lacking claw marks. The night was cold and starry, with coyote howls and owl whoops ringing out through the woods. As we talked around the campfire after a gumbo-and-French-bread supper, Orion the Hunter stole behind the treetops while the North Star looked on unmoved.

Heavy frost coated our canoes at dawn. Jeff made oatmeal with all the fixings. We built up the fire and drank coffee.

This was Sunday, so we passed around a camp testament, each reading a passage and commenting on it. I chose Psalm 19: "The heavens declare the glory of God; the skies proclaim the work of his hands. . . . In the heavens he has pitched a tent for the sun, which is like a bridegroom coming forth from his pavilion, like a champion rejoicing to run his course. It rises at one end of the heavens and makes its circuit to the other."

"So what are your comments?" Kemal asked.

I pointed to the riffling creek, the woods, the sun rising over the treetops ready to run its course. Those were my comments.

COASTAL MISSISSIPPI

If you want to know why the coast is such an inspirational place, ask Herman Melville, Jack London, Nordhoff and Hall, Robert Louis Stevenson, or Joseph Conrad. It's a glimpse of eternity. It invites rumination, the relentless whisper of the tide against the shore.

—JOHN COOPER CLARKE

The Mississippi Gulf Coast is a jigsaw puzzle of waterways. These coastal streams are typically short—In the space of a few miles they can expand from narrow creek to wide estuary. That's certainly the case with the Biloxi River and Jourdan River. Unlike most of Mississippi's coastal streams, which are more like estuaries, the Wolf is a real river, flowing eighty-one miles from the piney-woods interior of the state.

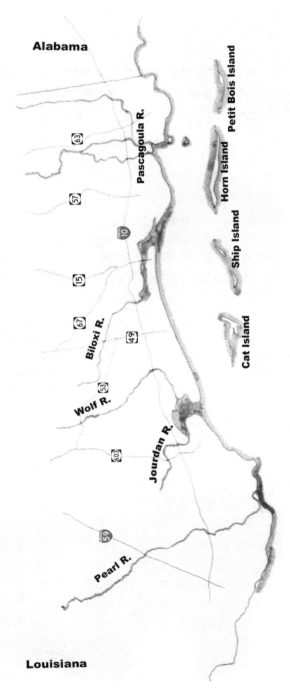

Navigable rivers and creeks of the coastal region and Gulf islands

BILOXI RIVER

> The presence of the sea gives the air and the light
> a very special quality that I absolutely adore.
>
> —CONNIE NIELSEN

If you cross the Biloxi River on Highway 49 north of Gulfport, you see a small, tumbling, woodland stream, but if you cross it on Interstate 10—barely ten miles away as the crow flies—you'll see a huge estuary of Back Bay of Biloxi. Back Bay is the western extension of Biloxi Bay, which is located between the city of Biloxi on the west and Ocean Springs on the east, with D'Iberville to the north. The Biloxi River enters from the far west of Back Bay, mingling with the marshy mouth of the Tchoutacabouffa (chu-ta-ca-BUFF) River, which is even shorter than the Biloxi and also expands from a tiny creek to a huge estuary in the space of a few miles.

> The name Biloxi comes from the Choctaw word *biluchi*, for hickory bark. Tchoutacabouffa is from *shuti kobaffi*, broken pots. The "Mad Potter of Biloxi," George E. Ohr (1857–1918), reportedly used the local clay for his handwork. Another renowned potter, Peter Anderson (1901–1984), founded Shearwater Pottery in nearby Ocean Springs. He was brother to the artist Walter Anderson.

The Biloxi River's main paddling stretch, ten and a half miles from Old Highway 49 to Three Rivers Road near Wool Market, offers a few hours of paddling or a day of lazing, with several miles of national forest and numerous sandbars. It's a beautiful float, but hard going in low water.

A Short Stretch to Paddle

The river is actually fifty-three miles long, heading up just south of Highway 26 between Poplarville and Wiggins. It remains creek-sized until it's joined by the Little Biloxi River, a mere eleven and a half miles from the mouth. Less than a mile downstream of Old Highway 49 is De Soto National Forest's Big Biloxi Campground, though there's little sign of it from the water since it's atop a bluff. It's a good place for a base camp but offers no access to the river without toting gear through the woods and down the bluff.

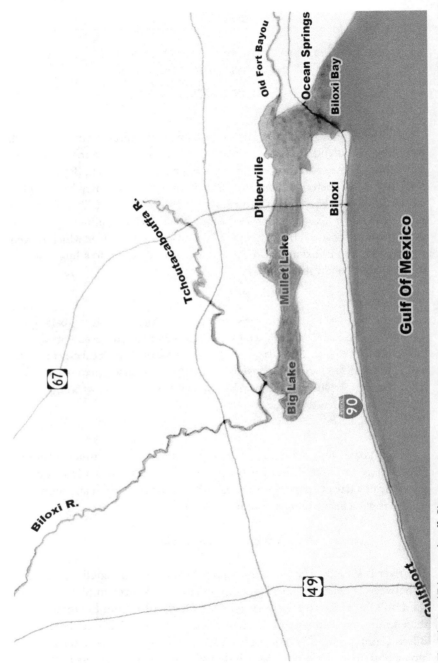

The Biloxi and Tchoutacabouffa Rivers

The first half of the stretch runs through national forest and is full of shoals and logjams. Don't even try it in low water. The Biloxi is, however, a classic bass stream. Redeye bass lurk in the upper stretches where the water is cooler, such as near springs. The creek also sports gorgeous, iridescent bluegill and chinquapin bream. The upper stream is great for wade fishing, using ultralight rigs or even fly-fishing tackle.

Piney woods continue outside the national forest boundaries, but development soon appears. A casino golf course stretches a long way down the west bank, scenic in its own way with its sweeping greenswards among groves of tall pines.

The Little Biloxi River enters from the west nine and a half miles below Old 49. The Biloxi is notably wider as it wends the final, slow mile to Three Rivers Road, where a huge stretch of sand beach lures crowds on weekends and summer days.

Paddlers can also venture upstream and float back down, thus avoiding pull-overs on the upper reaches and not having to bother with a shuttle. Although this is the outskirts of Gulfport, about all you'll see is woods. Above the mouth of the Little Biloxi, the Biloxi narrows considerably, with more current. Its tea-colored waters spout past sugarcake sandbars where wild blueberry bushes grow.

Populated Areas

Below Three Rivers Road, the river enters the heavily developed urban areas outlying Wool Market and Gulfport. In the six and a half miles from Three Rivers Road to I-10, it expands dramatically as it meets the brackish backwater from Back Bay. Here, fishermen have been known to catch both fresh and saltwater species.

At Back Bay, the Biloxi merges with the Tchoutacabouffa. In 2020, the city of D'Iberville opened the Tchoutacabouffa Paddling Trail and Nature Area at Riverside Park, providing a good way to enjoy the waterway. If there's sufficient water, the Tchoutacabouffa also provides a five-mile float through national forest from Highway 15 to C. C. Road. The catch is, it's hard to tell when there is sufficient water because the put-in, Hurricane Creek, is a small tributary, and the take-out is wide—what's in between remains out of sight. Several miles below C. C. Road, the Tchoutacabouffa widens into the huge estuary visible from the I-10 bridge.

Sailing and Rowing in Back Bay, by Ernest Herndon

Scott Williams untied the dock lines and cranked the outboard motor on his twenty-six-foot, two-masted sailboat named *Intensity*. I made sure the hull didn't bump the pilings as we eased out of the slip and maneuvered past rows of yachts and sailboats in Biloxi's Point Cadet Marina. We motored east along the breakwater and out into the Mississippi Sound, where a brisk southerly December breeze washed over us. Scott handed me the tiller and I felt the sleek, sea-green boat come under my control.

Although the entrance to Back Bay lay to port, we had to follow the shipping channel away from it before turning back to approach. The waters off the Mississippi Gulf Coast are so shallow that even a small sailboat has to stay in the channels between the red and green signs or risk grounding. We reached the turning point, and I swung us northwest toward the bay entrance.

Back Bay stretches ten miles long by roughly one mile wide behind Biloxi. Several waterways enter it, including Old Fort Bayou, the Biloxi River, the Tchoutacabouffa River, Bernard Bayou, and a man-made industrial canal. During Tropical Storms Isidore and Lili, Scott had to take the Intensity up into the Biloxi River for shelter. This time he wanted to make a slower tour of exploration.

We passed under the Highway 90 drawbridge, which was already up because a large shrimp boat was headed out to sea. The adjacent railroad drawbridge was likewise open. Past the drawbridges, we had the wide-open bay ahead of us, but the expanse was deceptive since we still had to stay in the channel.

The scenery was a mix of marsh grass, pine trees, houses, docks, and boatyards. A lineup of colorful deep-sea shrimp boats—greens, reds, blues—lay at anchor, noses pointed toward open water like hounds awaiting the hunters. Several bore Vietnamese-sounding names and paintings of dragons.

The skies were blue and sunny, the air cool enough for jean jacket or sweatshirt. A few fishermen in johnboats angled at the edges of the marsh.

The Interstate 110 bridge, flanked by a high-rise casino, towered before us. The interstate has a drawbridge, but it's sixty-five feet high and needed only by the tallest of vessels. The Intensity required a thirty-five-foot clearance, so we zipped under with no problem. With five miles of open water before the next drawbridge, Scott raised the mainsail and jib and turned off the motor. The boat sped on without slacking at a speed of between five and six knots.

"Sailing inland waters is some of the best sailing there is," Scott declared. On protected waters like this, you can enjoy the speed without turbulence, the motorless silence, the hissing wind, the slapping canvas, the swishing water. While a motor-driven vessel feels like a machine, under sail it comes alive, a horse galloping across a blue prairie. The catch is the narrow zigzagging channel. When it angles the wrong way, you can lose your wind. Get out of the channel and you're sure to run aground. As we would soon discover, such dangers were not just theoretical.

The thrill of sailing ended all too soon as we had to lower sails to pass under the Popp's Ferry Road drawbridge. Beyond that, we faced the last open water on Back Bay, called Big Lake. We hugged the south shore and ventured briefly up an industrial canal, where a towboat shoved a barge against the bank while a crane unloaded some kind of soil onto a conveyor. As we neared, the wash from the towboat's screws swept the Intensity in an alarming half-circle. We'd seen enough of the canal anyway, so instead of fighting it we headed back down the canal to the mouth of Bernard Bayou, another navigable waterway.

Here we made a critical mistake. Making the turn from the canal into the bayou, Scott edged too close to shore, and the depth shot from eleven feet to less than the depth-finder could register. The boat burrowed to a halt in bay-bottom mud. Grounded.

What had fooled Scott was the green channel marker standing in the shallows. He assumed the water on our side of the marker was navigable. Only then did we look at the chart, which said, "shallow point."

The risk of grounding is just part of the experience when sailing in Gulf waters, where the bottom can be wading-depth even far from shore. Scott, who's been grounded before, slung the mainsail boom out to starboard and climbed out on it to lean the vessel sideways. I gunned the motor in reverse, then forward, trying to wiggle us out. The hull swayed and twisted but couldn't get free. Then the motor began gurgling. A spark plug had fouled out. Scott replaced it, and this time the propeller freed us.

We motored cautiously up Bernard Bayou, a pretty little stretch of water with a park on the south shore where fishermen cast lines off wooden docks. We had to turn back at a road that lacked a drawbridge yet was too low to go under. The afternoon was early so we recrossed Big Lake and headed up the Biloxi River, the route Scott had taken when he fled Tropical Storms Isidore and Lili earlier in the year.

Houses—some ramshackle, some gorgeous—stood on the right bank amid pine trees and live oaks. A barge canal split off to a power plant on the left, and the Tchoutacabouffa River opened out on the right. Our chart didn't show depths in the Tchoutacabouffa, and there's not a marked channel there, so we stayed clear of it.

We motored north up the Biloxi River and anchored in a backwater, bow pointing downstream into the wind. Astern to starboard, the power plant puffed clouds of steam against the setting sun. Dead astern, a red Texaco star rose above the treetops. Off the port bow we could glimpse traffic on Interstate 10 through the foliage under a rising moon.

Sleep didn't come easily for a landlubber like me. I lay in a narrow bunk with no wiggle room. The wind blew all night, directing a squawky symphony of whaps, creaks, squeaks, thuds, whistles, and clangs—the normal sounds of a boat at anchor, but a racket to me. I probably got to sleep around 4:00 a.m., and we woke at first light to a golden strip of sky beneath low-hanging gray clouds that blossomed into metallic pink.

Soon we were headed back down the Biloxi River and across Back Bay. The breeze was stiffer today, with severe gusting winds, so Scott hauled in the sails and we relied on the motor.

The motor wasn't proving to be reliable. It kept gurgling like it had the day before when we were grounded. Scott finessed it for a while, but it conked out completely as we approached the I-110 bridge. Back Bay is no place to be adrift in a boat that needs four and a half feet of water. Lose power here and you'd better anchor fast or you'll be pushed into the shallows.

Scott let the anchor down and fetched his tool kit. He knows his way around a boat motor, so he soon had it working, and we skimmed under Highway 90, which offered thirty-six feet of clearance for our thirty-five-foot-tall boat.

Out in the Mississippi Sound, the seas were choppy. As we made the hard starboard turn toward Point Cadet, the boat pitched and wallowed in the water. Scott took the tiller from my inexperienced hand and eased us expertly into protected waters behind Deer Island and thence into the marina. Sheltered by a concrete breakwater, the marina was a picture of peace, with pretty boats in orderly rows, chimes tinkling, flags flying, and the wind a pleasant breeze.

WOLF RIVER

Wherever there is a channel for water, there is a road for the canoe.
—HENRY DAVID THOREAU

The Wolf River heads up west of Lumberton but doesn't become navigable until the Silver Run community southeast of Poplarville. It flows south by southeast until it crosses Interstate 10, after which it swings west and broadens into marsh as it empties into the east end of St. Louis Bay.

> The Wolf River, not surprisingly, was named for the red wolves that once roamed the South, including Mississippi. At forty-five to eighty pounds, red wolves are somewhere between the gray wolf and the coyote. Decimated by hunting and habitat loss, by the late 1970s red wolves were found only in southeast Texas and southwest Louisiana, mainly in coastal prairie and marsh. Numerous attempts by the US Fish and Wildlife Service to bolster the population, including releasing a pair on Mississippi's Horn Island in 1989, ultimately failed. By 2021 there were only fifty left in the wild, most of them in Alligator River National Wildlife Refuge, North Carolina. Around three hundred are held in breeding facilities around the nation.

The Wolf River is the showpiece of coastal streams, offering thirty-five miles of good paddling. It's also a microcosm of other Mississippi piney-woods streams. The ever changing Wolf has sections reminiscent of virtually every other river in the southern half of the state.

At Silver Run, the Wolf looks much like the Bogue Chitto River, but it's clear and tea-colored like Red Creek. Then it narrows and runs under big, overarching trees like Magee's Creek. Later it becomes wider but still shady like Bowie Creek, opens onto big gravel bars like the Tangipahoa River, with occasional logjams like the Amite, plunging rapids like Okatoma Creek, high mossy bluffs like the Chickasawhay, multicolored clays like Bayou Pierre, sudden drops like the Strong River, and wide, muddy reaches like the Leaf River.

Just when a paddler might feel overwhelmed by the constant sense of déjà vu, the Wolf takes on an appearance all its own, narrowing from one hundred feet wide to ten feet as it rushes down a clay chute. As with the weather, if there's a part of the Wolf you don't like, just wait: it will soon change.

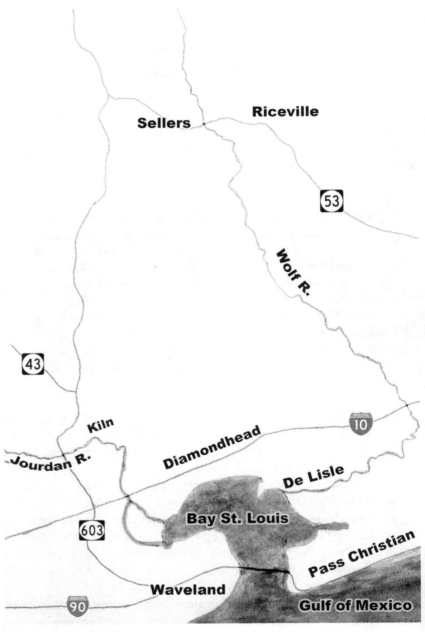

The Jourdan and Wolf Rivers

Exhilarating to Paddle

A sense of excitement begins when you launch the boat and slide away from shore. Multitextured smells, sights, and sounds surround the gloriously simple yet impossibly complex path of water through its tunnel of green forest and blue sky. In addition to the aesthetic qualities, the thirteen-mile stretch from Silver Run to Highway 53 is challenging—swift, crooked, narrow, and tricky. The ability to read a river is a much-needed skill on the Wolf, which frequently offers just one path for a paddlecraft to squeeze through. Paddlers can expect to bump logs, scrape over sandy shoals, and brush against bushes. It helps to take a maneuverable vessel on this creek, such as a river kayak or a canoe with a good rocker keel.

> Steve Cox made the mistake of taking a long, straight-keeled, seventeen-foot canoe down the Wolf River. As he and a buddy rounded a tight, sharp bend, the current barreled toward a sweeper, a chest-high horizontal log protruding over the water. If they had been in a more maneuverable boat, they might have avoided it. As it was, Cox's partner could only watch in horror as Cox prepared to have the top half of his body sheared backward. Did the McComb architect face decapitation, or merely a broken back? Fortunately he had good reflexes. He put his left foot against the log, which spilled both paddlers into the cold river and half-swamped the boat. Cox took off after his paddle while his buddy struggled to haul the canoe out of the current. "I didn't mind the dunking, considering the alternative of hauling Steve's carcass through the woods," his buddy said later.

The upper river features fine, small sandbars backed by thickets of muscadine, wax myrtle, red maple, and Chinese tallow trees (an invasive species that proliferates on southern waterways). Behind this green tangle rise giants like water oak, pine, and magnolia trees. Sandbars grow bigger below Highway 53. On a moonlit night, these expanses resemble a Colorado snowfield. But the morning sun can quickly change them into a reflector oven.

This upper part of the river also provides typical creek fishing: bream (bluegill and longear), bass, and some catfish. The Wolf is a great fly-fishing stream since it's shallow enough to wade, but those shallows can cause some drag-overs for canoers during the dry season, and they also enable the unfortunate habitat-destroying pastime of riding four-wheelers in the river, on sandbars, and down forest trails paralleling the stream.

Approaching the Coast

The river passes through a conservation easement on the stretch from Highway 53 to Cable Bridge Road, three hundred feet wide along each bank. The International Paper Company donated the land to the nonprofit Conservation Fund in 1999. The easement not only gives the public access to the stream-side land but prevents logging, gravel mining, construction, and other development that could damage the stream.

Below Cable Bridge, as the river widens, deepens, and slows, the canoeing feels more coastal. Gone are clay chutes and rapids. What's left is a contemplative paddle past big sandbars and through beautiful woodland and marsh scenery. Below Interstate 10 is Wolf River Canoe and Kayak, which rents boats and offers guided paddle trips through the marshes in and around St. Louis Bay. Bayou Acadian merges from the east just above Hampton Road.

There's plenty of opportunity for poking around in these marshes, even in the bay itself, wind and motorboat traffic permitting. But motorboats can be obnoxious on summer weekends and especially on holidays. Scott Williams was sailing in St. Louis Bay one Labor Day weekend and encountered aggressive, drunken speedboaters and personal watercraft users who made him fear for the safety of his vessel. One speedboater refused to give way in a tight squeeze under a drawbridge until ordered to do so by the drawbridge operator, and two personal watercraft users roared so close to the sailboat that their wakes drenched Scott and his companions. Nor are secluded bayous necessarily safe. One personal watercraft operator careened up Bayou Portage at top speed despite a no-wake zone and refused to pull over when a marina owner threatened to call the law. Unfortunately, paddlers are at the mercy of such people. On the other hand, on off-season weekdays you may find the entire bay virtually deserted, not to mention the backwaters. At such times, the area is bewitching.

JOURDAN RIVER

> Oh pull off your overcoat and roll up your sleeves, Jordan am a hard road to travel.
> Pull off your overcoat and roll up your sleeves, Jordan am a hard road to travel I believe.
>
> —UNCLE DAVE MACON, "JORDAN IS A HARD ROAD TO TRAVEL"

Bracketing the Mississippi coast is the vast Pearl River swamp on the west side and the Pascagoula swamp on the east. Between them lies a network of bays and estuaries. First is St. Louis Bay between the towns of Bay St. Louis on the west and Pass Christian on the east. Two rivers feed St. Louis Bay—the Jourdan on the west side and the Wolf on the east.

Continuing east along the coast past the cities of Gulfport and Biloxi, you come to Biloxi Bay. It stretches west inland to become Back Bay of Biloxi, which is fed by the Biloxi and Tchoutacabouffa Rivers. East of Biloxi Bay is the town of Ocean Springs, which provides entrance to Gulf Islands National Seashore.

Like most other coastal streams, the Jourdan River is scarcely a river at all, more of an estuary of St. Louis Bay. With virtually no current, it's just right for exploring from a base camp like McLeod Water Park. The park, located southeast of Kiln and operated by Hancock County, is the highest public access point on the river, yet even here the Jourdan is wide and deep enough for large motorboats. The river is born a few miles upstream from the park at the juncture of Catahoula Creek and Bayou Bacon. Farther north, where those streams cross under Highway 43 between Kiln and Picayune, they're just tiny brooks.

The Jourdan offers an interesting lesson in geography. If you take Interstate 12 east of Hammond, Louisiana, you're driving through mud and cypress country. But when you cross into Mississippi on I-10, mud turns to sand, murky waters run clear, and pine trees creep down to riverbanks. While Louisiana's Tchefuncte River to the west is muddy and brown, the Jourdan has clear water, sugar-white sandbars, and clean-smelling pines.

Maybe it's the artesian springs, or the shift from Mississippi River floodplain to coastal geography. Regardless, it makes for some interesting paddling—if you don't mind company. The Jourdan's biggest problem is its popularity.

This pretty, pine-clad stream is traversed by personal watercraft and water skiers as well as paddlers. McLeod Water Park is likewise overly popular, and understandably. Named for turn-of-the-century settlers, the 328-acre park is a comfortable, down-home place where you'll nearly always smell charcoal burning, see children romping—and hear radios playing. That can be pleasantly homey when the radios are at a distance, but not if you have the misfortune to be camped next to a crowd of teenagers in party mode.

> Albert and Virginia McLeod, for whom the park is named, ran a sawmill, general store, and turpentine plant in the early 1900s, employing some five hundred people. Mr. McLeod died in 1931, but his wife, known as Aunt Gin, operated the old store until her death in 1973 at age ninety-five. The park was developed in 1975.

The tent camping area is located on a sandy peninsula among pine and bay trees. You can launch a paddlecraft from virtually any site as well as a park boat ramp. To explore the Jourdan, just set off upriver—paddling is no problem against the slight current—where the scenery is best and motorboat traffic least. The park's one-and-a-quarter-mile no-wake zone helps slow big-boat traffic. Narrow side passages lead to oxbow lakes, and paddlers can poke into them to find quiet, lonely waters ringed by forest. The park encompasses an oxbow lake accessible by just such a channel. A nature trail also wends through the swampy forest around the lake if you want to explore on foot.

The park is so close to St. Louis Bay that the river rises and falls with the tides, making it a good place for both fresh- and brackish-water fish species. Fishermen may catch bass, bream, redfish, speckled trout, and flounder in one day on the same lure. Farther downriver, during September and October, bank fishermen throw cat food and rabbit food into the water to entice shrimp, then haul them in with cast nets. These shrimp can reach a foot long and are best stuffed or fried butterfly style.

> This used to be the heart of turpentine country. In the nineteenth century, turpentine collectors cut cavities in longleaf and slash pine trees near the roots, obtaining the resin in boxes but often killing the trees. In 1901, federal forestry officials developed a method similar to obtaining maple sap for syrup: collectors would use a V-shaped blade to cut the inner bark of a tree about once a week, gathering the resin in a cup without killing the tree. The resin was then distilled and stored in oak barrels.

The Jourdan hosts abundant birdlife, from massive ospreys to lanky great blue herons. Night is a good time to paddle to see other wildlife. Flashlight beams may pick up a beaver gliding nearby or a big-eared doe floundering neck-deep before climbing the low bank into the woods. It's also fun to cut the lights and use the dim reflection of night sky as guide. Dark forest lines either side, and the twisting channel sometimes leaves you wondering which way to turn, but not for long. The night thrums with crickets, the swish of paddles, the occasional sigh of a breeze. The backwaters look sinister in the darkness, a likely place for the Creature from the Black Lagoon, but it's a pleasant fear. Despite its monster mask, the swamp is benign.

Meanwhile back in camp, raccoons will clean your dishes for you if you set them back in the woods. They won't even wait till you go to bed; you'll likely hear them grunting and scuffling in the darkness. Flashlights will send them scurrying, at least temporarily.

St. Louis Bay

If you've ever looked at a map of St. Louis Bay or driven the Highway 90 causeway and glanced over at the six-mile-wide bay, you may have thought it would be ideal for sailing: spacious but protected from Gulf winds. Appearances can be deceiving. The bay is fine for shallow-draft boats like johnboats, not to mention sea kayaks, but for a seafaring vessel it's dicey. Most of the bay is just three to five feet deep, not enough for a blue-water hull, which may draw four feet or more.

Bayous and canals off the bay provide shelter for yachts when hurricanes approach. When Tropical Storm Cindy hit Biloxi on the night of July 5, 2005, Scott Williams was asleep on his sailboat in Point Cadet Marina. A sound like gunfire awakened him, and he sprang out on deck to find that the wind had demolished the sail of a neighboring boat. Not only that, but water had risen three feet over the docks, and waves were threatening to crest over the seawall.

He rode out the storm, but when Hurricane Dennis headed toward the Gulf Coast the following weekend, Scott took no chances. He weighed anchor and headed inland in the twenty-six-foot live-aboard.

Scott took his boat to Discovery Bay Marina (now closed) on the east side of St. Louis Bay. He planned to anchor in a nearby canal during the storm. Afterward, he would berth the boat at Discovery Bay instead of the more vulnerable Point Cadet.

Scott spent all morning motoring over from Biloxi. Already, shrimp boats had tied up in the canals to ride out the approaching storm. "Won't be the first time," a shrimper said as Scott passed by. Scott stopped in a piney-woods canal and set lines and anchors. Then he sat in the hot shade of the bimini, or boat awning, and made a pot of coffee as more boats arrived.

A sailboat pulled up, and the skipper ran the bow straight into shore—a bad move. The canal, though more than six feet deep in midchannel, was only about four feet along the bank, and the vessel got stuck. Scott paddled over in a canoe and helped try to free the mildewed, barnacle-encrusted boat, but it was too heavy. He volunteered to help anchor the boat, and the man handed Scott an undersized anchor. Then his cell phone rang. To Scott's amazement, he walked away, gabbing on the phone, as Scott stood in the bow of the canoe holding the anchor chain. Up until that point Scott had been planning to loan the man lines and anchors if necessary, and help him set them. But since his cell phone apparently took precedence, Scott left him to his own devices.

Now he faced a big problem. If the water rose—as it surely would if the hurricane hit—the neighboring boat would float free and pose a serious danger to adjacent vessels. Nor were its anchors big enough to hold in a real storm. The greatest danger to boats in storms is other boats. So Scott decided to move. He weighed anchor, headed up the canal, and turned into another canal, this one deserted. He and his buddy spent an hour mooring the boat, then headed to the marina restaurant for supper.

Protecting saltwater boats from storms isn't a problem confined to Gulf Coast residents. Plenty of inlanders—Scott lives in Jackson—keep boats on the coast. Bobby McGinnis, who used to run the Dry Creek Marine boat shop in Tylertown, said that "a lot" of Mississippians are in that situation. "They'll go down and a lot of them will either pull them home if they're trailerable, [or] if they're too big they'll go up. It is a hassle, but the people that love it, it's just something they've got to do. And all of them I know that go down to fish, they're hooked on it. . . . It's a routine and they know the routine. Yeah, it takes a whole day of maneuvering, sometimes two days, but they're just prepared for it."

Canoeing to a Stranded Yacht, by Ernest Herndon

Just prior to Hurricane Katrina on August 29, 2005, Scott moored his sailboat, the *Intensity*, at Discovery Bay Marina on the protected east end of St. Louis Bay. This was a remote area of piney woods, bayous, and derelict camps where he had sheltered his boat during previous hurricanes.

A few days after the storm, Scott and his brother Jeff went to the coast to look for the twenty-six-foot sailboat. They had already been to Jeff's house in Gulfport, which was reduced to a slab. Now they wanted to see what had happened to Scott's home away from home.

As they drove to the marina, a shrimp boat lay in the road, blocking their way. While Jeff waited at the truck, Scott launched his dinghy in a canal to go search.

Two men emerged from the woods and eyed Jeff and the truck, talking to each other. Then they approached, each stepping to one side.

"Why you wear gun?" the younger of the two challenged Jeff, who had a .45 strapped to his belt in light of the then-lawless state of the coast.

"Don't worry about it," Jeff said.

The man stepped toward Jeff and reached out with his hand. "You got fly on shoulder."

Jeff put his hand on the gun and stepped back around the corner of the truck. "Get on out of here—now!"

The men left, stopping to look back at him.

Meanwhile on the water, Scott rowed down eerily deserted canals, oars penetrating a slick of gasoline, diesel, oil, and who knows what else. The air stank of death. His boat was not where he'd left it, nor did he see it anywhere among the smashed vessels. He got out of there fast, and he and Jeff were glad to get away from the coast.

Then Scott enlisted me to go down there with him to help him find the Intensity.

With Hurricane Rita churning in the Gulf, we bypassed the interstates to avoid evacuee traffic. In Poplarville, cars mobbed gas stations, love bugs swarmed the wretchedly hot air, and sirens howled. I felt like we had entered the outer ring of hell. Traffic stopped as a fire truck, fire car, and ambulance screamed past. But they were merely responding to a minor accident, and soon we were back on open road, coasting south past smashed trailers, roofless houses, and piles of downed trees.

South of Interstate 10 we turned onto Arcadia Road, which winds through piney woods and marsh between river and bayou. Most of the pines were dead from the twenty-foot surge of salt water that had immersed them. The driver of a large truck stopped us. "You guys want lunch? We're handing them out." It was an American Red Cross disaster relief vehicle, prowling the back roads, trying to help.

We parked in the shade and ate the high-protein dinners: breaded chicken breasts, green beans, applesauce, bread, cookies, tea. We were going to need the energy.

On the road to Discovery Bay Marina, boats lay in the woods and along canals. Scott recognized some from the marina, half a mile away. Two massive shrimp boats blocked the road. To get past, we had to drive over a hand-lettered sign reading, "Keep out. Will shoot."

The marina building was a skeleton. Its restaurant was entirely gone. Boats were tossed about like bath toys. Tad Doolittle of Sea Tow, a business that recovers boats for insurance companies, tinkered with a motor on a skiff. "This is like nothing I've ever seen," said Doolittle. "Yesterday we pulled a boat through the woods, over the railroad tracks, across a three-foot ditch."

Scott and I launched a canoe and paddled slowly up the bayou, looking for his sailboat. There were vessels everywhere—big and small, upside-down, right-side up, on their sides, intact, or busted to smithereens. Shrimp boats, sailboats, power boats, skiffs, johnboats, catamarans, trimarans, yachts. We were looking for a green hull and white mast.

We followed a horseshoe canal around to the end, then got out to hunt on foot. An upside-down hull lay in the bushes. Across the marsh we saw the back side of the woods that faced the marina. From here they looked more open than they had from the water.

We crossed a quarter mile of marsh, our boots churning up a black-mud stench of rotten eggs and manure, well baked in the high-nineties midday heat. Boats lay everywhere in the piney woods. Humans couldn't have put them there like that no matter how hard they tried. But Katrina had no trouble. It just lifted them up on the surge, floated them out into the woods, then set them down wherever.

Scott and I split up. I picked morosely among the rubble amid the hot smell of pine straw. Then I heard his voice: "I found it!"

The Intensity was wedged between pine trees, surrounded by bushes. It was thirty-five yards to the nearest water. I was elated to have found our quarry. I could tell Scott felt otherwise.

"It's heartbreaking," he said. "You develop a bond with a boat." The Intensity had taken him many places: to and from Florida, out to the barrier islands, here and there in the Mississippi Sound and the Gulf of Mexico. A boatwright, Scott lived on the vessel when he had jobs on the coast. It was his second home, his security blanket, his ticket to adventure.

Putrid water floated inside the cabin. Someone had broken in and stolen a stereo, VHF radio, .22 caliber rifle, and other miscellaneous items. But the most valuable gear remained: anchors, lines, outboard motor, electronics.

I hiked to the canoe and paddled around to a point nearest the Intensity. We toted load after load of stuff to it, then ferried it over to my truck.

Even though the Intensity's hull was intact, Scott knew of no feasible way to salvage the seven-thousand-pound vessel. Nor was it insured. But he did save hundreds of dollars' worth of gear. And he got to say goodbye to an old friend, who went out in a manner worthy of its name.

GULF ISLANDS

> The isolation spins its mysterious cocoon, focusing the mind on one place, one time, one rhythm.... The island knows no other human voices, no other footprints.
>
> —M. L. STEDMAN

The Mississippi Gulf Coast is an almost continuous strip of towns from Waveland to Pascagoula, with casinos, hotels, restaurants, beaches, and traffic. But there are plenty of out-of-the-way places to explore. Prime among them is Gulf Islands National Seashore. This park provides canoeing opportunities at Davis Bayou and sea kayaking to the barrier islands of Ship, Horn, and Petit Bois. There are other islands as well, so options for coastal paddlers range from an afternoon's easy excursion to a saltwater expedition.

The park at Davis Bayou on the east side of Ocean Springs is a green pocket of marsh and piney woods barely a mile across but with winding bayous, a good place for casual exploring, as you can't venture more than half a mile in any direction without getting outside the park's boundaries, usually into residential areas. There are actually four bayous within the park, each a finger of the Mississippi Sound, which is the strip of salt water protected from the open Gulf of Mexico by barrier islands.

From the park boat ramp, Halstead Bayou wiggles west past the campground, Stark Bayou runs north to a park road, a smaller bayou meanders east beside the William M. Colmer Visitor Center, and Davis Bayou opens out to Biloxi Bay, with Deer Island barely a mile away.

You can drive to the visitor center or paddle up to it, and it's well worth a stop. The beautifully rustic, spacious building features boardwalks overlooking the bayou, Walter Anderson artwork, and a bookstore with a selection of titles on nature, travel, and history that will make you reach for your wallet.

> Infamously eccentric Ocean Springs artist Walter Anderson (1903–1965) would spend weeks at a time on barrier islands, where he immersed himself in art and nature. Anderson rowed to these islands repeatedly in a ten-foot dory. He capsized several times, but that never deterred him. Anderson is renowned for his beautiful art based largely on the Gulf Coast's marshes, beaches, and barrier islands, with scenes of herons, fish, crabs, alligators, and other creatures.

Davis Bayou

All four bayous are easy paddling except Davis, which is up to half a mile wide and subject to strong winds. But when the breeze is light, you can paddle inland to the east and north for several miles, past developed areas and Sandhill Crane National Wildlife Refuge, under a railroad trestle, and up to Highway 90. Sandhill Crane Refuge features a visitor center and short nature trail amid 19,273 acres of coastal savannah. The endangered cranes resemble great blue herons but are distinguishable by a red crown and long, curving tail feathers.

All told, the Davis Bayou area offers a neat sampling of marsh. Though rarely out of sight of houses or roads, it's home to ospreys, pelicans, and hermit crabs (not to mention mosquitoes and sandflies). There's fishing from a pier by the boat ramp, in the shallow bayous, or farther offshore. There are also picnic areas, a nature trail, and developed campsites in a lovely setting, which is unfortunately noisy at night because of the proximity of railroad tracks.

Deer Island

If you feel adventurous and the weather's calm, you can paddle to Deer Island, preferably in a sea kayak. From the Davis Bayou boat ramp, paddle south, then west onto Davis Bayou past a bird-crowded sand spit, and out into Biloxi Bay.

Down the coast to the right stand casinos and high-rise hotels. The island lies a short distance due south across a channel often plied by boats. You may see a shrimp boat churning out to sea dragging blue nets, a rip-roaring speedboat, or a graceful sailing yacht. It takes about half an hour of paddling to reach the five-mile-long island. A quarter-mile-wide strip of sand crowned by pine forest and palmetto, most of the island is state owned, uninhabited, and undeveloped.

The water around the island is remarkably shallow, which is advantageous for paddling since it's inaccessible to motorized craft, though sand flats can be troublesome even to paddlers at low tide. On the outside of the island, the pine forest blocks out most of the coastal urbanization. You may find bottlenose dolphins cavorting around you even though the water's only a few feet deep. Somehow the sight of dolphins suggests oceanic depths, not chest-deep shallows. Their big bodies glisten darkly, their blunt foreheads taper abruptly to narrow snouts, and each time they surface they blow with a low and contented sigh, accompanied by squeaks, squawks, and grunts.

To the west, casino hotels rise beyond the tree line. The scene grows magical in afternoon light. Crowds of seagulls spin confetti dances over the shoals at the western end of the island. A pelican soars past, heavy-bodied and smug.

Horn Island

It takes considerably more skill and courage to paddle to Horn Island, ten miles from Davis Bayou. It's amazing to consider that Native Americans canoed to Horn and other barrier islands without even an outrigger to minimize the chance of rolling. For us moderns, though, it's daunting enough even in a sea kayak or catamaran.

In addition to the difficulties of crossing, Horn Island, like all the barrier islands, has outrageously fierce biting insects, withering heat, and, in the winter, unvarnished cold. Such hardships are the price you pay to visit this astonishing wilderness of beaches, dunes, forest, marsh, and lagoons. Horn Island is a powerful experience for those who get there by whatever means—kayak, sailboat, or motorboat.

Horn Island is uninhabited except for a ranger's house mid-island. At night, the view of the coast lights from the barrier islands is enchanting, as is the view from the south side to the unlighted Gulf. Horn Island is home to wild hogs, bald eagles, ospreys, deer, rabbits, raccoons, snakes, and alligators.

> The Fish and Wildlife Service used Horn Island as a sanctuary for endangered red wolves from 1989 to 1997, producing numerous pups, which were transferred to other remote areas of the Southeast.

Only a few paths cross the island. You'd think a trail wouldn't be necessary on such a narrow island, but the interior is a wilderness of lagoons, marshes, and thickets. There are plenty of poisonous snakes, so watch your step. The trails lead through slash pine forest past swampy sloughs and emerge on the sprawling dunes of the south side. Here you can walk beside the clear water of the open Gulf, picking up shells and letting the smell of brine and the feel of sea breeze unlock—or create—memories. On both the blue Gulf side and the amber-green Mississippi Sound side, Horn Island boasts miles of empty beaches—empty, that is, except for washed-up detritus. But the views offset the rubbish—shrimpers and sailboats gentling in the breeze, low-flying pelicans in V formation, smooth-barked pine trees gnarled by wind. The setting sun unrolls your shadow down the beach, whose white sand turns gold with sunset, fading to silver and blue.

Evening beauty gives way to insect hell, though, unless you're camping in cold weather. And even a cold night may lead to a mild morning when swarms of mosquitoes bounce against the tent mesh, accompanied by no-see-ums and, later, biting flies. Such conditions make you glad to get out on the water.

Ship Island History

When French explorers led by Pierre Le Moyne, Sieur d'Iberville, arrived in 1699, one island offered a good enough harbor to earn the name Ship Island. Leaving his three vessels at the island, Iberville, his brother Jean-Baptiste Le Moyne, Sieur de Bienville, and some of the men took longboats around to the mouth of the Mississippi and rowed upriver.

The explorer René-Robert Cavelier, Sieur de La Salle, had already come down the Mississippi in 1682, and Iberville was following up from the lower end. After exploring upriver into what is now Mississippi and Louisiana, his group returned to Bayou Manchac and thence back to Ship Island.

> An Indian guide told Iberville that Bayou Manchac provided a shortcut from the lower Mississippi River to the Gulf, so leaving Bienville and the rest of the men to take the longboats on down the Mississippi, Iberville and a few others headed down Manchac in a pair of bark canoes. They found the bayou so logjammed that in one day Iberville counted fifty portages on a twenty-one-mile stretch. But the waterway did merge with the Amite River—which was swarming with alligators—and thence to Lake Maurepas, Lake Pontchartrain, and the Gulf. Iberville's team made it back to the rendezvous at Ship Island only shortly before Bienville's men. Before returning to France, Iberville built a fort at Biloxi Bay. He came back to the Gulf Coast late in the year to continue the process of exploration and settlement.

In 1859, US troops began building Fort Massachusetts on the west side of Ship Island to guard that back-door passage to New Orleans that Iberville had traveled 140 years earlier, but construction was interrupted by the Civil War.

> Before the Civil War, brown bricks were ferried over from the Slidell, Louisiana, area to be used in the construction of Fort Massachusetts. After the Confederacy seceded, the US Army had to ship red bricks from New England. If you visit the fort today, you can see the start of the Civil War clearly marked in the fort by a line several feet off the ground where brown bricks were replaced by red ones.

At one time, twenty-two thousand soldiers bivouacked on the island while sixty warships ranged in the surrounding waters. The fort was protected by eight-foot-thick walls and sixteen cannons with ranges of up to five miles. A top layer of sod allowed rainwater to percolate into pipes and thence into fifteen-thousand-gallon tanks for drinking.

The Confederates captured the fort briefly but lost it after a bloodless twenty-minute battle with Union ships. Unfortunately, all of the cannons but one were later sold for scrap iron. The remaining fifty-thousand-pound behemoth on top appears to guard the harbor.

In 1946, a hurricane cut Ship Island in two, but wave action filled the gap with sand. Then in 1969 Hurricane Camille split the island again much more emphatically. In 1998, Hurricane Georges washed completely over East Ship Island, clearing the underbrush out of the woods and lopping off the western end. In 2019, the Corps of Engineers reconnected the islands into one.

Such events are a few of the many that illustrate the changeability of barrier islands. Fort Massachusetts, for instance, was built five hundred feet from the western end of Ship Island; 130 years later, that shore extended more than a mile westward. Petit Bois Island used to be part of Alabama's Dauphin Island, which is now five miles east.

> The Mississippi barrier islands include numerous other islands besides the large, prominent Deer, Ship, and Horn. Round Island provides a good break point four miles out, slightly less than halfway to Horn. Part of this half-mile-long wedge of sand and pine trees is privately owned and part belongs to the City of Pascagoula. The city portion includes the site of an 1859 lighthouse that was blown apart by Hurricane Georges in 1998 and relocated to the mainland at Pascagoula in 2015. Three miles east of Horn Island lies the seven-and-a-half-mile-long Petit Bois Island—French for "little woods." Like Horn Island, it's a federally designated wilderness area. And 2,200-acre Cat Island is located about seven miles south of Long Beach. During World War II, the US Army used Cat Island in an unsuccessful attempt to teach dogs to track Japanese Americans in hopes of using them against enemy soldiers on the assumption that Japanese smelled different from Caucasians.

An Easier Way to Explore

Paddlers who want to experience a barrier island without a difficult and possibly perilous crossing can catch an excursion boat to Ship Island. In less than an hour from departure, passengers glimpse shimmering white beaches and the remains of Fort Massachusetts. On the picture-perfect south beach, visitors read, sleep, swim, sunbathe, toss food to gulls, fish in the shallows, and let the subtropical breeze blow their landlubberly worries away.

The rest of the treeless island remains untouched because few tourists care to wade through swamp crisscrossed by alligator trails. Behind the grassy dunes, tracks of raccoons and birds imprint the sand. Gator trails lead into the muck and grass-clogged water of the interior. The north side of the island has narrow beaches and is rarely visited. Here you can sit quietly, watch gulls gather in the shallows, and listen to the music the wind makes when it spills off the continent and strums the Mississippi Sound.

Five miles west of Ship Island and seven miles south of Gulfport lies Cat Island, named for its raccoons, which French explorers mistook for cats. Unlike the other barrier islands, which are linear, Cat Island is wildly irregular. The result is a number of coves that make it all the more interesting. The National Park Service owns some of the island as part of Gulf Islands National Seashore, which includes not only the Mississippi islands and Davis Bayou area but parts of Perdido Key, Alabama, and Santa Rosa Island, Florida.

Canoeing the Gulf Coast, by Ernest Herndon

It's impressive enough to canoe big rivers and lakes on a regular basis, but Mississippi River canoe guide John Ruskey has taken his vessel to even bigger waters: the Mississippi Sound and the Gulf of Mexico. In 2019 Ruskey, who runs the Quapaw Canoe Company in Clarksdale, took a canoe load of people and equipment to Horn Island, ten miles offshore, for a five-day artist's retreat.

Granted, this was no ordinary canoe. Ruskey's homemade wooden boat stretched twenty-nine feet and could hold half a dozen people and a mountain of gear. "It's made for waters like [the Mississippi Sound]," Ruskey said. "The French Canadian voyageurs used that design on the Great Lakes."

The campers found wildlife galore on the island. Pelicans, terns, gulls, and other birds put on dramatic diving performances. "There were lots of osprey—dozens of them, in fact, dozens of nests on the east side of the island," he said.

One day Ruskey was sketching when he realized he was "surrounded by ghost crabs." "I thought they were aliens," he said, comparing them to flying saucers with eyeballs. Another time, he encountered a seven-foot alligator crossing the island. Campers also saw a bald eagle, raccoons, rabbits, water moccasins, blue crabs, butterflies, and dragonflies.

"There were endless dolphins," Ruskey said. "All day long the dolphins were following us. They were leaping out all around us."

Ruskey also canoed on the lower Pearl River and the Wolf River during his visit to the coast. He said,

"I've been discovering a side of Mississippi I never knew."

INDEX

Bayou Pierre, 22, 73–84, 118, 166, 269
Big Black River, 4, 39, 89, 107, 160–70
Biloxi River, 261–68
Black Creek, 116, 166, 190, 201, 235, 247–49
Bowie Creek, 230, 238–40
Buttahatchie River, 180, 181, 182, 185

Chickasawhay River, 190, 205–12
Chunky River, 192, 205, 207, 217–21
Coldwater River, 38, 40, 44–47, 49, 52

Escatawpa River, 189, 192, 193, 201–4

Gulf Islands, 262, 279–85

Hatchie River, 171–72, 184
Homochitto River, 25, 73, 75–77, 85–95

Jourdan River, 261, 262, 273–78

Leaf River, 190, 205, 214, 217, 222–37

Okatoma Creek, 228, 230, 233, 238, 241–45

Pascagoula River, 122, 148, 189, 190–200, 214, 217, 223, 231
Pearl River, 3–5, 107–35

Red Creek, 137, 189, 192, 249, 257–60

Strong River, 107, 124, 136–42, 269
Sunflower River, 9, 31, 34, 41, 62–71

Tallahatchie River, 46, 49–53
Tangipahoa River, 73, 96–106

Wolf River (coastal Mississippi), 269–72
Wolf River (northeast Mississippi), 182–83

Yalobusha River, 32, 49, 53, 57–61
Yazoo River, 25, 31–43, 45–47, 63–66, 109, 117, 161
Yocona River, 54–56

ABOUT THE AUTHORS

Ernest Herndon is a longtime outdoor writer for the McComb, Mississippi, *Enterprise-Journal*. He is the author of seventeen books including two canoe guides and two adventure travel narratives. He has written for numerous magazines and won a long list of state, regional, and national journalism awards.

Photo by McComb Enterprise-Journal

Patrick Parker is a physiologist, naturalist, and travel/outdoor writer. His nature and adventure travel writing has been featured in *US News & World Report*, the *Washington Times*, and *Tanzania Today*, as well as local publications such as the McComb *Enterprise-Journal* and *Pulse* magazine.

Photo courtesy of the author